Further endorsements from leading experts and business people

'"Future Work" sounds seductive. But very few organizations have actually changed the way they really do work. Maitland and Thomson have painted a comprehensive and compelling picture of what is possible, going way beyond the typical hype about technology and GenY. And they have dug deeply to report many very human stories about how the future of work is happening today, and what it takes to transform the workplace. If you read this book and then put it aside without changing the way you manage, you will wind up watching the future of work from the sidelines.'
  – **James P. Ware**, *Executive Director, The Future of Work...unlimited*

'*Future Work* provides an invaluable guide to the kind of transformational leadership that will be necessary to make the best of all that this new world of work has to offer.'
  – **Dave Coplin**, *Chief Envisioning Officer, Microsoft UK*

'*Future Work* lays out a compelling business case for flexibility that offers essential guidance for leaders grappling with a changing workforce, globalization and continuous advances in technology. The authors challenge conventional attitudes with a powerful rationale on how work can be accomplished with more precision and efficiency, while simultaneously reducing costs and offering employees more control over how they work.'
  – **Michel Landel**, *CEO, Sodexo*

'*Future Work* is empowerment in practice!'
  – **Nuria Chinchilla**, *Professor of Managing People in Organizations, IESE Business School*

'The world of work is changing rapidly and the office is undergoing a radical redesign to accommodate twenty-first century work practices. This book captures these critical changes and identifies the leadership culture required to support them. It should be read by all managers who are striving to get the best results from their workforce.'
  – **Professor Ginny Gibson**, *Deputy Dean, Henley Business School*

'*Future Work* provides timely insight on the kind of culture organizations need to meet the expectations of today's workforce. It will be useful for executives who want to learn how business must adapt to the revolution in work practices now being fuelled by incredibly rapid technological and social changes.'

– **Stewart D. Friedman**, *Practice Professor at The Wharton School and author of Total Leadership*

'Alison Maitland and Peter Thomson's book is where every board member and senior executive should start when thinking through the best way to future-proof their organizations.'

– **Lucy P. Marcus**, *CEO, Marcus Venture Consulting, and non-executive board director*

'Alison and Peter have successfully navigated the future of work to explain why this is now a critical issue for all business leaders. Their book is essential reading for anyone wanting to gain a glimpse of the future and understand the new world of work.'

– **Philip Ross**, *CEO, Unwork.com*

Praise for the first edition of *Future Work*:

'I have devoured your book and I am sharing your brilliant wisdom with many. Your book is a much needed resource if businesses want to succeed. Brilliance from cover to cover.'

– **Lolly Daskal**, *Founder, Lead From Within*

'Thanks for writing this excellent book – the best I've read about current changes in work style & culture.'

– **Barbara Josef**, *Corporate PR, Citizenship and Media Spokesperson, Microsoft Switzerland*

'We had considered that we were good employers, even having won an award for being "family friendly", but your book has pointed out that we are not going far enough. Thank you for being the catalyst for change.'

– **Julie Coward**, *CEO, Basel Trust Corporation*

'I just finished reading your book *Future Work* and felt compelled to write to thank you for getting this challenge/opportunity in print! I am a senior leader in a large multinational, I work in a very flexible way, and truly integrate my life with two small children and my work. However, I feel "unusual" and unconventional and sometimes question how all this works. I'm not sure how seriously I am taken in terms of career these days, but I find myself very productive and motivated with this working approach. My small team work this way too and we enjoy great "virtual" interactions and lots of autonomy. Thank you for your book – it truly "validated" my approach and I feel more compelled to realize my potential because I work this way and not in spite of it!'

– **Senior leader**, *global manufacturing company*

Changing organizational culture for the new world of work

Future Work

2nd edition

Alison Maitland

and

Peter Thomson

First published 2014 by
PALGRAVE MACMILLAN

Palgrave Macmillan in the UK is an imprint of Macmillan Publishers Limited, registered in England, company number 785998, of Houndmills, Basingstoke, Hampshire RG21 6XS.

Palgrave Macmillan in the US is a division of St Martin's Press LLC, 175 Fifth Avenue, New York, NY 10010.

Palgrave Macmillan is the global academic imprint of the above companies and has companies and representatives throughout the world.

Palgrave® and Macmillan® are registered trademarks in the United States, the United Kingdom, Europe and other countries.

ISBN 978–1–137–36715–0

This book is printed on paper suitable for recycling and made from fully managed and sustained forest sources. Logging, pulping and manufacturing processes are expected to conform to the environmental regulations of the country of origin.

A catalogue record for this book is available from the British Library.

A catalog record for this book is available from the Library of Congress.

Typeset by MPS Limited, Chennai, India.

For David, Eleanor and Isabel
(AM)
For Zac, Eva, Willow and Indie
(PT)

Contents

List of Illustrations, Figures, Tables and Case Studies

Illustrations

Figures

Tables

Case Studies

Foreword

For me, it was a toddler's exercise class that brought home the importance of workplace flexibility. It was 25 years ago, and the toddler was my two-year-old son. I was at a Gymboree class in our neighborhood – with my son and 24 mothers and their kids – because my wife had suggested our son would benefit from going, and that I would benefit from taking him. So every Wednesday morning, from 9 to 11, through the busiest time of year at the office, I was there in a track suit, playing, not working.

As the only father in the class I was a curiosity. Three weeks in, one of the mothers asked me what I did for a living. What job was so flexible that I could spend every Wednesday morning with my boy? When I told her I was an accountant she was shocked.

Why should she have been so surprised? I could organize my week around a Wednesday morning class. Even during our busiest period I could meet my deadlines, spend time with my son, and be happier, more productive and more well-rounded because of it. But 25 years ago, taking advantage of flexibility was an oddity.

I had another lesson about the importance of flexibility ten years ago. I was in my role in Ernst & Young and we had a problem: women were leaving us at a much higher rate than men. We did all kinds of research to find out why. Was it pay? Benefits? Was our culture sexist? No. The biggest factor was that women felt that our workplace needed more flexibility.

So we changed. If people wanted to work different schedules we stopped asking them 'why?' and started asking their managers 'why not?' Flexibility became more a 'right for all', not a 'privilege for few'. The results were dramatic. A year later we were retaining far more women. But we were retaining far more men, too, and more of our highest performers among both.

I'm convinced flexibility will become ever more important. The members of Generation Y joining the workforce expect it. They are highly committed workers – but don't want to be chained to their desks.

As Alison and Peter point out in this important book, organizations that give their workers more control over their time, provide them with more autonomy and empower them to use their skills and knowledge will be the winners in the twenty-first century. For many organizations and managers this requires a shift in culture and mindset. For those who are wondering where to start, I recommend this book.

James S. Turley – former Chairman and CEO, Ernst & Young (EY)

Authors' Preface and Acknowledgments to Second Edition

In the two years since the publication of the first edition of *Future Work*, we have seen yet more evidence that there is a revolution in working practices on the way. We have had encouraging feedback from many readers saying how the messages in the book ring true and we have observed companies, large and small, moving further towards autonomous working practices. So, we were pleased to say 'yes' when Palgrave Macmillan asked if we would like to write a second edition.

The economic climate over the last two years has had a noticeable effect on working patterns. In a downturn, it might be thought that organizations would revert to 'safe' traditional practices and abandon agile working as a luxury. There was the high-profile case of Yahoo abandoning its home working program and some reversal of other innovative practices in the US, which we address in this new edition. But these have been exceptions. Even in the financial services sector, we are now seeing companies adopting progressive working practices as illustrated in three new case studies, Credit Suisse, RBS and Swiss Re.

The first edition provided guidance for leaders and managers, pointing out the cultural and organizational changes involved in implementing future work. In this edition, we have included an extra chapter with more practical advice on implementation, particularly helping individuals to make the change. This reflects the fact that the leading exponents of future work have two more years of experience under their belts and can show the positive impacts on their business as well as their workforce.

We may be two years further along down the road towards future work, but the blockages to progress remain firmly in place in many organizations. We hope that the new evidence of enlightened practices in this edition will persuade more leaders and managers to challenge the traditional model of work, with its long and often unproductive hours, and to embrace work innovation and autonomy as essential elements of their business strategies for sustainable future growth.

Both editions have been enriched by the experience of the many executives and experts who generously gave us their time, and we also thank all the people who helped arrange interviews. We are grateful to those leaders who shared their personal stories about challenging and changing their own assumptions and then tackling resistance in others.

We would also like to thank the people who have helped us in many other ways, including: Shirley Borrett at the Telework Association; Fleur Bothwick at Ernst & Young; Janine Duchar, David Learmond, Sara Murray, Rebecca Ray and colleagues at The Conference Board; Ellen Galinsky, Carol Bryce-Buchanan and Kelly Sakai at the Families and Work Institute; Alison Gregory, Sarah Williams-Gardener and colleagues at IBM; Kate Grussing at Sapphire Partners; Sarah Jackson at Working Families; Kate Lister and Tom Harnish at the Telework Research Network; Anne Madden and colleagues at the Equality and Human Rights Commission; Colin Maitland; Professor Ian Maitland at the University of Minnesota's Carlson School of Management; Peta Payne of IWE; Caroline Turner; Caroline Waters, formerly of BT; Women on Boards Australia; and Stuart Woollard at King's College, London. Roger Beale's cartoons add a delicious twist to our messages.

We are grateful to Cass Business School and Henley Business School, to which we are respectively affiliated, for their great help in disseminating our survey to their alumni networks. We would like to thank Lindsay Allen and Margrete Resellmo for their useful advice and assistance with the survey during their MBA studies at Henley and Cass.

The team at Palgrave Macmillan have been strong supporters of our project from the start, and we are most grateful for their enthusiasm for both the first edition and this second edition.

Finally, and most importantly, we thank our families for their support, patience and love during the long months of researching, writing and editing. We hope this book will benefit people currently at work of every kind, as well as future generations.

Alison Maitland and Peter Thomson

CHAPTER 1

Time for change

Bram Meulenbeld and Martijn van der Linden, two Dutch men in their 30s, started out in traditional high-flying corporate careers, working for ING bank and Philips among other employers. During the global economic crisis, each concluded it was time for a change. 'I didn't want to go to an office all my life,' says Martijn.

The two friends heard about a young firm called Amplify Trading, in London's Canary Wharf, recruiting people to trade financial futures electronically from wherever they were located. They moved to a remote chalet high in the Austrian Alps, enjoying mountain sports in the mornings and switching on their computers in the afternoons to earn a living by trading shares on the New York stock exchange. They worked for as much or as little time each day as it took to make enough money.

A year later, they returned to the Netherlands to embark on new careers in sustainable development. Bram set up a consultancy and website and Martijn turned to writing a book, both working mainly from their homes.

Bram says he is grateful that he can work in a way that would not have been possible 20, or even 10, years ago. 'I decided that "structured" life in an organization did not meet my requirements. I moved to Austria to benefit from two valuable things in life: a very interesting and challenging job and at the same time being able to fully benefit from all the things I value in life.

> *'Now, as I'm working from home, I can offer lower hourly tariffs because I don't have an expensive office. I use all kinds of online tools – Skype, Dropbox, Prezi – to work with others, while having all the freedom that I want around my work.'*

> *Martijn coordinates the Platform for an Economy based on Sustainability and Solidarity and chairs the Our Money (Ons Geld) foundation which campaigns for reform of the financial system. He still works mostly from home, collaborating with a wide range of people in the Netherlands and abroad. 'We share information and knowledge online instantly between international specialists,' he says. 'It's a competitive advantage for those who are involved.'[1]*

We are living in a time of exponential technological change. All around us there is evidence of digital breakthroughs. Whether it's an octogenarian ordering groceries online, a celebrity encouraging a mass protest through Twitter, or a young man reconstructing his past through Facebook after illness wiped out his memory,[2] the Web and its applications have rapidly and fundamentally altered our lives. They are having a profound effect on the way we communicate, learn and socialize. You may well be reading this book electronically on a Kindle, iPad or other e-reading device.

As the experience of Bram and Martijn illustrates, there is enormous scope for the way in which we work to change as well. Many people have choices unimaginable a decade or two ago. Some companies are responding by radically rethinking how they organize and manage people. They are at the forefront of a revolution in how we work.

Many organizations, however, remain stuck with a model of employment and management practices that were appropriate for work in the nineteenth and twentieth centuries, but are no longer so for the twenty-first. People are still expected to be present at their workplace for fixed periods of time and are paid by the hour, day, week or month for turning up. Long hours are often required and rewarded without any measure of the productivity involved. Getting the job done in half the time and going home early, instead of winning people praise, is more likely to see them sidelined as 'slackers'.

Yet there is overwhelming evidence that employees are more productive if they have greater autonomy over where, when and how they work. It should not be surprising to find that people feel motivated to produce their optimum when they are trusted to manage their own work patterns. There is nothing new in the concept of empowering employees. Progressive management thinkers have been preaching this since the middle of the last century.

What is new is that we now have the technology to enable a major shift in the way people work. It has already transformed how hundreds of thousands of self-employed individuals carry out their jobs. But many large organizations are struggling to make the transition to more efficient business, better working lives and a healthier planet.

Fifty years ago, Douglas McGregor, the MIT management professor, wrote in *The Human Side of Enterprise*: 'Many managers would agree that the effectiveness of their organizations would be at least doubled if they could discover how to tap the unrealized potential present in their human resources.'[3] Managers often pay lip service to his proposition that people tend to be self-motivated and that management by empowerment is more effective than command-and-control (McGregor's Theory Y versus Theory X). When it comes to putting it into practice, however, old habits die hard.

In this book, we challenge those old habits. We explain why they have to change if companies are to keep pace with the competition in the networked world. Drawing on a wide body of research, and on interviews with organizations at the leading edge, we reveal the culture, approaches and skills required to make the transition to more effective ways of managing people and to organizing work for the overall benefit of business, individuals and society.

The new workforce

There are powerful reasons why companies and managers need to think differently about people and work. Tectonic shifts are taking place in the composition of the workforce, and in attitudes in wider society, which demand a response from any organization that wants to secure talent for the future, as we explain in **Chapter 2**.

Women now make up between 40 percent and 50 percent of the workforce in most developed countries,[4] as well as half or more of the employees inside many organizations. They represent the majority of the educated talent pool – around six out of ten graduates coming out of universities in the developed world, and a rising force in many parts of the developing world too.[5]

As women's earning power grows to equal or even outstrip that of their partners, the other side of the coin is that more men are taking on greater responsibility for childcare and are willing to be active fathers. In the US, the conflict between work and family commitments, felt acutely by working women during the late twentieth century, is now shared by men in dual-income families.[6] In the UK, fathers and mothers who were questioned about what would most help in achieving a better balance in their lives wanted 'a wider range of flexible job opportunities in all types of jobs' – a finding mirrored in the Shriver Report, A Woman's Nation, in the US.[7]

The fact is that the traditional male career model – which assumed people would have an unbroken full-time career and a steady rise to a peak of performance and earning power in their late 40s or 50s, followed by retirement around 60 – does not fit the new majority of the workforce.

Our aging societies pose both a huge challenge and an opportunity for better ways of working. From Japan and Australia to Italy and Germany, countries are grappling with how to support a generation of old people, as the population of working age shrinks and fewer young people enter the workforce. The extension of working life is now inevitable in many parts of the world to maintain pensions and old-age care at acceptable levels.

Fortunately for governments and employers, this lengthening of working lives coincides with a desire on the part of many mature people to work past traditional retirement age, whether for financial reasons or to stay active and fulfilled. Many of them do not want to work in the old way, however, with fixed, full-time hours. Research shows, for example, that American baby boomers who continue working want greater control, autonomy and choice about where, how and when they work.[8]

This is a desire they share with others, notably the youngest people in work. This youthful cohort, variously called Generation Y, Millennials or digital natives, takes the greater flexibility afforded by technology for granted. They have grown up with the means to connect with their peers anytime anywhere, and they expect to be able to work this way too.

Young 'knowledge workers' are as likely to want to work while munching a sandwich over their laptop in a wireless-enabled café as behind a desk in a traditional office.

Many companies are inadequately prepared for the cultural changes that will take place as these younger workers move into leadership roles. According to one survey, over two-thirds of senior executives think their organizations are too reliant on male CEOs from the baby boomer generation and only 41 percent say they are ready for the coming demographic changes.[9] 'Companies which don't change are always vulnerable,' says Richard Boggis-Rolfe, chairman of Odgers Berndtson, the executive search firm that commissioned the research.[10] 'But they will change, the successful ones will.'

Motivation is more than money

Demographic shifts, globalization and cost-cutting have already led to significant changes in the contractual models between employer and employee, with the growth of temporary agency work and the rise in part-time jobs in regions like Europe. The economic downturn following the global financial crisis saw an increase in insecure employment such as 'zero-hours contracts' in the UK and 'mini-jobs' in Germany, which earn less than the tax threshold.

At the same time, new web-based companies are springing up to challenge incumbent, or 'legacy', organizations by offering competitive rates based on their relatively low overheads and lack of hierarchy. These firms often assemble individuals or teams to work on specific projects and then disperse and regroup, giving the workers a high level of autonomy but lower job security than traditional employment contracts.

As economies become more knowledge-based, there will be a decline in permanent employment, predicts Denis Pennel, managing director of the International Confederation of Private Employment Agencies (Ciett). The future, he suggests, may look like a throwback to the past – to before the Industrial Revolution when most workers, such as farmers, artisans and shopkeepers, were self-employed and responsible for their own output. 'They will have work to do but with several different employers,' he said in a *Financial Times* interview.[11] 'Technology enables this. It means people can be based anywhere and gives organizations access to global expertise.'

One of the chief preoccupations of business leaders is how to attract, motivate and retain skills and talent. The excesses uncovered by the global financial crisis triggered a fundamental questioning of reward and motivation, management styles and dominant models of work. It is perhaps no coincidence that the investment banks at the heart of the crisis were among the most extreme proponents of command-and-control management, short-term results and huge rewards, with the expectation of exceptionally long hours and 'face-time'.

Since the crisis, there has been widespread questioning of the conventional view that success is measured solely by the size of one's salary or bonus. Public discontent, even outrage, continues to be expressed at the high compensation that many executives receive. There has been a powerful backlash against 'rewards for failure', especially when contrasted with the impact on ordinary people of government measures to reduce public spending and budget deficits.

A new branch of social science, the economics of happiness, is attracting increasing interest. Ever since Abraham Maslow introduced his Hierarchy of Needs in 1943, psychologists have been studying how people gain satisfaction in life. As Richard Layard points out in his book *Happiness*,[12] we are no happier now than we were 50 years ago, even though our incomes have doubled. The 'Happiness Index' produced by City & Guilds, a UK vocational education body, underlines how money does not buy happiness.

'For the last five years, sky-high salaries have rated pretty low on our list of reasons for feeling fulfilled and satisfied in our careers,' it says.[13]

Given the urgent need for talent and skills, many organizations are worried about the big challenge they face in keeping employees motivated and committed. Only 40 percent of employees in North America are fully 'engaged' with their work, according to a report by the global consulting firm BlessingWhite.[14] Engagement levels range from 42 percent in India to just 22 percent in China, with Europe at 31 percent and Australia and New Zealand at 37 percent.

Research indicates that both baby boomers and the young workers of Gen Y, particularly in advanced economies, place at least as much importance on having flexible work, high-quality colleagues, recognition and access to new challenges as they do on financial rewards.[15] The new generation joining the workforce is also much more concerned about environmental issues and likely to look closely at the 'green' credentials of a potential employer before applying for a job.

Rewarding work, not time

An important way to motivate people is to trust them with greater autonomy over how they get work done. Doing so will reap dividends for managers and organizations, as the many case studies in this book demonstrate.

What we are proposing goes beyond arrangements typically known as 'flexible working'. Since the turn of the twenty-first century there has been a surge of interest in alternative working practices. The topic is moving from being a curiosity represented by a few supposedly quirky companies such as Semco in Brazil or Happy Computers in the UK to being part of mainstream human resources management.

The trouble is that most cases of flexible working have simply been grafted on to existing management practices without reviewing or changing the underlying model of work and careers. This has resulted in an uncomfortable coexistence between traditional management attitudes and pockets of greater flexibility, as we describe in **Chapter 3**.

Practices such as part-time work, compressed working weeks, job shares and term-time working do not challenge the prevailing, but now outdated and unsuitable, model of work. These cosmetic adjustments are introduced as an employee benefit and are commonly viewed by operational managers as a cost and an imposition. They are not seen as a business initiative to increase competitiveness and improve the bottom line.

So, in the second decade of the twenty-first century, we still live in a world where the predominant form of employment is 'fixed time and place'. This was established at the time of the Industrial Revolution to meet the demands of a manufacturing-based economy, and it lingers on today as if the Information Revolution had not happened.

This model is based on time: If you give me your time to perform a job, I will reward you per hour. If you are a 'part-time' person and work less than the normal hours, you will be rewarded pro rata. The hours of work are set down in a contract issued by the employer, accepted by the employee and enforced by managers.

Many employers now offer varieties of 'flexi-time', allowing employees to vary their starting and finishing time around a set of core hours. But this is still a time-based relationship where the commodity being purchased is hours. What is achieved during those hours is of secondary importance. In many business cultures, people are expected to work far longer than the contracted hours. By doing so, they are seen as 'loyal', 'dedicated' and 'hard working' and are rewarded and promoted for this.

The concept of paying for time implies that people give up their freedom in exchange for money. They no longer have control over what they do between 9 a.m. and 5.30 p.m. from Monday to Friday – or 7 a.m. and 9 p.m. if they work in a high-pressure job. They need permission to go to the dentist, attend a funeral or take a holiday. They have the impossible task of taking their children to school at the same time as they are supposed to be getting to work and they end up in traffic congestion caused by everyone else trying to do the same thing.

No wonder that in Britain, for example, self-reported work-related stress, depression or anxiety accounted for an estimated 10.4m lost working days in 2011/12.[16] Or that in Australia, 60 percent of working women and nearly half of working men feel consistently time-pressured, and most workers would rather have two weeks' extra holiday than an equivalent pay rise.[17]

Paying people by the hour is the opposite of rewarding productivity. If you work slowly to perform a task, you will get paid more than if you work quickly. If your lawyer takes two hours to sort out your legal problem, you will pay her twice as much as if she fixes it in an hour. If the plumber takes three hours to mend a leak, he gets paid more than the efficient one who does it in an hour.

This system even encourages people to slow down their rate of work during 'normal' hours so that a job runs over into 'unsocial' hours and they are paid a higher rate to compensate for the extra hours. What's more, when people are paid for a fixed number of hours per week, as happens in the vast majority of organizations, working efficiently and completing tasks quickly results in being given more work to fill up the hours.

So, while 'flexible working' is a step toward a more sensible approach to work, it misses a fundamental point. Who is responsible for making sure that work gets done? If it is up to management to divide work into jobs and allocate these to people in return for a number of hours of their labor, we will remain stuck in an Industrial Age model of work. If a group of people agree on what they are going to achieve, then each carries out the tasks necessary to provide the results required, we have a new approach to work and management.

This new approach is well-suited for what Gary Hamel, the influential business thinker and writer, calls 'the creative economy', in which ideas are the basis of competitive advantage and management is about creating an environment in which people feel free to take the initiative, make connections and seize opportunities without waiting for direction.

It involves a radical change in the way work is done, rewarding people for their ideas and output, not for their time. Some organizations that have already made the change, or are in the process of doing so, call this 'smart' or 'agile' working because it makes sense for business as well as being good for people. We call it 'future work', because it represents the way that successful businesses will operate in the future, not just in terms of the technology that supports the change, but also crucially in terms of the way that work is organized and people are managed.

It often takes longer to move organizational cultures and attitudes than it does to introduce smart technology or create futuristic workspaces. It is much easier to build a 'future work'-ready company from scratch than to change long-established organizations, where there will be resistance and a tendency to fall back on command-and-control management in tough times.

However, it is not an option to stand still and resist the change happening all around. We feature organizations of many types throughout the book, including household-name companies, which are pointing the way to the future.

Capturing hearts, minds and wallets

A key argument in favor of new ways of working is that they improve productivity, a point we demonstrate in **Chapter 4**, where we examine why future work makes business sense. Countless surveys have shown big improvements in output when people have greater autonomy over how, where and when they carry out their work to meet their objectives.

This is a persuasive argument for managers to use in countering doubts about the new work model. As long as practices such as working from home are seen simply as an employee benefit, they will not be treated seriously, especially by business leaders. However, when it becomes clear that they are major contributors to business success, attitudes change. As John D. Finnegan, CEO of Chubb, the US insurance group, told the *Financial Times*, he was initially skeptical about reported benefits but then changed his mind. 'As most CEOs would, I saw it as an employee accommodation program with a cost. I didn't know you could at the same time maintain or increase productivity.'[18]

The trigger for making a radical shift in the organizations we have studied is usually a business need – the soaring cost of real estate, a drive to improve customer service or a focus on reducing high rates of employee turnover. The benefits do not have to be confined to 'knowledge work', although this type of work is easiest to transform through communications technology. Jobs in many sectors, such as health care and retailing, have to be done in a fixed location, while others, in manufacturing for example, require people to be available at fixed times of the day or night. But even these jobs contain tasks, such as form filling and record keeping, that are susceptible to far greater autonomy than is currently exercised.

In addition to productivity, the business benefits of future work include major cost savings on real estate and on employee turnover and absenteeism, extended customer service cover and the ability to enter new markets faster. There are less obvious advantages, such as a lower risk of business disruption and more transparent succession planning. There are also important benefits for the environment and wider society, which in turn contribute to the green credentials and public image of the organization.

Productivity can be combined with greater well-being. Flexible working interventions that increase worker control are likely to have a positive effect on health, according to a study of ten research projects.[19] Another report, looking at over 24,000 IBM employees worldwide, found that those with workplace flexibility could work an additional 19 hours per week before experiencing the same level of conflict between their work and personal lives as their office-bound counterparts.[20]

The global economic crisis brought urgency to the drive for change. Organizations have been forced to focus even harder on costs. Many resorted to shorter working weeks on reduced pay as a way to preserve jobs during the recession.

Natural disasters, such as the 2011 earthquake and tsunami in Japan and Hurricane Sandy that hit the Caribbean and North America in 2012, have underlined the importance of new, technology-enabled work practices. Companies that equipped people to work from home or on the move experienced far less disruption than the rest.

In the post-crisis period, the savings associated with a shift to future work offer employers a further opportunity to improve growth while keeping a lid on costs.

Leadership for the future

Much has been written about collaborative technology – the web of devices, services and applications that enable organizations and people to work together more efficiently in the internet era. Cloud computing is the next stage of this evolution that is changing the way we work. Technology often provides the essential underpinning, but the key to moving to a more efficient and healthier working model is a change in culture, led from the top of the organization.

This book is about the human side of the transition to future work. It is aimed at leaders and managers who want to equip themselves with the thinking and skills needed to meet the challenges of the new world of work. It also provides practical advice for individuals seeking to rebalance their lives and at the same time work more effectively.

The global crisis triggered fevered debate about the leadership of our largest institutions, particularly in the financial sector. The economic repercussions of the financial earthquake left trust in business leadership at a low ebb. According to the BlessingWhite survey, only half of employees in Europe and 57 percent in North America trust the people at the top of their organization, who represent the culture and values and who need to inspire performance and commitment.[21] Rebuilding this damaged trust will take innovative approaches as well as time.

Leaders must also face the fact that trust is ebbing away from institutions. Research by Edelman, the international public relations firm, points to a democratizing trend, with people trusting their peers or experts nearly twice as much as government officials or chief executives. 'The hierarchies of old are being replaced by more trusted peer-to-peer, horizontal networks of trust,' says CEO Richard Edelman.[22]

Many of today's senior managers rose to the top by working long hours in full-time jobs. They have reaped the rewards of that system. The not so subtle message to others is that if they want to climb 'the ladder' of success, they too must follow traditional career paths and make the necessary 'sacrifices'. The mantra is that senior jobs in high-performing companies require near total commitment of body and soul, and that balance at these high levels is virtually impossible.

Yet the crisis has demonstrated more clearly than ever how essential it is to have balanced, responsive leaders at the top of companies to avoid a repeat of the disasters that brought whole institutions crashing to oblivion. The prevailing work model at the top is not a healthy way to live, to lead or to maintain perspective – witness the surveys showing high levels of stress among managers, as well as staff. It also sends a negative message to many aspiring leaders: don't expect to have any control over your lives if you choose to climb the ladder to the executive suite.

Will the talented individuals joining the workforce today be prepared to play this game? There is increasing evidence to show that they – and many of those already in the workforce – will not. This will leave an ever-shrinking pool of potential leaders, with more skills and talents leaking out of larger organizations.

'Leadership in the past was built on organizational power and the ability to dish out money,' says Damien O'Brien, head of Egon Zehnder, the executive search firm. 'This new generation coming through will have less deference to organizational power and for many of them money will be less of a driver. They will come to work if they are inspired. The successful leaders of the future will be those who enable their people to release their creativity, rather than trying to control what they do.'[23]

The biggest component missing from leadership today – especially in the corporate world – is women. If diversity in the leadership team really is a strategic objective, as more and more business leaders claim it is, then the requirement of 'total commitment' will undermine it. It will perpetuate the exclusion, or self-exclusion, of a large part of the talent that companies need to survive and thrive. This, in turn, will encourage 'groupthink' – the pressure within a homogenous group to go along with the prevailing arguments rather than rock the boat – and the damaging fallout that we saw during the global crisis.

Christine Lagarde, managing director of the IMF and former French finance minister, is a strong advocate of more power for women, and she also argues for a more responsible, equitable approach to global finance. 'We need a financial sector that is accountable to the real economy – one that adds value, not destroys it,' she told the 2013 World Economic Forum annual meeting.

Research shows that female management skills are well attuned to the more democratic workplaces of the future and to the needs of the younger generations X and Y.[24] 'They're more participative in their leadership style, they have a sensitivity to risk, they're less hyper-competitive, and all those things align themselves with a more democratic, participative workplace,' says Professor Cliff Oswick, head of the faculty of management at Cass Business School in London.[25]

A fresh approach to leadership is essential if organizations are to break free from the old rules of work. In our research for this book, we found a growing band of women and men who have had the courage to challenge and change these rules, not only by encouraging future work in their teams but also by remodeling their own career and work patterns. Future work is for everyone. It is important that leaders, including those responsible for running large businesses, show how it can be done, as they are the most powerful agents of change. We tell the stories of seven trailblazing leaders in **Chapter 5**, and feature others through the book.

Leaders and managers who set goals for people and trust them to achieve those goals will encourage others at every level to take on responsibility and generate positive outcomes for the organization. This will lead to power being distributed through the company, rather than simply being concentrated at the top. Diversity, as research studies show, is important to creativity and innovation. Future work will enable a more diverse group of people, from different backgrounds and with different perspectives and talents, to flourish and move into leadership positions.

Under new management

For many of today's managers, these shifts are likely to be a challenge, since they require a willingness to examine and probably change aspects of their own management style, as many of those we interviewed have done. It may feel uncomfortable. But it produces significant results and it is already happening in companies at the forefront of the new world of work. In **Chapter 6**, we explore the role of location in future work, and the implications for management methods as teams become dispersed across locations and time zones, and as offices change from being workplaces to meeting places.

Traditionally, managers have been responsible for the allocation of tasks to their people. They have decided what needs to be done, by when and by whom. They have monitored progress and used various motivational techniques to encourage their staff to perform effectively. The whole process has been based on the assumption that the manager knows best and has the authority to tell people what to do.

Yet for the past 50 years, respected management writers have been arguing that motivation is about giving people responsibility and creating an environment where they can use their skills to achieve something satisfying. Maslow, Frederick Herzberg and McGregor were preaching this in the 40s, 50s and 60s and Charles Handy, Peter Drucker and Tom Peters were pushing the same messages in the 80s and 90s.

As Dan Pink puts it in his enlightening book *Drive*, recent behavioral science studies show that 'autonomous motivation promotes greater conceptual understanding, better grades, enhanced persistence at school and in sporting activities, higher productivity, less burnout and greater levels of psychological wellbeing. Those effects carry over to the workplace.'[26]

It is about trusting people to get on with their work and giving them real freedom of choice as to how they do the job. It is about rewarding success, not punishing failure. In summary it is about treating people as adults and not as children.

We carried out a survey of international alumni of Cass Business School and Henley Business School in the UK, as well as other managers around the world, to investigate what kind of organizational cultures enable future work to thrive.

Our key findings are that:

- A majority of managers expect there to be a revolution in working practices in the next decade

- Most managers think their organizations are not adapting fast enough to new ways of working

- A majority want more freedom to let people manage their own work patterns

- More than half believe new ways of working would benefit their business

- Organizations that enable future work tend to have a strong culture of trust, to value individual creativity and input and to treat people as self-motivated

Based on these findings, we explain in **Chapter 7** what kind of culture organizations need to foster to adapt and thrive in the new world of work. We also see how countries and regions vary widely in their openness to new working practices, although the desire for a different deal from work is not peculiar to employees in advanced industrial societies.

The number of hours worked each year gives an indication of the differing approaches to work among developed nations. According to OECD figures, people work an average of 1381 hours per year in the Netherlands while at the other extreme in South Korea the average is 2090 hours.[27] This means that more than three Dutch workers are needed to match the hours worked by two Koreans. There is a distinct difference in approach between many European Union (EU) countries, which are restricted by the Working Time Directive, and the US, where there is no regulation. Both genders in the US work on average 41 hours a week. In Europe, women work just over 30 hours, compared with around 38 hours for men.[28]

In addition to our unique survey, we have interviewed over 70 executives and experts in global companies, medium-sized firms, online businesses and public sector organizations around the world. There have been notable developments since our book was first published in 2011, which we have incorporated into this second edition. The controversial decision by Yahoo to ban working from home in early 2013 was interpreted by some as a sign of a wider backlash against autonomy for employees. However, we have encountered more and more companies that are keen to adopt new working practices and want to know how. The Yahoo move triggered a useful debate about collaboration in the new world of work and the importance of getting communication right in virtual and dispersed teams.

Drawing on our research and our knowledge of what works, we write about strategies for change in **Chapter 8.** We set out the main principles – we call them the 'TRUST' principles – and the key skills that leaders and managers need to develop for future work.

This book is about a twenty-first century model of work and management that starts from the principle that people are involved in the process. It recognizes that employees have lives outside the workplace and allows for this in the creation and design of jobs. It is empowerment in practice.

The ultimate empowerment is self-employment. This gives an individual the freedom and the responsibility to get work done however they choose. So this is a good place to start when designing jobs for the future. Can the work be given to an individual who is totally self-managed, who charges for his or her output and who is responsible for his or her time? There may be good reasons to keep the work in-house and give it to employees. If so, can it nonetheless be done by people who manage their own time?

If your organization starts from the basis that work is done in the office between fixed daytime hours, then you still have something close to a traditional work arrangement. If you believe that work – or at least parts of people's 'jobs' – can be done anywhere at any time, then you are moving toward future work.

In **Chapter 9**, we guide organizations on how to put this approach into practice. Leadership from the top is crucial, so it is important for senior management to understand and commit to the business case for change in their organization.

Managing by results, rather than micromanaging the hours people work, is another key step for organizations to take. Anand Pillai, senior vice president at HCL Technologies, the Indian IT services company that advocates putting employees first, says that it is an insult to their intelligence to recruit and train the best people and then tell them what to do. 'They have the knowledge, they have the resources, we

just have to empower, engage and enable them to use it. That's the beauty of an intrapreneurial organization – people taking responsibility for doing the things we have entrusted them to do.'[29]

By agreeing what needs to be achieved, managers can set their employees free from the constraints of 'presenteeism' – the belief that they must be present in the workplace, often for long hours, regardless of whether there is work to do – and allow them to work more productively.

Trusting people to act as adults, and enabling them to decide the best way to do their job, including the 'where' and 'when', is the secret of success. Organizations that have discovered this are now reaping the rewards. Those that have not are in danger of being overtaken by events.

For individual managers, the experience of implementing future work will depend heavily on the organizational culture, as our research shows. **Chapter 10** provides advice and practical examples on how managers, teams and individuals can make the changes work. Using the fact that people are more productive when they have control over their own work patterns, for example, the team can discuss how to achieve their business goals as well as healthier, more balanced lives.

If you work in an environment where experimentation is encouraged and managers are able to try new ideas, it will be a positive experience. If complying with the status quo and maintaining corporate norms is the route to success, it will be an uphill battle. This should not stop you from trying, since by doing so you will be helping your business to adapt and thrive.

In the final **Chapter 11**, we gaze over the horizon at how jobs, careers, workplaces and hierarchies are likely to evolve. Change is happening fast, faster than any other major changes in the history of work, and technology-enabled future work will not wait for those who fail to seize the opportunity now.

CHAPTER 2

How work has evolved

In a few hundred years, when the history of our time will be written from a long-term perspective, it is likely that the most important event historians will see is not technology, not the Internet, not e-commerce. It is an unprecedented change in the human condition. For the first time – literally – substantial and rapidly growing numbers of people have choices. For the first time, they will have to manage themselves. And society is totally unprepared for it.

Peter Drucker, 2000[1]

A historical shift

With his usual prescience, Peter Drucker, the father of modern management, foresaw the really important trend underlying the information age. At the turn of the twenty-first century, he recognized a historical shift in management and the place of work in society. He saw that people were faced with career choices unavailable to previous generations, and women in particular had opportunities that never existed before.

Thanks to technology, we can now work in ways unimaginable 30 years ago. Social attitudes to work and life are shifting fast. Economic pressures are forcing employers to review the productivity and effectiveness of their human resources. The world of work is ripe for radical reform.

Yet, as Drucker said, we are unprepared for this shift toward self-management, which is a central element of future work. Over a decade after his prediction, much of the mainstream world of work still relies on Industrial Age working practices, and management practices reflect this. There are hierarchies, career paths and compensation plans to meet corporate targets. The underlying logic is clear: management knows best. Direction is set from the top and managers transmit the orders down the line. Employees are a resource to be used by the business to achieve its aims, typically to maximize the bottom line. Companies refer to people as 'human resources', but in practice struggle to find ways to account for them as assets rather than liabilities.

The last time work underwent a major transformation was the move from a world governed by the seasons and daylight to one ruled by the factory whistle and clock. In the middle of the nineteenth century, 90 percent of white men in the US worked for themselves as farmers, merchants or craftsmen. The biggest company in Britain in 1850 had only 300 employees.

The next 50 years saw the rise of the first of the massive corporations that served us well during the twentieth century. Leaders perfected hierarchical, command-and-control management processes based on the examples set by the Army and the Church. Businesses improved efficiency by gaining economies of scale, standardizing work processes and introducing the production line. Work had moved from being an activity using an individual's skill, producing an output of value, to a job performing a narrow set of tasks in exchange for a salary.

Henry Ford's legacy

The model of work that developed over the past century reflects the thinking of Henry Ford. Whether people are employed in a factory, office, hospital or school, they are part of a production process. If the same product can be obtained with fewer people or lower pay, unit costs are reduced and profits improved. Companies have worked hard at reducing the cost of labor and increasing output. They standardized jobs to make them easily repeated, reduced the variety of tasks to increase the reliability of output and studied activities to the finest detail to eliminate waste and improve efficiency.

This worked for a while. The production line was the driver of industrialized economies, and people were prepared to carry out routine work for low pay. Large corporations thrived and nations prospered, as long as economies of scale gave some competitive advantage. But 'Fordism' produced boring work, reduced to the simplest tasks, with the minimum possible discretion exercised by the worker. This bred militant unions who defended powerless employees against exploitation and even led to deliberate sabotage just to relieve the boredom.

'If there was a single question that obsessed twentieth century managers, from Frederick Taylor to Jack Welch, it was this: How do we get more out of our people?' writes Gary Hamel in *The Future of Management*.[2] 'At one level, this question is innocuous – who can object to the goal of raising human productivity? Yet it's also loaded with Industrial Age thinking: How do we (meaning "management") get more (meaning units of production per hour) out of our people (meaning the individuals who are obliged to follow our orders)? Ironically, the management model encapsulated in this question virtually guarantees that a company will never get the best out of its people. Vassals and conscripts may work hard, but they don't work willingly.'

In the age of what Hamel describes as the creative economy, knowledge work drives advanced nations. It is no longer necessary to gather people together in large organizations every day to ensure the smooth running of the wheels of commerce or the functions of government. Yet this is what still happens, because current management methods are based on an increasingly outdated model of work.

Technology is not a panacea

The last 20 years have seen an explosion in the technologies available to support new ways of working. It is easy to forget how fast and dramatic these changes have been. The personal computer, invented in the 1980s, had limited use until the 1990s, when the advent of the Internet and the World Wide Web opened up the possibility of genuine personal computing. Yet today the PC has already become rather 'last-century' as it cedes territory to the touchscreen tablet and smartphone.

The first generation of cellular mobile phones was launched in the 1980s, but it was not until the 1990s, when digital networks arrived, that usage really took off. Then, in 2002, with the first 3G networks, it became practical to use cell phones for surfing the Internet and sending emails. Now we are into the era of 4G, and the technology continues to race ahead of our ability to change working habits. So we should not be too surprised that innovative working practices enabled by these technologies are still in their infancy, with a long way to go to reach their full potential.

People have been able to work at home using dial-up technologies to exchange data since the 1970s, but it was not until the turn of the twenty-first century that broadband communications arrived. In the 1980s, there were a few teleworking pioneers, mainly in the rapidly expanding IT industry, who were experimenting with alternative work styles. Computer programmers were able to work from home and send their coding across a standard phone line via a modem. Some saw this at the time as a forerunner of the way most people would work in the future.

What has happened in reality has not lived up to the boldest predictions of the 1980s. The growth of full-time home-based work has been relatively slow, but the expansion of part-time teleworking has been rapid in some countries. This shows that home working is a very useful part of a mixed pattern of work but not a permanent solution for most people. According to the UK's Office for National Statistics, the total number of teleworkers in the UK increased by 46 percent in the decade leading up to 2012.[3] In the US, telecommuting by employees several days per week increased 73 percent from 2005 to 2011, though the rate of growth slowed during the recession.[4]

What has clearly changed from the early days of telework is the availability of technology to support a wide variety of jobs. Anyone involved in 'knowledge work' can now take advantage of affordable laptops, smartphones and broadband connections. We have moved rapidly from the pioneering days of computing, when the only users of IT were the technical specialists, to the age of universally available tools. People have also adopted the Web as a resource in their personal lives, for everything from finding information and shopping to organizing street protests. Surfing is done on the Internet as well as the waves, browsing on websites as well as in bookshops and chatting through social media as well as face-to-face in real cafés. Leading employers are now embracing social media and using applications such as Yammer to help their employees share ideas.

Yet we are far from mastering technology, either in terms of workplace innovation or in the way our work is integrated with our personal lives. For one thing, communications technology in the home has advanced much more rapidly than in most workplaces. Look at the technology being used by the under 25s: at home they will be chatting to friends on Facebook, having live conversations with them via internet applications such as Skype, sending text messages, watching the latest uploads to YouTube and keeping an eye on the people they follow on Twitter. But when they go to work, they may well find that their employer is one of those where communications have barely advanced beyond email, that social media are discouraged or even blocked and that discussion forums are confined to the water cooler. There is a growing disparity between these organizations and those that are leaping ahead and adopting social media for the benefit of the business.

The variety and choice of technology that has revolutionized our consumption patterns is now forcing the pace of change at work. An increasing number of employers are adopting a 'Bring Your Own Device' (BYOD) policy, realizing that individuals have their own preferences in the way they access data, collect emails or 'chat' to colleagues. Combining a BYOD policy with a 'cloud' based IT strategy gives employees freedom to work with technology in their own way and not be forced into a standardized solution based on outdated kit.

These developments are further blurring the boundaries between work and personal territory, a trend welcomed by some but feared by others. Our ability to connect people at times and places hitherto out of reach has meant that additional working time has simply been layered onto what was already required. Customers can contact their suppliers at any time to demand a better service, just as employees can be tracked down at weekends or on vacation to deal with 'urgent' business.

When email capability arrived on handheld devices, conventional working hours started to stretch. In 2006, the new term 'Crackberry', depicting the addictive qualities of BlackBerrys and other handheld devices, was nominated word of the year by the staff at Webster's New World College Dictionary.[5] The BYOD trend means employees have constant access to both work and personal communications at the same time, unless they choose to keep them separate on two different devices.

The technology itself is neither the hero nor the villain in these developments. It can liberate individuals and give them more balanced lives – or it can extend work into times and places that people would prefer to reserve for leisure. It can be a catalyst for empowering new work styles, but it can also be an instrument for the employer to monitor and control employees more closely. It improves communications, speeds up business processes and increases efficiency – but it can also turn jobs into boring, repetitive tasks. Call centers, for example, can resemble nineteenth-century factories where employees mindlessly follow instructions.

So it is not the technology that changes our working lives for better or worse, it is the way people choose to use it. A lot depends on whose finger, physically or metaphorically, controls the 'off' switch.

Changing expectations

The rapid development of technology has run in parallel with major shifts in society. Attitudes to work and careers have evolved dramatically over the past 30 years. For many employees, especially in higher-paid jobs in developed countries, life no longer revolves around work. Employers cannot just assume that people will accept standard conditions of employment and take working patterns as a given. If the job can be done without sticking to a rigid pattern of time and place, employees will expect flexibility to be on offer. If it is not, they are likely to look elsewhere.

A survey by PricewaterhouseCoopers found that the top benefit sought by professionals across the UK was flexible working, with almost half putting it at the top of their list.[6] Interestingly, it was given fairly equal priority by men and women.

Other countries are seeing similar trends. A survey of hourly paid workers in the US found that flexibility was an important factor in deciding to take the job for 83 percent of workers who had joined in the last two years. The survey by Corporate Voices for Working Families[7] also found that 60 percent of the workers said it was likely they would leave the company if they did not have the opportunity to work flexibly.

Today's workforce inevitably has different expectations of their employers than previous generations had. They know they are unlikely to get job security and a safe pension in exchange for lifelong service. If they are fortunate to have a choice of jobs, they are looking for fair rewards, flexibility and engaging work.

Notions of what constitutes a successful career are changing too. The PricewaterhouseCoopers survey revealed disillusionment with the traditional career working for a major employer. Exactly half the respondents said they would prefer to work for themselves. Almost a third wanted to be employed by a company whose values matched theirs, while the remaining 20 percent said they wanted to work for an elite company that employed only the best.

A survey of over 3200 Generation Y finance professionals in 122 countries found that lifestyle factors outweighed contractual ones in their choice of job. 'Perhaps the preference towards lifestyle factors is in part due to a changing definition of success,' says the report by ACCA, the professional accountants' body, and Mercer, the consulting firm. 'Our survey suggests the historical view of career success being defined by more money probably rings less true for this generation. This is a generation that seeks a much broader range of benefits from working life, and actively seeks out organizations that can deliver this.'[8]

The economic downturn that hit Western countries hard in the wake of the global financial crisis has shrunk the choices available to many people, particularly in the younger generation that has been saddled with high unemployment levels. For them, getting paid work of any kind has become the overriding challenge.

Sarah Jackson, chief executive of the UK charity Working Families, which campaigns for greater work flexibility, describes the gap between progressive and laggard employers and managers. On the one hand, 'the understanding has developed enormously that it's not about compliance but about how you build a better business, where the needs of the employee and the business are aligned. There is also increasing recognition that it's about the quality of leadership, that managers have to be trained, and that you need to keep communicating about it.'

On the other hand, some managers and organizations are trampling over employee rights, she says. 'If you're at the bottom of the food chain, the state of the economy is having a very nasty effect on your ability to work flexibly. People phoning our helpline are having a miserable time. People are suffering from unilateral changes to their contracts and there is increasingly blatant maternity discrimination. People are being demoted, expected to take pay cuts, or losing their jobs.' She notes double standards too: many callers to the helpline work for organizations with supposedly great policies on flexibility.

What matters is choice and good management. Recession brought a growth in insecure 'zero hours contracts', which do not guarantee any work and only pay for actual hours worked. If they are managed well, and people have a choice, they can be a convenient form of flexibility for both individuals and employers. If they are forced on employees against their will, they amount to exploitation.

The role of gender

A generation or two ago, the world was arguably a much simpler place. Everyone knew where she or he belonged. Men went to work, but rarely did women pursue careers outside the home. Despite the vital role played by women when they took many men's jobs during two world wars, they were largely back at the hearth in the 1950s. Then came the Pill, the women's liberation movement, a raft of equal rights legislation and women's journey toward parity with men in the workplace.

It has been a long road. In the UK, the 1919 Sex Disqualification (Removal) Act allowed women to become lawyers, vets and civil servants. Even then, only single women could get a job in the British Civil Service and it was only after the Second World War that they were allowed to stay once they married. It was not until 1961 that Barclays Bank removed its marriage bar and it was still perfectly legal in the UK until 1975 to dismiss an employee for becoming pregnant.

Women in the US gained voting rights through the Nineteenth Amendment to the Constitution in 1920, but only in the 1960s were several federal laws passed improving the economic status of women. The Equal Pay Act of 1963 required equal wages for men and women doing equal work. The Civil Rights Act of 1964 prohibited discrimination against women by any company with 25 or more employees.

Within the lifetime of a senior manager, we have moved from a world where women were legally and socially treated as second-class citizens to one where they have equal employment rights and nearly equal representation in the labor force of many advanced economies. In countries with generous maternity benefits compared with paternity provisions, it can be argued that women have overtaken men in certain entitlements. Sex discrimination in employment is illegal in most Western countries and many have equal pay legislation to counteract the legacy of low-paid 'women's work', although this has failed to eradicate the pay gap.

The introduction of maternity leave and the right to return to work in the same or equivalent job is almost universal,[9] even though some employers still blatantly flout the law.

The US is one of the few countries in the world that does not mandate paid maternity leave, a fact that led the campaigning organization Human Rights Watch to publish a report in 2011 accusing it of 'failing its families'. The US Family and Medical Leave Act of 1993 provides for parental leave for serious medical conditions, but this is unpaid and does not cover all workers. Many countries provide paid paternity leave, but the US does not. Yet countries that have paid family leave programs show productivity gains, reduced turnover costs and health care savings, according to Janet Walsh, deputy women's rights director at Human Rights Watch.[10]

The 1980s and 1990s saw a series of legislative changes in most Western countries that made employment fairer and increasingly 'family friendly'. These reflected changing attitudes in society toward work. No longer was it a male preserve. Women could have a career and a family. They could take their maternity leave and still return to their former position in the hierarchy. It seemed we were moving into a truly gender-neutral world of work.

Sadly, reality has not kept up with the ideals. Ironically, the very legislation that was designed to ensure fairer treatment for women reinforced some of the old stereotypes. Women had to be given 'special' treatment so they could take time off work to have children. Men might have the right to a few weeks of paternity leave if they were lucky, but maternity provisions were longer and more generous. This has strengthened the notion that it is primarily women who have children, not women *and* men together. It has reinforced some employers' beliefs that it is a disadvantage to hire women of childbearing age.

Women are still underrepresented in many professions and in the ranks of senior management, despite over 40 years of equality legislation. It will be an uphill battle to achieve real equality as long as employment legislation and HR policies imply that mothers need special treatment and fathers do not. If societies stop assuming that 'men have careers and women have children', we will achieve faster progress.

Scandinavian countries such as Norway and Sweden are leading the way, with generous parental leave for both mothers and fathers. Introducing parental rights that are shared completely would go a long way to breaking through the remaining prejudices. It would encourage fathers to take an active role in childcare and adjust their work patterns to accommodate family responsibilities. Employers would in future have to assume that any employee, male or female, might need to take a substantial amount of time for parental responsibilities at some point in their (increasingly long) working lives.

It does not help that maternity leave and flexible working legislation are often classified together as 'family friendly'. Employees in the UK, for example, were given a legal right to request flexible working from their employers in 2003. Over the following decade, this right was confined to parents and caregivers, who were identified as needing special treatment and requiring the weight of the law to persuade employers to listen to their requests. In a welcome move, the government proposed in 2012 to extend the right to request flexibility to all employees, from 2014.

We do not quarrel with the need for legislation to protect vulnerable employees from unscrupulous employers and to provide a baseline from which good employers can build far better practices. However, legislation that frames flexibility as an employee accommodation requiring a change to 'normal' working patterns reinforces the prejudice that regulation obliges employers to act against their best interests and interferes with managers' ability to get their job done. As we shall see in Chapter 3, this is the opposite of what actually happens with new ways of working. There is such strong evidence that changing the way we work can benefit business, that governments should be selling this as a positive measure to boost economic competitiveness, as well as environmental sustainability and 'work-life balance'. That should be a more powerful way to persuade laggard employers to change their tune.

We also need an urgent reframing of careers and career development, because women's career paths tend to be very different from the traditional male model that still prevails in many organizations. Companies cannot afford to continue losing so much female talent. According to UNESCO, more than half of the students now in universities worldwide are women.[11] In North America and Europe, a third more women than men are on campus. Latin America, the Caribbean and Central Asia also show high rates of female enrolments. In a number of countries, at least two females graduate for every male. These young women are going into employment and becoming well established in their careers before even thinking of starting a family. By then they may be earning more than their male partners, as is now the case in junior management positions in the UK, according to the Chartered Management Institute.[12]

Family patterns are shifting. Already in the UK, nearly one in three working mothers with dependent children are the primary breadwinners for their family,[13] while mothers are the sole or primary providers in a record 40 percent of US households with children under 18.[14]

There has been a big shift in men's attitudes to family and work, in parallel with women's increasing participation in the workforce. In the US, employed fathers in dual-income couples are now significantly more likely to experience 'work-life conflict' than mothers, according to a report by the Families and Work Institute. Significantly, it found that the probability of this conflict increased with high job pressure, but decreased when men had greater autonomy in their jobs and greater support from their supervisors.[15]

Another study by the Pew Research Center found that about half of all working parents in the US with children under age 18 feel it is hard to balance their job and family responsibilities, and there is no significant gap between mothers and fathers. However, fathers are much more likely than mothers to feel they are not spending enough time with their children. Some 46 percent of fathers say this, compared with 23 percent of mothers.[16]

Far more is known today about the importance for children's well-being of bonding with their fathers as well as their mothers. Sixty percent of parents in the UK think fathers should spend more time with their children, a survey by the Equality and Human Rights Commission found.

Asked if they spent enough time with their own children, 44 percent of men and 23 percent of women said they did not. Half of fathers, and nearly a third of mothers, thought they spent too much time at work.[17]

'The way we "do" family has changed – not only because mothers are more likely to go out to work but also because today both mothers *and* fathers want close relationships with children as they are growing up,' says Dr Caroline Gatrell of Lancaster University Management School, who has researched the subject of fathers, work and family life for the charity Working Families.

Work and life across generations

Awareness of the tension between work and the rest of life has grown in recent decades in parallel with globalization, women's rising participation in the workplace and legislative developments. 'Work-life balance' was not in the management vocabulary until the 1990s. How people chose to spend their time outside work was not the business of their managers. Employees were used to fitting their personal lives round the fixed commitments of their jobs. For good employers, that has all changed. With the 24/7 demands of business, they know they have to make allowances for employees' lives outside work if they want to attract and retain the best people.

We live in a shrinking world. Telephone enquiries from customers in the US and Europe are likely to be answered by call center staff in India or the Philippines. We take it for granted that we can shop for almost anything at almost any time. The Internet has delivered services to the home and revolutionized the retail sector and personal banking. Totally new ways of buying and selling products have emerged through channels such as eBay. So it is hardly surprising that young people in particular expect the way we work to be different too. If I can shop any time I choose, why can't I work any time I choose?

Inevitably some views about work differ across the generations. The contrast in life experience between baby boomers and Generation Y is obvious. People born in the decade after the Second World War went through school, university and their first jobs without ever seeing a computer, except behind the doors of an air-conditioned room. Yet people born since 1990 have never known a world without computers, cell phones and the Internet at their fingertips.

However, these 'bookend generations', as economist Sylvia Ann Hewlett and colleagues describe them, share some common views about work, apparently in contrast to Generation X sandwiched between them. Their research found that both generations are seeking a 'remixed' set of rewards. They prize meaning and choice over money. 'They are shedding Industrial Age conceptions of work and demanding control over when, where and how work gets done.'[18]

The baby boomers include many people who no longer want to fully retire. It may be that they feel they are just not ready for retirement at 60 or 65. However, it is increasingly likely that the pension fund they hoped would keep them going through their old age is grossly inadequate. We are emerging from the 'golden era' of pensions that guaranteed a percentage of final pay. Individuals increasingly have to take responsibility for saving for their retirement. Employers and pension providers are slowly waking up to the fact that the traditional 'cliff edge' between full-time work and full-time retirement no longer makes sense. Why should someone who still has a wealth of experience to give to their employer not continue to do so, at least on a flexible basis?

Tapping into mature talent

B&Q, the UK's largest home improvement retailer, was an early mover in recognizing the value of older workers. Faced with the challenge in the late 1980s to recruit and retain talent during a period of rapid expansion, it recognized that an ageing population had a commercial fit with its business. Older workers were more likely to be home-owners with experience in DIY and likely to be able to work non-traditional hours. In 1989, it made a bold statement by opening a store staffed by over-50s and was immediately surprised by the results.

The retailer had a phenomenal response for vacancies and found that assumptions about older workers needing more training or struggling with the computer systems were unfounded. An independent study by Warwick University showed that, compared with other stores, profits were 18 percent higher, staff turnover was six times lower and absenteeism was reduced by 39 percent. Now 28 percent of B&Q's workforce is over 50 and its oldest employee recently celebrated his 90th birthday.[19]

Life expectancy continues to grow rapidly, even without any major anti-aging medical breakthrough. In the UK, there are now more people of pensionable age than under-16s, and the government estimates that 35 percent of the babies born in 2012 will live to be 100.[20] As economist George Magnus points out in *The Age of Aging*, this is a phenomenon already felt acutely in Japan, Germany and Italy and soon to affect most Western countries as well as the economic powerhouse of China. He points out that the median age of the world's population (where half the population are older and half are younger) will rise from 28 now to 38 by 2050. It will be 47 in Europe by that time, 45 in China and about 41 in North America and Asia.[21]

How can we provide for an aging population out of the taxation revenues from a shrinking younger generation? One answer is an increase in retirement ages, which is already happening. If people are fit to work into their 70s, then why should they expect to stop when they are 60 and live for 20–30 years on a combination of their savings and government support? This has been difficult to achieve in a world where work consists of fulltime jobs, but new work styles will make the idea of gradual retirement both possible and normal.

In Australia, employers are being urged to 'get flexible' in order to attract and retain older workers, particularly older women who are severely underrepresented in the workforce. This is often because they cannot combine inflexible working hours with caring responsibilities, according to recent research.[22] 'We are ignoring the huge pool of talent and experience represented by older women,' says Susan Ryan, age discrimination commissioner. 'This is a terrible waste of human capital, undermines the national imperative of growing the economy and results in significant loss to businesses. It also impacts the financial, emotional and physical wellbeing of the many women who are consigned to unwanted early retirement.'

Future work for all sectors

As we show throughout this book, leading employers have started to realize that modernizing their work practices is essential to running an effective organization. The **high-tech** sector started the trend, with some professional services firms following on, but we have found examples of future work leaders in many different industries and countries, and in both private and public sectors.

One global company in the consumer goods sector that has embarked on the shift to future work is **Unilever**. It launched an 'Agile Working' strategy, driven by business objectives. 'Agile Working is a simple but powerful concept,' says CEO Paul Polman. 'It affords everyone at Unilever the opportunity to work with maximum flexibility and minimal constraints, enabled by technology and specially designed office facilities.' This increases productivity, reduces the need for travel and its associated costs and helps people to achieve greater balance in their lives, he adds.

The company has made the connection between business success and new ways of working. It has recognized that this is a way to increase the diversity of its organization at every level, drive productivity and engage its people. It understands that this involves a change in culture. We look at how Unilever is doing this at its futuristic offices in Hamburg in Chapter 6 and we analyze the lessons of the agile working strategy in Chapter 8.

Some sectors are more reluctant than others to embrace change. **Manufacturing** companies, for example, may think that new work styles do not apply to them. But as pioneers emerge in these industries, others will follow suit.

In the **finance** sector, there is still an addiction to extremely long working hours. Law firms and investment banks, the pillars of the world's major financial centers, are among the most conservative sectors when it comes to new ways of working. Post-financial crisis, anecdotal evidence suggests that the opportunities for flexibility in many firms have become even more limited, with teams stretched due to cutbacks and employees feeling under pressure to put in face-time to preserve their jobs.

'Extreme hours are less about getting things done and more about showing commitment,' according to Professor Andre Spicer of Cass Business School in the City of London. 'Large firms need to ask themselves just how productive and healthy long hours actually are. If they hope to be sustainable and attractive to employees, they need to tackle the extreme hours culture.'[23]

Chris Hobbs, partner and deputy head of compliance at law firm Norton Rose Fulbright, is unusual in working four days a week, one of them at home, in such a senior position, and he is held up as a role model of how things can be done differently. 'Law firms tend to lag behind other parts of business and industry,' he told a Working Families conference.[24] 'We're pretty traditional and conservative in approach. There's a culture, particularly in big City firms, of working all hours, being chained to the desk 24/7 serving clients.'

If this 24/7 office culture remains the rule in the financial heartlands, there are signs of change, albeit tentative compared with organizations leading the way in some other sectors.

External pressure, including from clients, is forcing the pace in the legal profession, says Denise Jagger of law firm Eversheds, who has worked on a three-day week basis as a partner since joining in 2004.

'The hourly rate remains the basis of fee charging in the overwhelming majority of law firms, which results in a focus on input rather than output,' she says. 'Nonetheless, clients are adopting more enlightened and flexible working practices and therefore many expect their law firms to do the same, not least as they know that if they don't they will not attract some of the best talent.

'They are increasingly asking questions in pitches relating to diversity, and they expect their firms to be able to field diverse teams. Unless firms adopt more flexible working practices they will score poorly on diversity statistics, particularly relating to gender, which will ultimately affect clients' purchasing decisions.'

She says that women and the younger generation of lawyers do not want to work to the exclusion of everything else. 'To continue to attract the best and to retain and motivate a skilled team of lawyers, law firms are at last waking up to the need for flexible working.'

Despite this awakening, many firms still think flexibility is fine for some disciplines but not for others, she says. 'Corporate finance still suffers from an image of long hours and inflexible styles partly, in my view, because people confuse flexibility with part time, which it is decidedly not. As a former corporate finance practitioner, I recognize the need during a particularly large or complex transaction for a senior lawyer to be available. But this doesn't always mean in person. And, after a protracted spell of long hours on a deal, work could be allocated to ensure a lighter period of work or a sizeable break.'[25]

A Danish solution to long hours in law firms

An example of how a new generation can change things is **Sirius**, an all-purpose Danish corporate law firm launched by eight young lawyers who left their firms to try to replace the conventional 60–70-hour weeks with a culture of fewer hours and greater flexibility for all staff.

'There's been an enormous shift in the approach of young lawyers,' says Birgit Gylling Andersen, an employment lawyer and founding partner. 'Now it's both male and female lawyers who discuss over lunch how to handle the kids, and both who take days off or leave to look after the children.

'If you go through our office at 6 p.m., it's very rare that there's more than one or two people left, and they are normally partners. If you do have to work long hours on a case, we say: "Take some time off". It's very important for our employees that they know it's acceptable to have personal wishes.'

Clients understand, she says. 'They also have their personal needs. And we attract clients that also wish to work in a different way.'[26]

There are other examples of how the legal sector is changing below, and in Chapter 5.

The events in recent years affecting the financial markets have 'changed the way that people in this sector are recognized', says Michelle Mendelsson, co-head of diversity and inclusion for Europe, Middle East and Africa (EMEA) at **Credit Suisse**, the global investment bank. 'We have to look for other ways to motivate and retain employees and enabling them to work in a way that suits them can help to raise levels of engagement.'

The EMEA diversity and inclusion team used the 2012 London Olympics, when the authorities encouraged financial firms to let employees work from home to cut down on traffic congestion, as a way to demonstrate that 'agile' working was possible. 'The feedback from the business areas was generally very positive. That was the tipping point from a cultural perspective for both managers and employees who then recognized that this can be done.'

With support from the CEO of Credit Suisse EMEA, a plan of action to embed agile working across the bank was agreed by the EMEA diversity council, which comprises senior managers.

Implementation was set for autumn 2013, with training for managers and employees. 'We have completely moved away from presenteeism and agile working is just another way for employees to find the most appropriate way of working for them and to be supported to do that,' says Mendelsson.[27]

New types of work contract

The last decade of the twentieth century brought a rapid growth in the flexibility of employment contracts. Part-time work, staggered hours, condensed working weeks and 'flexi-time' spread. Remote and home-based working increased with the introduction of mobile technologies. But these were mainly just variations of the permanent, full-time job.

The following decade saw an expansion of the 'contingent workforce'. Organizations kept hold of a core of essential talent but contracted out peripheral activities to save costs and increase flexibility. This paid off during the recession when many businesses shed temporary staff but managed to hold on to their permanent staff ready for the upturn. The trend toward a more flexible model of work has raised the question of whether organizations need to be burdened with liabilities for 'permanent' employees at all. Even in the public sector a permanent job offer is no longer necessarily a lifetime commitment.

The Internet has given birth to a new type of organization that can tap into the talent of individuals without taking over their lives. The network business, the virtual corporation and the e-enterprise are versions of this emerging entity. They contract with individuals to supply their services, but not through a conventional employment contract. They pull together collections of individual contributors to achieve a common aim. These individuals are 'free agents' who can choose a lifestyle without the ties and constraints of conventional employment. The world they inhabit has much in common with the pre-industrial era. They are more likely to be working from home, some perhaps in a rural setting, and building social relationships in their home community rather than in the office. As work evolves into a new era, future generations may reflect back on the 200 years of Industrial Age working practices and see them as a passing phase in our social history.

Here are three examples of these new types of business:

Six years ago Simon Harper was a partner in a major London law firm and recognized that the profession was ready for change. Lawyers had been working the same way for years serving the business community and he felt there was a gap to be filled with an alternative structure.

'I had a hunch that more and more lawyers were open to working in a different way,' says Harper. 'They were rejecting the options that were currently out there, whether that was the construct of a traditional law firm and moving into partnership or the hierarchy of an in-house team. For a variety of reasons they were open to doing things differently. Either they were in a job and were unhappy with the way it was working for them or they'd left the law behind, not because they hated law but they just couldn't find a way to practice it.'[28]

So he set up **Lawyers on Demand** (LOD) as an alternative legal services provider. They now have over 100 self-employed lawyers who have autonomy to work the way they choose, and LOD acts as the link with the client. 'It's not an agency, it's a different way of working,' explains Harper. 'For us it's about being a hub between the lawyers and the clients. Our relationship with the lawyers is a business one. Half our energy goes into working with them and half goes into working with the clients.'

Initially, they expected the interest to come from female lawyers with young children, but they quickly found they appealed to a much wider group. Harper's view is that having children is just one catalyst that makes people stop and think about how they are running their lives.

'People used to need to have an excuse to work differently, now more and more people just want to work in a different way. I see it as a move towards the individual economy rather than the employed economy. People are doing their own thing and LOD assists them in doing that.' LOD is not alone. Others, such as LawEvo in the US, are rejecting the traditional law firm business model and setting up as lower cost 'virtual' alternatives.

Based in Santa Clara, California, **LiveOps** uses a dispersed workforce of around 20,000 independent agents, mostly working from their homes across the US, to provide virtual call center services on demand for businesses. The agents include a high proportion of women, as well as retired people and students, and many have caring responsibilities.

Pay depends on their performance and the volume of service they provide. Some clients pay a simple rate, generally 25 cents per minute of talk time, some pay a base rate in addition to a bonus for commission and some pay entirely on commission.[29] Such 'e-lance' businesses are open to criticism over their pay rates and lack of employment rights, benefits and job security. However, LiveOps says that 'an average agent can make well over minimum wage' and points to the flexibility that freelance operators have.

Agents can choose where they work, although calls can only be routed to their regular business line, not re-routed if they are traveling. They can choose when to provide their services, which can be in blocks of just 30 minutes, and it is up to them whether to develop their skills or not.

The company says this work model does not replace existing models but creates opportunities for people who do not want to, or cannot, work in the traditional way. With a large dispersed and independent workforce, it seeks ways of building 'a self-sustaining community'. It provides the contract workforce with access to resources to interact as a community, motivate each other and self-regulate their own businesses' performance.[30]

At what might be considered the other end of the work scale, **Eden McCallum** is a UK-based management consulting firm that draws on a pool of more than 400 independent consultants and matches them to clients' projects, but does not employ them directly. Launched in 2000, it has attracted highly qualified professionals who want more control over their working lives while maintaining their earning power. About half the consultants previously worked for big firms such as McKinsey, Bain and Boston Consulting Group.

As founding director Liann Eden explains, strong interpersonal skills are as important as ever in managing the consultants, even though this network model is based on looser affiliations than the traditional employer–employee contract. They still need feedback, reinforcement and a sense of belonging. 'Being very clear in our communications is very important in this network model,' she says. 'We've got very good at setting clear expectations about the frequency and nature of the work up front. They know exactly where they stand. They know our standards.'

To ensure effective communication, the firm uses a contact management system that records every contact with each consultant, every project they have done and every client they have worked with. It also captures all the information about and feedback on the consultant from interviews, references and project debriefs. This means that the in-house team can interact knowledgably with the consultants, almost as if they were staff.

The firm also runs regular information and training events for the consultants to meet, exchange experiences and stay on top of developments.

'That's where they get a sense of identity,' says Charlotte Cameron, the partner leading the firm's consultant-focused activities. 'People say it's great to feel part of something. We also get consultants together to tell them what we're planning for the future of the firm. It's about sharing information with them so that we as an organization are not a black hole.'

Trust is a big part of the relationship, as the firm's founders discovered. After they launched in 2000, they were worried that some of their growing pool of consultants might bypass them and seek work directly from their client companies or vice versa. They required them to sign a contract saying they could approach the clients only through Eden McCallum. 'Two to three years in, we realized that the consultants and clients aren't interested in one-off transactions,' says Eden. 'The consultants want to work with us as a conduit to lots of interesting clients and projects. Clients want to work with us to solve many different issues, not just what one consultant can do. Over the past 13 years we've done over 1200 projects and I can count on one hand the number of times someone tried to go behind our backs.'[31]

In summary

We are on the cusp of the next big transformation in the model of work. Today technology allows us to work very differently than we did even a decade ago, and the new generation joining the workforce is not the only one demanding a new deal. Demographic and social trends, particularly the changing role of women, all point to the need for a fresh approach to work. We are poised for a revolution in how work is done. Fabio Rosati, chief executive of Elance, an online employment platform, predicts, for example, that at least 10 per cent of all work will be online and piecemeal, or 'fractional', by 2020. 'Currently it's less than 1 per cent,' he said in a *Financial Times* article. 'It's a nascent industry and we're about a decade behind e-commerce.'[32]

In Chapter 3 we show how future work is emerging as a product of the many changes described above, built on a model of individual autonomy and a culture of trust and responsibility.

CHAPTER 3

Turning convention on its head

Organizations that remove the artificial boundaries around how, where and when work gets done are those that are winning in today's marketplace. They are more flexible, more efficient, and better able to respond to rapid change.

Fiona Laird, co-lead, 'Agile Working' program, Unilever

Which of the following two companies sounds more like yours?

FlexCo offers its employees a range of 'flexible work arrangements'. Reduced hours, flexible start and finish times and compressed weeks (four ten-hour days instead of five eight-hour days) are all available. The HR department encourages individuals to talk about their personal situation so that the management and the individual can find a response that suits both. Employees can have paid time off for personal needs and can take it in one-hour slots, for example to attend a school event or have a longer lunch. Chair massages are available when peak work demands push up the stress levels. 'Our employees tell us how grateful they are that we offer these arrangements,' says the head of HR.

FutureCo has invested in the latest technology so that all employees can access work databases from anywhere, using their own favourite device if they wish. By encouraging remote working, it has retained talented people who have moved to the other side of the world and, in some cases, it has gained new business through them. It has abolished the traditional definition of paid time off. People can take any number of days' break, provided they meet their objectives and customers' requirements. Everyone on the staff, from senior professionals to junior assistants, is able to arrange their work around other priorities such as family care, volunteer work, or training and development. The company says that this kind of flexibility is a business survival tool.

We suspect that, if you are a lucky Westerner, you probably work for an organization like FlexCo. However, we will show in this chapter why FlexCo's approach involves only a small tinkering at the edges, and no fundamental change to the standard work model that we have described as outmoded and unsuited to the twenty-first century. FutureCo, on the other hand, represents the future, because it has made the essential shift from controlling and measuring the time people spend at work to measuring and rewarding people based on how well they perform and what results they produce.

There is a wide spectrum of jobs in the world today and both these examples are at one end. They both attempt to provide an environment in which employees will be motivated to perform. Although their approaches are very different, they are built on the assumption that caring about people is a good business investment.

Sadly, there are still many employers around the world that appear not to care much about their employees' motivation or welfare. They treat people as disposable assets that are simply units of production in a business process, expecting them to clock up excessively long hours, often doing repetitive, mind-numbing work.

From time to time, when things go badly wrong, labor conditions in the factories churning out goods for Western consumers make the headlines and force big brand names to take action. In one of the world's worst industrial disasters, a garment factory in Bangladesh collapsed with the loss of over 1100 lives in April 2013, drawing attention to the dismal treatment of many of the four million, mostly women, workers in that sector. The government closed a further 16 factories soon afterwards and committed to inspect every factory in the country. In response to the disaster, a group of 20 North American retailers, including Wal-Mart and Gap, set up the Alliance for Bangladesh Worker Safety to improve working conditions in their suppliers.[1]

Big consumer electronics brands have also been in the spotlight over labor conditions in plants that manufacture their goods in China. Such was the case in 2010, when a spate of worker suicides put the spotlight on Foxconn, which makes electronic devices in China for big brands including Apple, Dell, Nokia and Sony. Supplier codes of conduct were established, but in 2013 another company Pegatron, also used by Apple, became the focus of attention. The US-based China Labor Watch found 86 violations of labor rights, from the staff recruitment process, to conditions on the factory floor, to the state of workers' dormitories.[2] Apple said it had audited Pegatron sites 15 times in six years and would investigate all the claims thoroughly.

The scourge of the 'long-hours culture'

Compared with such labor issues in emerging markets, the stresses involved in high-powered jobs in Western multinationals might pale into insignificance. But they do have some common features. In both cases, people are expected to sacrifice their personal lives for the good of the company and work in often highly pressurized environments. For some, the high rewards and challenges make this acceptable. But others burn out, or quit for a saner life.

As one executive who left his job with a global technology group told us: 'When the expectation is to be available 24/7 *and* be at the office each day for no productive reason, then insanity occurs.'

His team, who had to support internal customers in other time zones, had been used to working from home because their job involved long hours, primarily late at night. Then the new boss above him decreed that they should also commute into the office during the business day. 'When it became a requirement for employees to sit at the office during business hours for the sake of being there, many felt completely defeated. The "flexible" work environment was not so much a way for employees to work more effectively and with more flexibility, but as a way for the company to extract every extra bit of productivity out of each employee without having to pay for it.'

International business executives who operate in a time zone different from the headquarters country often experience some of the most extreme demands of all. Take the case of Katrin, a highly experienced senior executive based in Europe working for a US multinational, who had to travel two or three weeks in every month between continents as her responsibilities grew. She hardly saw her children. When she was back at base in Europe, she regularly had to take part in teleconferences at 8 p.m. or 9 p.m. to accommodate the US team, thus missing dinner with the family, and then her inbox would be full of 'urgent' emails first thing in the morning. Exhausted and demoralized, she was eventually diagnosed with burnout. She quit for a senior job at another large company that gave her back control over her schedule and her life.[3]

The long-hours culture often goes hand in hand with 'presenteeism', where people feel they have to be in the office regardless of whether they have something productive to do. If being seen to be working is a good thing, then being seen to be working for longer is better. Making sure your car is still in the car park when your boss leaves the office is a sound route to promotion. Hanging an extra coat on the back of the chair to show you are there, even if you have actually popped out for a sandwich, is extreme, but it happens.

It is hardly surprising that the long-hours culture has become ingrained in some sectors and countries such as the US and UK. People are often well rewarded for those extra hours. Some employees will be paid for every minute past their allotted time and, if this is deemed to be at 'antisocial' times, they will be paid a premium. So there is every incentive to slow down work during weekdays to ensure there is some left over for evenings and weekends. This is a sure recipe for low productivity. The salaried employee may not be paid directly for the extra hours, but their 'dedication' will still be noted and the reward will come eventually.

There is now increasing evidence that the hours spent in the office are not being used effectively. A study by Kansas State University showed that when the average worker is on the internet they spend 60–80 percent of their time 'cyberloafing' on non-work activities.[4] As long as employers choose to reward effort and not results, long hours will persist.

The trouble with flexible work arrangements

Flexible working has been around for 40 years in various forms. It started with 'flexi-time', which gave people the opportunity to vary their hours within strictly limited boundaries. Employers defined the 'core hours' and then allowed some choice outside those times, such as a two-hour window for people to vary their arrival and departure times.

These schemes allowed employees to fit in other commitments at the beginning and end of the working day but were problematic for managers because people could change their flexi hours on a day-to-day basis and 'bank' hours to take as extra days' holiday. Meetings had to be restricted to core hours or negotiated with employees weeks in advance.

While flexi-time schemes are still popular in some countries, they can also undermine productivity because people are more likely to stop work when their paid time is finished if they are recording their hours and 'clocking in and out'. So where employers have adopted innovative approaches to work, this form of flexible time is being replaced with something more predictable and less likely to lead to clock-watching.

Another popular version of flexible working is compressed hours. One example of this is the 'nine day fortnight' where each working day is lengthened slightly and, by the end of nine days, the employee has worked the equivalent of ten. This is usually a fixed pattern, so is more predictable than flexi-time, but brings its own difficulties. Friday is by far the most popular day for people to choose as their 'day off', which is not a problem until the demand cannot be met. Then Fridays off have to be rationed.

Today, if an organization employs people on any contract other than the conventional one, whether it is part time, job sharing, term-time work and so on, it is likely to be labelled 'flexible working'.

However, these various flexible hours options simply shift the time that the work is performed. People are still expected to work for a set number of hours per week or month and are paid accordingly. Part-time workers are paid pro rata, and job sharers are paid their share based on the split in time, even though, in practice, they are often more productive than one full-time person. Home workers frequently have to log in to a time-management system to count their hours. Flexible time has been pasted on to conventional fixed work patterns without any fundamental change in the work model, but with a lot more complexity.

Flexing time and place

Many flexible working schemes have been bolted on to conventional working patterns and have ended up lengthening the working day. Employers are happy for their staff to use laptops to work on the move and to have flexible hours as long as they are still available at their desk for the eight-hour day. 'Flexibility' has allowed work to invade personal time and space without giving any concessions in return.

So what is the solution? Turn convention on its head, as FutureCo did, moving away from defining work by time and location. Most 'knowledge work' today can be done completely independently of both time and location, while many other jobs are much more restricted by one or the other, or both. Yet even these jobs can often be fundamentally rethought, drawing on the knowledge of those at the front line, as we will show.

A wide spectrum of working styles can co-exist within a single organization, as demonstrated at **Vodafone UK**'s modern headquarters outside Newbury, west of London. At one end are the mobile teams, such as sales staff, who are out most of the time but in the office for team meetings once a week. Mid-way along are the staff who are based in the office but who can work remotely; when they are there, they pick a free desk, or meet at a table in the canteen, and their hours are not monitored. At the other end is the network operations center, which has to run with military precision 24 hours a day, 365 days a year. Everyone here is dressed in uniform black, a stark contrast with the casual dress code elsewhere in the building. Center staff have no choice over the location of their work, but they have a degree of flexibility over timing: they work in shifts that are self-rostered, with management guidance when needed.

Looking at jobs in terms of their dependence on time and place gives a clear picture of the options available for new ways of working. **Figure 3.1** shows four quadrants representing the options, as depicted in a report by Britain's Equal Opportunities Commission (now part of the Equality and Human Rights Commission).[5]

It shows that even people who are unable to vary the hours or location of work can still have some flexibility in their choice of shift. Hence they are categorized as 'Shift-shapers'. Examples are health care workers and police officers who have to be in fixed places for much of their work but who

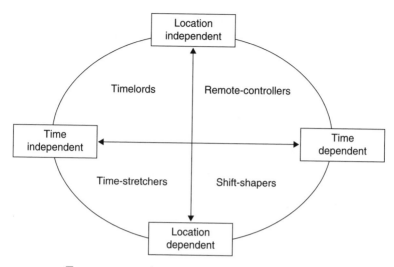

FIGURE 3.1 Categories of workers

also have tasks such as planning and administration that could be done at home or in another location.

People with flexibility over both time and place are described as 'Timelords'. Those with some flexibility in time but with a static location for their work are 'Time-stretchers', and those with fixed times but variable locations are 'Remote-controllers'.

The Commission mapped all 353 occupations in the UK government's standard classification of jobs on to this diagram and estimated that about 60 percent of workers were in the occupations in the bottom right of the chart, where time and location flexibility are traditionally less available. It points out that about 45 percent of these people are in the bottom quartile of jobs, typically the lowest paid, and often have the least control over their working lives. But their conclusion is that despite the business realities of these occupations, models are possible that increase the degree of flexibility so that people gain some control over their work.

The Commission found that one in seven employees fitted the Timelords category, people who have substantial control over when and where they work. Men account for six out of ten employees in these occupations, and around three-fifths of the occupations in this quadrant are in the top-quartile, highest paying jobs.

So, varying a combination of time and place of work can be the most rewarding pattern for employee as well as employer. This is because it gives autonomy to the individual while boosting productivity for the employer.

Up until relatively recently, most work had to be performed at the employer's premises, and this happened under the watchful eye of a supervisor or manager. If employees were at their workstation, they were deemed to be working. Where the job was part of a production line, this made some sense. But it has little relevance to today's knowledge work.

If someone is sitting at a desk, or in a meeting, there is no guarantee they are working productively. Yet their employment contract almost certainly does not mention productivity. It defines the hours they are expected to work and the compensation they will receive. If they turn up for work and are busy doing something that appears to be useful, they are paid at the end of the month.

Today's low productivity model is ready for reform. Tomorrow's model is a high productivity work process that gives better satisfaction to the individual and the manager. It supports the organization's goals, improves output and gives employees more manageable lives, all at once. That is what 'future work' is about.

Future work

Future work is based on the simple principle that work is an activity that produces a desired result. It is performed to achieve outcomes which contribute to the enterprise that has engaged the worker, whether as employee or contractor.

The tasks carried out in the name of 'work' are useless if they have no detectable output. Yet many organizations have lost sight of this. Managers turn business requirements into a job description and person specification, run it through the job evaluation system and recruit someone who appears to meet the criteria. They pay for the time of the employee at a rate calculated according to the skills needed for the job. Somewhere in this process, the direct relationship between work and output gets lost.

A new approach is emerging to challenge this. It is called results-based working and is a core element of future work. It challenges convention by asking the following questions:

- Instead of paying for inputs, regardless of their usefulness, why not pay for outputs?

- Instead of rewarding long hours of low productivity, why not reward shorter hours of high productivity?

- Instead of encouraging people to be seen at the workplace at defined times, why not encourage people to work where and when they are most productive?

Getting results

Measuring results in itself is not new. 'Management by objectives' was a management fad in the 1960s. Most organizations have a performance appraisal system and many have bonus schemes based on achieving targets.

What is new is the introduction of systems that just look at results and ignore other traditional management constraints. So the amount of time you put into achieving the result is irrelevant; it is what you achieve that counts. Where and when you do the work does not matter; producing the outcomes to the right quality and on time does.

Some innovative and successful Fortune 500 companies have embraced this model as an essential business strategy, say consultants Tom Harnish and Kate Lister in their report, *Results Based Management*.[6] 'They've learned that when they ignore the where, when, and how work is done, and focus on results, their people are more productive, more creative, and more successful.' They also argue that this new way of working allows companies to do more with less – fewer buildings, less pollution, less overtime and less waste. Their employees are doing more with less too – fewer distractions, less stress and less commuting. 'For companies, that all translates into greater loyalty, engagement, and productivity.'

One such system is the Results-Only Work Environment, known as ROWE[SM]. This disconnects the value of someone's work from the effort that they put in. There is, therefore, no pressure on people to turn up to work, attend meetings and impress the boss with long hours of dedicated effort. As long as they achieve the required results, employees have the freedom to work any way they want. They are also encouraged to challenge established practices. If they do not think a meeting is useful, then they do not need to attend. 'Every meeting is optional' is one of the guideposts laid down in the scheme. 'There is no judgment about how you spend your time' is another.

The approach is described in detail in *Why Work Sucks*[7] by Cali Ressler and Jody Thompson, who introduced it at **Best Buy**, the US consumer electronics company. It started in a small way in 2001 as a move to make the company an employer of choice. In 2003, it was named ROWE and, based on its success, spread across the corporate staff so that, by 2008, 80 percent were in the scheme. Five years later, at least 13 other companies had officially completed the ROWE migration process and many more have been experimenting with the system.

However, as the price of PCs fell and competition from online retailers increased, Best Buy reported poor financial results and a new CEO, Hubert Joly, arrived in 2013. One of his first decisions was to put the brakes on the ROWE scheme, which he felt had gone too far. Explaining this decision he said: 'This program was based on the premise that the right leadership style is always delegation. It operated on the assumption that if an employee's objectives were agreed to, the manager should always delegate to the employee how those objectives were met.' In his view, the right leadership style may be coaching, motivating or directing rather than delegating, depending on the individual. He said that a leader had to pick the right style of leadership for each employee, not a one-size-fits-all as the ROWE program would have suggested.[8]

The same year, Yahoo's CEO, Marissa Mayer, banned working from home as part of her drive to reverse the fortunes of the ailing internet company, saying that people collaborated better in an office. While these developments in the US may seem like a backlash against giving people greater choice and autonomy over work, they do not amount to a trend. Ironically, Maynard Webb, Yahoo's chairman, has been a strong supporter of home working and is the author of *Rebooting Work*, a book that extols the virtues of new ways of working. As he explains in the book, 'The things that people don't like about work – toiling away so many hours in office buildings, spending too much time in cars commuting to work, and ceding control to a company – no longer have to be facts of work life.'[9]

Eric Severson, senior vice-president of HR for Gap Inc., says his company has seen big benefits from a results-only work environment. 'I can't speak to the experience of Yahoo, Best Buy, or other companies that have experimented with workplace flexibility. What I can say is that at Gap we have five years of quantitative and qualitative evidence proving the substantial business benefits of ROWE.

'It has also been extensively studied among thousands of employees in real workplace environments by researchers from the University of Minnesota in partnership with the US National Institutes of Health (NIH) and the US Centers of Disease Control (CDC). The results, published in peer-reviewed journals, have proven ROWE's statistically significant positive impact on operating outcomes and employee health.' (See Chapter 8 for the full Gap story.)[10]

At BDO USA, another company featured in this book (Chapter 4), Stephen Ferrara, the chief operating officer, went on record after the Yahoo move to stress that BDO remained as committed as ever to its flexibility program, which 'continues to be an important business strategy for our firm'.[11]

We examine the questions that are often raised about giving people greater autonomy and choice, and provide the answers, in Chapters 9 and 10.

It's all about culture

The real success of future work lies not in a set of rules about results-based working but in a change in the culture of the organization and the way managers treat people as a result. Just introducing a results measurement system into a conventional management culture is unlikely to have much impact. In fact, there is likely to be a negative reaction from managers.

A pure results-only system relies on a relationship of trust between a manager and employee. It is based on the belief that when people are given a clear goal to achieve in a supportive environment, they will be motivated to do so without having to be monitored, supervised or forced. It assumes that most people will make good use of the freedom to manage their own work. They will choose to get things done in the way that best suits them and is most productive. They will want to achieve the best results, but in the shortest time practical, rewarding themselves with the extra time to use as they wish. This is the opposite of the usual 'pay for hours worked', which encourages and rewards long hours.

From 'sweatshop' to award-winning workplace

Ryan is a global tax services firm founded in 1991 by its current CEO and chairman, Brint Ryan. Now the firm ranks as the largest indirect tax practice in North America, and the seventh largest corporate tax services firm in the US. Its 1600 employees serve over 9000 clients in 40 countries, generating annual revenues in excess of $350m.

As the company broke through the $100m mark in 2005, it was quickly developing a reputation as a highly skilled, if well paid, sweatshop. Employees had to log 50 hours a week, with a minimum of eight hours each day. In theory, an employee who worked 60 hours over four days to complete a project would still be expected to log an additional eight hours on the last day of the week. When it came to compensation and promotions, the one metric that mattered most was hours logged.

Ryan's workplace environment was not only making it difficult to recruit talent, it was also making it challenging to retain employees with young families or other personal demands. Employee turnover was close to 20 percent and the issue of work-life balance kept resurfacing as a key reason why employees were leaving.

So Delta Emerson, then head of HR, enrolled Ryan in a best workplace survey to develop some baseline measures of employee morale, camaraderie and work-life balance. 'I knew we weren't going to win,' she said, 'but this is a company that's driven by data and so I knew we'd need to get the data in before we could start to address any of these employee issues.' As expected, Ryan scored low on all of the employee-satisfaction measures.

The data had a profound impact on Brint Ryan who, as founder-CEO, had created the hard-driving culture of dedication to work hours. In 2006, the company formed a workplace effectiveness committee and he challenged it to examine an approach in which employees could work anywhere at any time, as long as they achieved results.

The result was the MyRyan program, which celebrated its fifth anniversary on 1 August 2013. It is intentionally straightforward. Employees can work anywhere, any time, as long as the work gets done. There are no hour requirements, no location requirements and no schedules. For salaried employees, Ryan dispensed with vacation policies – employees, in concert with their teams, are their own judge of how much time to take off and when to take it.

The results are impressive, according to Delta Emerson, now chief of staff. 'We have won over 100 workplace excellence awards in recent years, including the coveted Fortune "Great Place to Work" award, in both the US and Canada. Ryan employees treasure flexibility and it has helped us become a "talent magnet" and reduce turnover. Additionally, the other metrics that any CEO cares about – client satisfaction and revenue – have skyrocketed. Flex is a business imperative – not a nice-to-have.'[12]

Putting theory into practice

To progress beyond 'flexible' working to future work requires a fundamental review of the role of management. Managers need to understand how people are motivated and how to get the best out of them. To do this they need to put into practice lessons about motivation that have been around for over 50 years. It helps to take a fresh look at how a few outstanding businesses have been getting 20–30 percent improvements in output from their people and ask why this is not happening everywhere.

In 1960, Douglas McGregor posed a key question to managers: What are your assumptions (implicit as well as explicit) about the most effective way to manage people?[13] His own answer was that there were two models, which he named 'Theory X and Theory Y'. Summarized simply, Theory X assumes that people have to be forced to work by constant management control while Theory Y contends that people are self-motivated and can be left to manage themselves.

Many more recent management gurus, such as Warren Bennis and Peter Drucker, have been influenced by McGregor's work. But his ideas are not just theoretical. They have been put into practice with positive effect by inspired CEOs who have recognized that traditional management is heavily 'Theory X' while their own beliefs about people are firmly 'Theory Y'.

In 1958, Bill Gore set up **W. L. Gore & Associates**, the company that makes Gore-Tex, the material used in many applications from outdoor clothing to artificial arteries. He established a structure and culture based on communication and cooperation rather than authority and hierarchy. Any person was allowed to make a decision as long as it was fair, encouraged others and made a commitment to the company.

Consultation was required only for decisions that could potentially cause serious damage to the enterprise. Furthermore, new associates joined the company on the same effective authority level as all the other workers, including Gore himself. There were no titles or bosses, with only a few exceptions, and commands were replaced by personal commitments.

This flat 'lattice' organization, which still tries to limit units to about 150 people, has stood the test of time. Not only has W. L. Gore been outstandingly successful financially, it still ranks highly among employees, appearing consistently near the top of the charts of the best employers. The reputation of the company has spread far and wide. It has been studied and admired by leaders of other organizations. Yet very few have been able to replicate the success. Why is this?

The challenge that proves insurmountable for most of those trying to emulate W. L. Gore is to remove the hierarchical structure and thinking in the organization. If managers see their role as directing employees, the

Gore system won't work. It relies on a genuine belief that people are self-motivated and that by being empowered to control their own work they will flourish and produce great results.

But to put this into practice takes away managers' power to make decisions, delegate work and exercise their authority. It also strips them of the physical trappings of power and status. These are hurdles that are now being tackled by leaders in a range of other companies, and we will see in Chapters 5 and 6 how they are breaking through the barriers of 'macho management'.

W. L. Gore & Associates is so called because the people who work there are treated as associates who collaborate to achieve the company goals. There are no salary bands. It is rare for a manager to be recruited from outside, apparently because of the difficulty they would have in adjusting. Associates rank each other in annual surveys and earn the right to manage others based on the abilities they have demonstrated to their peers.[14]

Bill Gore also introduced 'dabble time' – half an hour each week which associates could spend as they wished as long as they were still meeting their main commitments. A few other organizations have versions of this scheme. **Google** allows its engineers to take 20 percent of their time to work on their pet projects, provided they can enlist a team of colleagues to collaborate.

A matter of motivation

Our proposals for future work are built on the principles laid down in McGregor's Theory Y and repeated in varying forms over the last half century by motivation theorists and management professors. The idea that people will respond willingly to being trusted and treated as adults fits in with Herzberg's motivation theory, Maslow's hierarchy of needs and the views of leading management thinkers of the late twentieth century, from Peter Drucker to Charles Handy, from Tom Peters to Gary Hamel. Empower your employees and you will reap the reward. If you believe people will react responsibly to being given freedom, don't just talk about Theory Y as a theory, manage as if you mean it.

Hamel states this succinctly in *The Future of Management*.[15] 'To a large extent, managers play the role of parents, school principals, crossing guards and hall monitors,' he says. 'They employ control from without because employees have been deprived of the ability to exercise control from within. Adolescents outgrow most of these constraining influences; employees often aren't given that chance. The result: disaffection. Adults enjoy being treated like 13-year olds even less than 13-year olds.'

Why do managers persist in treating people like children? The command model of management appears to be blind to the evidence that ranges from academic research to highly successful employers. Assume people are responsible, give them the freedom to manage themselves, treat them like adults and watch them flourish.

Hundreds of research papers point to the same conclusion. 'Human beings have an innate inner drive to be autonomous, self-determined, and connected to one another. And when that drive is liberated, people achieve more and live richer lives.' So says Daniel Pink in *Drive*,[16] his excellent review of the theory and practice of motivation. He questions how much real autonomy people have under today's management practices. We may talk about 'empowerment' and 'flexibility' but current management still revolves around control. 'This era doesn't call for better management,' Pink says. 'It calls for a renaissance of self-direction.'

The epitome of self-direction is self-employment. Running yourself as an enterprise and charging your customers for your services means deciding for yourself how best to do the work. Many managers will happily engage a consultant or subcontract work to an individual without worrying about the working hours involved. They will leave the individual to do the work their own way and pay for the results when they are delivered. If this can be achieved with the self-employed, then why not engage employees on a results-only basis? In both cases, they are delivering a product through a self-managed process.

Autonomy at work

The best indicator of true autonomy at work is control of time and place. In a future work organization, the control is with employees as far as possible. They choose how to get the job done in the best way. They make informed, intelligent decisions because they are trusted to do so. They know what results they need to achieve and are motivated by the intrinsic satisfaction of doing a good job. If the job allows, they decide whether and when they need to go to the employer's premises to get work done. They work when they are at their most productive, not just when their manager wants to see them. The results of our survey (covered in detail in Chapter 7) show that organizations moving toward future work are most likely to have a culture of trust and empowerment.

Most work can be expressed in the form of results, but as we showed above there are still many jobs that have to be done at a fixed time and/or place. So results-based systems will not replace conventional employment contracts where jobs necessitate working at specific times. However, what is done within those times can still be measured and rewarded on output as part of the mix of compensation.

Employees with limited choice of time and place of work may be involved in customer service that has to be provided in person or they may be part of a continuous process that needs to be operated at all times. The delivery of care to the elderly or nursing of the sick cannot be done remotely or at a time totally at the discretion of the employee. Yet in the UK, the National Health Service gives autonomy to groups of nurses to organize their own shift times, and NHS Direct, a telephone help service, answers five million phone calls a year and employs 1400 trained nurses working remotely from their patients. A joint US–UK study of over 1700 patient care cases estimated that 45 percent of US patient care could be handled by telephone diagnosis and advice, or 'telemedicine'.[17]

Technology is enabling more tasks to be done remotely in a way previously unthinkable, removing the constraints of location for both the worker and the customer (or patient). Remote surgery, in which surgeons operate on a patient in a different location by controlling robotic arms, is one such example. As defined by Wikipedia, 'remote surgery is essentially advanced telecommuting for surgeons, where the physical distance between the surgeon and the patient is immaterial. It promises to allow the expertise of specialized surgeons to be available to patients worldwide, without the need for patients to travel beyond their local hospital.'

A report on police innovation cites an initiative in the Dutch port of Rotterdam where police stations have been closed, saving money, and replaced by conveniently located contact points with two-way audio-visual technology to enable members of the public to speak to officers. Max Chambers, editor of the report, called it a modern version of the Tardis box from the *Dr Who* television series. 'You'd be able to go into a police box and make a statement, report a crime, talk to the police officer through a screen where you'd have a conversation as if you were in the same room as an officer.'[18]

These are glimpses into how technology will fuel greater flexibility and choice in the future. A well-documented example of long-standing autonomy is **Semco** in Brazil. In his best-selling book, *Maverick*,[19] Ricardo Semler explains how he took over the business from his father and totally changed the company culture. He abolished organization charts, job titles and trappings of power. He empowered employees to recruit their peers and their managers. He gave his workers as much freedom as possible, with influence on every decision the company made, from how the plants should look and where each section should be positioned to letting them set their own working hours and schedules as well as their pay.

In creating a real democracy with power resting with the employees, Semler would stand out as a brave and inspired leader in any environment. Managing to do this in Brazil at a time of economic chaos and destructive labor relations in the 1990s makes it more remarkable. Semco, which has survived through Brazil's economic downs and ups, has been used as an example of inspired leadership across the world, but very few organizations have been able to match the radical approach of Ricardo Semler. And many have indeed viewed him as a 'maverick'.

This approach to running an organization is seen as a threat. What is left for managers to do if employees are allowed to get on with the job under their own steam? How does the boss exercise authority if employees are coming and going whenever they choose? Those are the fears. In fact, we think managers still have a very important role to play, but it is different from the one that prevailed in the Industrial Age working model.

Employees as micro-businesses

Two managers who have successfully adopted an autonomous working model are Julian Wilson and Andrew Holm of Matt Black Systems. Their company, based in the UK, designs and manufactures aerospace products. It has gone through a radical transformation over the last five years, driven by their belief that there must be a better way to run a business than a traditional functional structure.

While engaged in a 'lean manufacturing' program, they started by splitting the workforce of about 30 people into two autonomous teams (or cells), each responsible for their own business process, from sales and marketing through to production and delivery. This did not have the desired impact on 'QDP' (quality, delivery and profit) so they divided the teams again, giving each one full responsibility for running its own profit-making enterprise within the business. Soon they were down to teams of two, each running a separate enterprise within the business, with Wilson and Holm acting as landlords and bankers but not providing any of the traditional top-down management direction. With each further subdivision, QDP measures improved, but not dramatically.

The real breakthrough came when they decided to go to the logical conclusion and make every employee a separate micro enterprise within the business, with its own profit and loss account and balance sheet. For most of the existing employees, this scrutiny was a step too far. Some did not have all the skills to run a solo business and others did not want the responsibility. As people left, they were replaced by newcomers who were keen on the challenge. Typically these were engineering graduates with technical design ability who were able to learn other business skills quickly.

The employees pay themselves a basic salary and take a further 20 percent of the profit that they generate, against a strict grade assessment they carry out for themselves. A further 20 percent goes into their individual risk capital account to deploy however they see fit. Of the three remaining 20 percent slices of the original profit, one is paid out as corporation tax, another as a dividend to the shareholders and the last retained as collective risk capital on the company's balance sheet.

Because Wilson and Holm have given almost total autonomy to their people, they have a 'hands off' leadership style. They both work from home, only visiting the factory occasionally, and they employ an auditor who keeps a close eye on the adherence to procedure of each employee's business. They see the company as a 'social enterprise' that has dispensed with unnecessary management overhead.

The results are impressive. Income per employee has increased by 300 percent since they implemented the scheme in full and the company needs only half the space and working capital to achieve the same turnover. They say customers are pleased with the arrangements as they deal directly with the person designing their product who is committed to delivering it to the highest quality and on time. The only limitation on the success of this model appears to be finding people willing and able to take on the responsibility. For the right people the rewards are good. Wilson reckons that their young graduate engineers are earning twice as much as their peers in conventional jobs.[20]

Happy Computers is a UK training company that has won a stack of workplace awards. Its visionary founder and CEO, Henry Stewart, has written a nine-point manifesto for a great workplace, including 'Give freedom within clear guidelines' and 'Select managers who are good at managing'. The latter is a simple principle, often ignored. 'Make sure your people are supported by somebody who is good at doing that, and find other routes for those whose strengths are elsewhere,' Stewart says. 'Even better, allow people to choose their managers.'[21]

Managing in a future work environment is about supporting people and enabling them to perform to maximum effectiveness. It is not telling people what to do, but helping them to see what is needed. It is about sharing goals and inspiring people to achieve them. It is about listening to employees and using their ideas and energy, not telling them to do what they are told. It is about trusting people to make their own decisions about how they get the job done, not watching their every move. It is about enabling them to work anytime, anywhere, as far as possible.

It is also about adapting work to the new majority workforce, for whom the old model does not fit, as we showed in Chapter 2. The restrictions of 'part-time' work, compressed hours or other flexible work arrangements currently hold back people's career progression and access to leadership roles, even though working this way is usually at least as productive, and often more so. Switching to the FutureCo model described at the start of this chapter renders categories such as 'full-time' and 'part-time' irrelevant.

As this new model spreads, it will become easier for both women and men to fit work around personal responsibilities and to have better access to leadership roles without being saddled with career-limiting labels.

In summary

It may take a new generation of managers to make future work a common reality. Companies such as W. L. Gore and Semco have benefited from enlightened CEOs whose values are reflected in every management action in the business. Others, such as Ryan, have changed their working practices through a fundamental shift in their management culture.

To make this shift successfully, managers must:

- question their own assumptions about the most effective way to manage people, not expect their employees to be present for fixed hours to prove they are working
- adopt Theory Y thinking
- allow their people to define when and where they do their work
- manage people by results
- let go of the reins and allow people to flourish

It's a big help in getting future work off the ground if you have a complete grasp of the business benefits. In Chapter 4 we will examine how some organizations have achieved great results by changing the way they manage their people. They have provided an autonomous working environment and trusted their staff to manage themselves. In return for their faith in their employees they have seen dramatic improvements in performance. Your organization could be next.

CHAPTER 4

Why it makes business sense

If implemented successfully by business leaders, workforce agility can offer sustainable business performance and engaged employees. Creating an agile workforce has helped us to compete in the global market.

Letter from 21 business leaders to the Daily Telegraph[1]

A group of leading businesses, including BP, Ford, KPMG and Tesco, joined forces in the UK in 2013 to declare that they had gained significant and tangible financial benefits from having an 'agile' workforce. In a big step forward by the business community, they launched the 'Agile Future Forum' to persuade other organizations to follow suit, saying this would be in the interests of the country's economic competitiveness.

How exactly does future work make sense for business? Here's how. When **BDO USA**, the accounting firm, moved its New York office from Madison Avenue to Park Avenue, it was able to cut the space per person by 20 percent and achieve cost savings of $1.5m to $2m a year by encouraging teleworking. Not bad for a prime spot in Manhattan, where office rents average more than $70 per square foot.

In the UK, the supermarket chain **Sainsbury's** recorded a 65 percent jump in bread sales at a major London store after it involved its bakery staff in working out a schedule to meet customer demand for fresh bread throughout the day instead of only first thing in the morning.

US insurance company **Chubb** halved the number of complaint calls, and extended the time employees were available to customers, when it asked teams to devise their own working patterns to meet targets for improved performance.

How did these three very different businesses do it? By handing people greater autonomy over how they work and how they achieve their business objectives. In the case of BDO, the big reduction in office space is the result of a US-wide 'Flex Strategy' that encourages work practices such as telecommuting as a way to 'do more with less'. The firm gives people a large degree of control over where and when they work. Since this is a business strategy, not a human resources program, it measures the impact on the bottom line.

'Measuring was really important to show business leaders in the firm that it wasn't about being nice to employees but was essential to operating in the new world of global client demands,' says Marcee Harris Schwartz, director of the Flex Strategy.[2]

Sainsbury's scored its sales success at the Camden store in north London by the apparently simple, but often neglected, means of empowering frontline employees. Ziggie Singh, the store manager, invited the bakery team to devise a response to the change in shoppers' requirements. There was no flexibility about where they baked the bread, but there had to be flexibility about who did it at what time. Instead of imposing new working hours on them, as happens in many businesses, Singh asked them what *they* would do if they were in his shoes. The team came up with a system of rotating shifts that meant they could produce a regular supply of fresh bread while taking account of their varying personal and family commitments. 'It was more of a pull than a push style of management,' said Singh. 'Being involved in the whole process made the bakers more enthusiastic about the change.'[3]

Chubb did something similar with teams in various parts of the business across the US. The teams, who were jointly accountable with their managers for meeting the new business goals, worked collectively to find more efficient ways of doing their jobs that also accommodated their preferences, in this case for both working hours and location. Some started work earlier or finished later, thereby extending customer service cover; some opted to work from home several days a week to cut commuting time, while others chose to stick to a regular 8 a.m. to 5 p.m. office schedule, as a *Financial Times* article described.[4]

As well as the direct business outcomes – cost savings, increased sales, higher productivity – all three organizations reported a rise in employee satisfaction and motivation. So not only did the companies achieve improvements in financial performance, they also found that the approach they took to achieving these business goals had a direct and positive impact on how people felt about their jobs.

At Chubb, the business results from one such program involving 120 employees in the Chicago insurance claims department included: an increase from 90 percent to 100 percent in benefit payments made on time; a rise in the percentage of customers contacted within 24 hours of making a claim; and productivity increases of at least 5 percent.

What's more, employees began to come up with more ideas for improving customer service and increasing market share. Here are some of their comments about the improvements they experienced:

> 'I feel less stressed and I am more focused on results'
> 'I am more excited to come to work and I feel my ideas are being heard'
> 'I can now put my kids on the bus'
> 'I see change as more positive, more opportunity'[5]

As we explained in Chapter 3, these approaches go beyond traditional flexible work arrangements, which are designed first and foremost as an accommodation of employees, and which tend to be granted only on request to certain individuals or groups. In traditional schemes, any positive outcomes tend to be ticks in the human resources box: greater staff loyalty; higher retention; lower absenteeism. While these are important, it is often difficult to measure the direct cause and effect. Not surprisingly, the link with the wider health and prosperity of the organization is often poorly understood.

Future work takes a more radical approach. It starts with business goals: to gain a competitive edge; to attract the best talent; to keep costs under control; to respond to rapid shifts in customer demand. It usually uses communications technology to make working practices more efficient and productive. It requires a culture of trust and empowerment, in which people are treated as adults and measured by results, not by the hours they work.

Cutting-edge companies are already demonstrating what this means for business. Companies that outperform their peers in terms of innovation and expansion into new markets are three times more likely to have adopted 'smarter working practices', according to an IBM survey of 275 senior executives around the world.[6] These practices include enabling people to stay connected by allowing them to work productively 'regardless of location, time or device'. In other words, giving them the tools and letting them get on with it.

By putting future work at the heart of the way the business operates, other organizations can also start to reap the performance gains that are demonstrated by the case studies in this chapter. Some of these gains have an immediate and tangible effect on the bottom line. Others emerge over the longer term and are harder to measure directly, but have the potential to make an even greater and more sustainable impact on a company's success.

To understand better the range of benefits your business could experience from future work, we categorize them as tangible and intangible.

Tangible gains include:

- Higher productivity
- Improved customer service
- Cost savings on real estate, utilities and services
- Cost savings on business travel
- Lower staff sickness and absenteeism
- Lower staff turnover
- Resources better matched to customer demand
- Faster response to market changes
- Faster access to new markets
- Reduction in CO_2 emissions

Intangible gains include:

- Reduced risk of business disruption
- Higher employee morale and loyalty

- Healthier workforce, less prone to burnout

- Increased creativity and innovation

- Greater customer loyalty

- Better access to key contracts

- Stronger management skills

- Lower management overheads due to employee self-management

- Retention of knowledge and skills

- More transparent succession planning

- Access to wider sources of talent

- More diversity in senior management

- Enhanced employer reputation

- Contribution to environmental sustainability

It is tempting for finance directors to look at the tangible savings that can be made, particularly in real estate, and see future work as a cost-cutting exercise. Getting better use of buildings by more efficient use of space is a sensible business goal. It is easy to see and measure the savings when a building is vacated or a floor sub-let. But the real financial impact comes when the issue of productivity is addressed. For most organizations, getting 10 percent more output from their employees – or saving 10 percent on employee costs – would eclipse all the space savings they could possibly make.

By focusing on outcomes, future work forces managers to value productivity. If they are going to reward people for their achievements, not their hours, then they need to measure these, as shown by the case studies in this chapter.

On top of these gains for individual organizations, more efficient working offers wider environmental and social benefits. By adopting future work, you can help to save the planet by reducing commuter and business car journeys and air travel, building and running smaller offices and thus cutting CO_2 emissions. There are huge long-term social benefits in having a healthier labor force that is better able to balance family and personal time with work requirements and that includes people who might otherwise be unable to do paid productive work, for example because they have disabilities or are caring for children or elderly relatives.

We will now look at some of the business gains in detail, with examples from a range of organizations, large and small, private and public sector, which have already reaped the benefits.

Productivity gains

There is a large body of evidence that giving people autonomy over where and when they work tends to boost their output. This is partly because they have fewer distractions from office meetings and interruptions. People concentrate better if they can work at least some of the time in a quieter location, escape the stress of a long commute, or be freed of worries about how to manage both work and personal commitments. Trusted to get on with the job, people tend to be more motivated to do so, especially if they gain more time as a result. They may actually be working a few hours longer without realizing it, because work is more integrated into the rest of their lives.

Cisco, the leading international producer of networking equipment, might well be expected to record the business benefits it derives from remote working – and it does. Eighty-five percent of its employees telecommute, and no one except call center operatives has a set work schedule. In a study of employees who use its 'Virtual Office' equipment to work from home for part of the week, they reported being nearly 50 percent more productive than in the office. The average employee using this equipment gained 2.75 productive work hours per week, which would typically have been spent commuting.[7]

These findings are remarkably similar to those of a productivity survey by the UK Telework Association. In this study, 85 percent of people who worked from home for at least part of each week reported an increase in how much they achieved. A quarter of those who were able to measure their output said they were over 50 percent more productive. Only 5 percent thought they were less productive at home.

The main reasons they gave for their higher productivity were fewer interruptions, the ability to fit work alongside other commitments and time saved on commuting, at least some of which was then devoted to work. A third of respondents also cited loyalty and repayment of trust as a reason for their improved productivity.[8]

In our own survey of 366 managers, covered in more detail in Chapter 7, 88 percent of the respondents agreed or strongly agreed with the statement 'I believe people are more productive given autonomy over their working patterns', and 84 percent said they believed new ways of working would benefit the business.

Likewise, in a national survey by Microsoft, in the US in 2010, 71 percent of employees said they were more productive when they were working away from the office. Only 11 percent said they were less productive, while 18 percent thought their output was about the same in the office as away from it.[9]

Telework payback

The initial investment in technology to support a telework program produces a return of between 200 percent and 1500 percent, according to analysis by the US government's **General Services Administration**, the agency responsible for federal facilities. This return takes the form of increased productivity, reduced absenteeism, lower real estate costs and reduced recruitment and retention needs.

'Our experience is also backed up by a pilot (GSA) program that we recently ran out of our Kansas City office,' said Martha Johnson, former administrator of the GSA, in a speech to the US Telework Exchange. 'This 90-day project moved 42 employees to telework. Two-thirds of them had the option to telework five days per week. Our results were great. Seventy-seven percent of participants reported that their productivity had increased. Sick leave went down 69 per cent, saving on average 14 hours of work time per employee. Peer-to-peer communication increased almost 55 per cent.' There was also a predicted reduction of 30 metric tons of CO_2 due to reduced commuting.

Johnson said that telework 'is best when an entire group does it together, when they are empowered by collaborative technologies, and when there is a "water cooler manager" who facilitates social networking. There needs to be a "just do it" attitude across the organization.' We cover the US federal government's initiative in more detail in Chapter 6 and give further guidance on effective management techniques for future work in Chapters 8, 9 and 10.

Bringing it all back home

As part of its 'Work Smart' strategy, **BT**, the UK communications group, introduced 'homeshoring', cutting back on call center premises and moving the jobs to individual agents' homes. These home-based operators are up to 30 percent more productive than those based in physical contact centers, partly because they can respond to the daily fluctuations in incoming calls, says Dave Dunbar, head of BT flexible working services.[10]

'We're moving more and more people into home-based contact centers, for example in the Thurso area of the Scottish Highlands,' he says. 'We've always wanted, from a business perspective, to have split shifts because there are natural peaks and troughs in customers' needs. The peaks tend to be morning, at lunchtime when people are ordering things or ringing in and saying that something isn't working, and in the early evening when people are coming home. Employees aren't going to drive into work for part of the day, go back, and then come back in again later. But if they're at home they can productively use the troughs to get on with their lives, even having essential health services such as kidney dialysis, and then "return to" work when they are most needed.'

In the US, BT has introduced on–off shifts lasting 40 minutes for home-based 'call minders' for its teleconference services. These employees guide callers through the teleconference process. The shifts are long enough to cover a typical teleconference. They then take a break before the next shift. While this has proved helpful for people with caring responsibilities, such as looking after an elderly relative, Dunbar cautions against stereotyping home workers, saying: 'The demographic of our home workers matches the workforce as a whole.'

He says home workers are on average about 20 percent more productive than their office-based counterparts in the same functions.

Does this additional productivity decline over time as employees get used to home-working mode? No, says Dunbar, the increased productivity has proved constant over time. 'The 20 percent we quote is a mature figure that has been measured after things have settled down, and it has been found across many thousands of people. You do see some much higher figures for productivity quoted but these are often in a smaller population which is fresh to home working.'

Employees in the UK estimate that they could gain on average five productive hours per week through better ways of working such as avoiding the daily commute, according to a study by the RSA, a charity that seeks innovative solutions to social challenges. This equates to around £4200 per employee per year.[11]

Another study carried out by Stanford University in 2012 measured the effect of home working in a Shanghai call center over a nine-month period.[12] The researchers asked the 996 employees whether they would be interested in working from home four days a week, with the fifth day in the office as usual. About half (503) of the employees were interested, particularly those who were married, had children and faced long commutes to work. Of these, 249 were qualified to take part in the experiment by virtue of having at least six months' tenure, broadband access and a private room at home in which they could work. Those with even-numbered birthdates were selected to work at home while those with odd-numbered birthdates stayed in the office to act as the control group.

Office and home workers used the same IT equipment, faced the same work order flow from a common central server, and were compensated under the same pay system, which included an element of individual performance pay. The only difference between the two groups was the location of work.

The output of the home workers increased by 13 percent over the nine months of the experiment. This improvement came mainly from a nine percent increase in the number of minutes they worked during their shifts, due to fewer breaks and sick days, and a four percent increase in the number of calls per minute worked. Meanwhile, the performance of the control group remained static. In interviews, the home-based workers attributed these gains to the quieter working conditions reducing distractions and allowing them to spend more time on the phone per shift.

In addition, attrition fell sharply among the home workers, dropping by 50 percent versus the control group. Home workers also reported substantially higher work satisfaction and had more positive attitudinal survey outcomes.

However, higher productivity does not depend exclusively on being able to work away from the office or spend time at home. Simply having greater autonomy over one's working day can boost efficiency.

A two-year study of formal and informal flexibility in seven large UK-based companies found that most flexible workers, as well as their colleagues and managers, rated the quality and quantity of their individual work as being as good as, or better than, when they had worked standard schedules. They were also more committed than their peers to their organization.

These employees worked a variety of patterns, from having control over their start and finish times, to occasional working from home, through to more formal reduced-hours arrangements. 'I probably wouldn't be doing this job if I couldn't do it the way I am,' said one respondent in the study by Cranfield School of Management and the charity Working Families.[13] 'I would probably have left the company.'

Another interviewee highlighted the efficiency gains from rethinking how work gets done. 'I started focusing on only going to the meetings where I could get something out of it, or the company would get something out of it,' she said.

Cost savings

Companies have to control costs during economic upswings as well as downturns. However, the global financial and economic crisis that began in 2007 put a particularly severe squeeze on costs, even in the most financially robust companies, and led to massive cuts in both public and private sector jobs and services in many economies around the world.

For managers anxiously seeking ways to do more with less, future work provides two important solutions: it can reduce the amount spent on fixed costs such as office premises, and it can lower spending on recruitment, training and emergency cover by reducing staff turnover and absenteeism.

Efficiencies on office space are achievable both immediately and over the longer term, and they can be substantial. **IBM**, a pioneer of new working practices driven by business need, says it saves more than $100m a year on office space by operating a highly flexible, mobile workforce.

Seventy percent of the technology company's 400,000-plus employees work from home at least once a week. About 40 percent are classified as 'mobile', which means they have no fixed office and work at home, at client sites, in airport lounges and trains, or at hot desks in IBM locations.

BT says it has cut its property running costs, such as rent, heating, lighting and security, by £550m per year since 2000, reducing office space by more than 40 percent, and moving to flexible and mobile working.

Over 75 percent of the 79,000 non-engineer staff in the UK have flexible schedules. 'Each of our 9,500 full-time home-based workers saves us £6000 a year in office desk costs,' says Dave Dunbar.

The freed-up space in BT's 1960s headquarters building near St Paul's Cathedral in London has been turned over to new activities. The basement now houses a large auditorium, a film studio and editing suite, an area to showcase new technology and a 'touchdown' zone for visiting staff. This innovative use of space saves costs, while the ability to demonstrate new products and services generates revenues.

Improved customer response

Giving people autonomy and responsibility to make decisions without constantly having to refer upward can accelerate the business process. It can enable a faster response to customer needs, as BDO USA found when it wanted to move into new territory (see case study at the end of this chapter). In rapidly shifting markets, reacting quickly can be critical, as Guy Laurence, head of **Vodafone UK**, explains when talking about the open environment in which employees, including the directors, work, with no private offices, no personal desks and virtually no paper. 'The way to operate faster as a company is to move to this way of working rather than in a traditional closed office environment,' he says. 'The time to market is a prerequisite of success. As a consequence, companies have got to speed up. It used to take us 90 days to change a price plan. Now we do it in four days.'[14]

When teams are given the opportunity to work out their own schedules to suit their personal needs and those of the business, a common result is an extension of 'opening hours' or customer service cover. This is what **Chubb** found in the example at the start of this chapter. There were unexpected benefits as well: people learned how to do each other's roles so that they could cover for them when they were not in the office. They also took more initiatives themselves to ensure customer service, and jumped in if there was an unexpected absence.

Business continuity

Terrorist attacks, influenza pandemics and natural disasters all threaten serious disruptions to business. Official advice suggests that large organizations should plan for an extra 15 percent of staff being absent at the peak of a flu pandemic, and that small businesses should plan for 30 percent absence.[15]

Businesses are regularly exhorted to draw up contingency plans for this and other types of disruption, such as Iceland's volcanic ash cloud that shut down big sections of European airspace during the spring of 2010. In these circumstances, efficient future work practices help to keep businesses going.

One London-based investment bank introduced working from home in one of its operations as contingency planning when a deadly outbreak of swine flu in Mexico disrupted business travel and forced some air passengers into quarantine.

Previously, there had been a stigma attached to working at home. However, the manager of the operation decided that it made sense for people to do this, rather than to work together at an expensive remote location, especially in the event of a contagious illness outbreak.

Each team had to have one in five members working from home for a week at a time over several months to understand the benefits and address any challenges. Feelings of isolation were overcome by creative use of technology, such as instant messaging. Managers, too, were required to work from home at least one day a month or lose their remote access to office computer systems.

Swiss Re, the global reinsurance company, decided to introduce a new style of working partly to ensure it could keep operations going in the face of natural disasters such as the Japanese earthquake in 2011 and Hurricane Sandy in 2012. (See full case study, Chapter 10).

Healthy, motivated people

Work in itself is generally good for people's health, but relentlessly long hours of work can lead to major health problems. A recent study of middle-aged British government workers, published online by the *European Heart Journal*, found a 60 percent greater risk of a heart attack or other serious cardiac disease in those who regularly worked 10–11 hour days, compared with those working a seven-hour day.[16]

Much has been written in the past decade about the increasing incidence of work-related stress and 'burnout'. Sylvia Ann Hewlett of the Center for Talent Innovation in New York has described the proliferation of 'extreme jobs', involving 70-hour weeks, heavy travel and intense performance pressures. These jobs are particularly prevalent in financial and professional services firms but also in senior roles in many large companies. Interestingly, though, 75 percent of respondents to her research survey said they loved their jobs: the pace, the financial rewards, the recognition and the intellectual challenge.[17]

What motivates employees and keeps them engaged – or does the opposite – is a complicated matter. But we know from research that having control over one's work is a crucial factor. A 2003 study of workers in Sweden found that those with highly demanding jobs and very little latitude over how they carried out their work had an increased risk of long-term illness.[18]

In a nine-year longitudinal study in Japan, researchers found that lack of control at work was a predictor of suicides among male workers. They concluded that this finding 'implies that job redesign aimed at increased worker control could be a worthwhile strategy in preventing, or at least reducing, the risk of suicide death'.[19] As our economies become increasingly reliant on people working long beyond traditional retirement age, it will become more important than ever to address the causes of work-related physical and mental illness.

Progressive organizations have a shrewd understanding of the importance of employee motivation, or engagement, in improving customer service and thence the bottom line. They also know that winning contracts, especially in the public sector, increasingly depends on being able to demonstrate that they treat their people well and respect their needs for balanced lives.

Those companies that have bothered to measure it have found that levels of engagement are linked to the degree of autonomy people have at work.

'Flexible workers have some of the highest scores in **IBM** around the work environment,' says Gary Kildare, human resources vice-president for IBM Global Technology Services. 'They're generally more satisfied with their jobs and they have a greater sense of accomplishment. They tend to rate the company more highly as an employer and they're often the least likely to leave.'[20]

Creativity and innovation

Confidence grows in the innovative value of flexible working the more it is experienced, according to a study which surveyed over 2800 employees and senior managers in the UK. 'The most common view is that working out of the office is often much more productive from a creative point of view,' says 'The Flex Factor', published by the RSA.[21]

One survey respondent shared an example of how remote working led directly to a new product, saying, 'I have personally developed software to allow staff at our company to print documents or spoolers from the server to their local/home printer no matter where they are. This software has now been sold to users. Without home working I would never have even thought about the need for it.'

This kind of engagement and drive from having autonomy is something that **Google** has turned into a distinct source of innovation among its large workforce of engineers. Competition for jobs at the world's biggest internet company is fierce, and it seeks to recruit already highly motivated self-achievers who are capable of working collaboratively. People are judged on results, not hours, says Matt Brittin, vice-president for northern and central Europe. 'Our engineers can work whatever hours they like, assuming they coordinate with colleagues and deliver what they've agreed. They can be nocturnal.'

Engineers have a large degree of latitude and control over their work, with the option to spend 20 percent of their time on a project of their own devising. Gmail, the internet mailing service, and Google News were two services that resulted from this practice. It can be frustrating for managers when engineers go off to work on their own ideas, admits Brittin. 'But it's not having 20 percent time of your time to muck about. It's mainly for engineers to be able to be creative and pursue their passions, and to do that within Google rather than having to leave.'[22]

Saving the planet

As we described in Chapter 1, many people are motivated to work by factors other than the financial reward. There are employees of all ages, not just in Gen Y, who want to feel part of an organization that cares about its environmental impact and about addressing wider social challenges.

Future work practices make organizations more attractive institutions to work for or be connected with. They also produce big environmental benefits.

BT has calculated the savings in terms of petrol and carbon emissions. In a single year, it avoided 11m km and 2,800 metric tons of CO_2 from company car, rail and air travel through the use of conferencing technology and smart working policies. 'Our research suggests each one of our home workers reduces their annual carbon emissions by 1.4 metric tons per year,' says Dave Dunbar.

Cisco also measures the environmental gains. Employees who use its Virtual Office software avoid 36.4 commuting miles on average for each work-at-home day, totaling 47m miles a year, it says. This means a reduction in auto emissions of 22,710 tons of CO_2 annually, saving nearly $126,000 per year in reforestation project costs necessary to offset the automobile carbon footprint.[23]

Studies by the US Telework Research Network show the environmental benefits that would result if the 40 percent of Americans who could work away from the office actually did so for half of the time. 'Each person could save an average of $362 on gas per year [at $2.40 a gallon],' says the Network's Kate Lister. 'At the national level, that adds up to over $15bn in savings a year. It would reduce US greenhouse gas emissions by about 53m metric tons – that's the equivalent of taking more than 9.6m cars off the road for one year.'[24]

Lloyds Banking Group runs a 'No Travel Week' in the UK for one week in every month. During this period employees are encouraged not to travel unless it is business-critical. Since 2011 the bank has eliminated 96,000 business journeys. The bank says the policy has changed its business travel culture, with a cost reduction of 39 percent in travel and associated costs since the end of 2010. The environmental benefit has been a drop in CO_2 emissions of more than 25 percent.[25]

O2, the mobile phone operator, asked the entire workforce in its head office in Slough in southeast England to work away from the office for one day in February 2012 as an experiment. This meant that a quarter of its 12,000-strong workforce operated remotely for the day as the doors were shut and lights turned off at the 200,000 sq ft office.

Employees avoided 2000 hours of commuting time, about half of which they spent working instead. This saved approximately 12.2 metric tons of CO_2 (for the purposes of comparison, this is equivalent to the CO_2 emissions from driving 42,000 miles in a medium-sized diesel car).

Other results were that water use at the building fell by 53 percent and electricity consumption was down 12 percent, but gas use went up slightly 'probably due to the loss of body heat in the building', the company reported.

Ben Dowd, business director, said the pilot was a good start in promoting remote working. 'We're educating people about the whole future of work here and there's still work to be done.'[26]

Adding it all up

Few organizations currently measure the business benefits of future work at all, let alone in any detail. **BDO USA**, which we featured at the start of this chapter, is unusual in having collected a large amount of data on a wide range of business and people benefits, including cost savings, increased speed to market, productivity gains and improved employee morale.

We examine these under the two headings: tangible and intangible benefits. As a case study, it neatly encapsulates many of the advantages that we have covered in this chapter.

Tangible business gains:

- Real estate savings: The firm's new offices in big urban centers are making creative use of office space, telecommuting and coordination of team schedules to help manage the high cost of real estate. In addition to the Manhattan example, the firm's chief financial officer, Howard Allenberg, calculates that annual savings from individuals who work exclusively from their homes or clients' offices, compared with having dedicated BDO office space, amount to $500,000–$700,000 a year in reduced facility and equipment rentals, maintenance and related occupancy costs.

■ Rapid moves into new markets: The firm says it entered and grew faster in new markets, such as Austin, Texas, by making flexible use of telecommuting rather than taking on physical office space at the start. Professionals who lived in Austin but worked at the Houston office began to work from their own or each other's homes or clients' offices in Austin to help develop the business quickly, says Marcee Harris Schwartz of BDO. This saved about $1.6m in office overheads in the first three years until the business was solid enough to justify opening physical premises.[27] More recently, the firm expanded its operations in various east coast states, drawing both on professionals living locally and others living further afield who were set up to work from home offices.

■ Extended service cover: The new working models are not confined to accountancy professionals at BDO. Some administrative staff work part of the time from home or do shifts so they come in and leave at different times, says Harris Schwartz. 'Three admin assistants in the Dallas office do a rotating schedule, each working a compressed week every third week, which involves four 10-hour days, while the other two do normal eight-hour days.' This not only benefited them but also provided extended cover for the partners, and it saved money because the firm did not have to pay the staff overtime to stay extra hours. The IT department used flexible schedules and telecommuting to extend its Help Desk user support from the traditional 7.30 a.m.–7.30 p.m. Eastern Time to any time of the day, regardless of where users are located.

Intangible business gains:

It is harder to isolate the impact of the Flex Strategy on things like hiring and employee turnover. However, BDO surveyed its people to gain feedback in building the business case for the strategy in 2009. They said the approach to flexibility positively impacted:

■ Their work-life balance (72 percent said it did)
■ Their desire to stay with the firm (71 percent)

- Their productivity (70 percent)
- The firm's ability to recruit talent (83 percent)
- The firm's ability to keep talent (82 percent)
- The firm's ability to compete in the global market (74 percent)
- The firm's ability to serve clients (65 percent)

In a more recent employee survey in mid-2012, 93 percent said that having the right 'fit' between their work and the rest of their lives was extremely, or very, important to them, and 85 percent said they had used flexible practices in the past six months.

BDO has found ways to do better business in a highly competitive sector. As Harris Schwartz says: 'It's a reality for anyone working in the professional services industry that clients want access when they want access. But I don't think that means one individual has to be available to them at all times. We have examples of teams being more thoughtful about creating multiple relationships with clients so that they can extend their availability, for example by offering the clients the possibility of reaching one of three people.'

Crucially, the firm's senior people are committed to the strategy. When Wayne Berson was elected CEO in 2012 on the retirement of Jack Weisbaum, a strong advocate of flexibility, he immediately made clear his own intention to continue the policy.

In summary

Future work goes beyond traditional flexible work arrangements by starting with business goals. These are both tangible gains such as higher productivity, cost savings and improved customer service, and intangible gains such as a reduced risk of business disruption, healthier and more motivated employees and lower environmental impact.

In Chapter 5 we look at the crucial question of leadership and how senior people in highly demanding jobs in different industries around the world are showing that future work makes business and personal sense for them and their teams.

CHAPTER 5

Leaders for the new world of work

At his home in California's Santa Cruz mountains, nearly two hours' drive up winding roads from San Francisco, Slade Fester is living proof that people can hold down a senior job regardless of where, when and how they do their work.

Thanks to technology, an enlightened employer and an adaptable personal style, Slade, a partner with an international accountancy network, is able to satisfy the competing demands of his clients, his team of 20 auditors and managers and his young family. He even finds time to pursue his passion of ocean surfing when the swell hits the Pacific coast.

'In some respects, I'm working round-the-clock because a lot of my clients are international companies – I do a lot of calls and emails in the evening, which is beneficial because I'll get an answer from someone in Europe or China while I'm sleeping,' he says. 'Within that 24-hour day, however, I'm also getting really valuable quality time with my family and surfing. Sometimes I'm out on the ocean four to five times a week.'[1]

No two days are the same for the 51-year-old. He works a day or two from home each week. On the other days, he drives to visit clients or to see colleagues at the San Francisco and San José offices of his firm, BDO USA.

Living and working so remotely (even the nearest store is 20 minutes' drive from the house), he makes it a priority to strengthen relationships with people during his city visits. 'I'll do whatever it takes to show up *face-to-face for the key meetings,' he says. 'In the office, I roam the floor and drop in to see people in their cubes.' Unlike more traditional office-based colleagues who spend most of their time at their computers, he does his concentrated work at home, often after his children have gone to bed.*

Can there be life at the top?

This chapter is about the type of leadership that organizations need to thrive in the new world of work, illustrated by the stories of women and men we have encountered who practice such leadership in their daily lives.

There's a powerfully prevalent view in the business world that holding down a senior executive role is incompatible with 'having a life'. This belief is perpetuated by many of those who wield power. Here's what John Rowe, the then CEO of Exelon, a large US energy company, told a conference of diversity professionals: 'If you're going to have a very senior job at a very high-performance company, it requires a near totality of commitment. There's some level in most government or corporate structures where balance becomes near impossible.'[2]

Conventional flexible working arrangements, typically based on the number of hours or days worked per week or year, remain a 'no-go' area for executives in many organizations. According to one survey, three-quarters of European Union companies have no part-timers in highly qualified or managerial positions.[3] Another study found that managers in Britain and other countries were often excluded from 'part-time' jobs. Nearly one in five UK employers in the retail sector – which could not function without flexibility from its employees – made 'full-time' work a condition of managerial posts. Not surprisingly, managers were found to be less likely than other employees to ask to reduce their hours, and if they did, they were more likely to be turned down.[4]

'Flexibility in senior jobs is the most difficult area,' says Caroline Waters, former director of people and policy at BT, a UK communications company that was early to adopt mobile, flexible and remote working. 'There are a lot of extreme jobs in industry. We need more senior people sharing jobs and working part time to create the role models that will make this a more common solution right across industry. The question companies need to ask is: "Do we want this extremely able person for some of the time, or not at all?" because they may very well go elsewhere if we cannot give them that flexibility.'

Companies also need to ask why they still judge senior people on presence and hours worked, rather than performance. There's no doubt that people running large organizations need to be driven, focused and hardworking. It is illogical, however, given the latitude that technology allows in the way we work, to equate these requirements with having to sacrifice any semblance of a personal life.

There's a danger that these myths about the need for body-and-soul commitment to the corporation will undermine the future success of business. This is because they risk alienating people with the leadership skills for a world in which operations and teams are dispersed across regions and time zones: balanced leaders who encourage collaboration, understand people and know how to motivate them, and are open to innovative work practices.

Fortunately, there are signs of change. We're seeing more examples of senior people adopting innovative work patterns that offer them a degree of balance. Some are doing this with the support of their organizations, others against the grain of their company's culture. More of them are also speaking out, recognizing that they are standard-bearers for the next generation of leaders.

In 2012, a UK jobs website, Timewise, collected examples of 50 leaders from different sectors who worked less than a five-day week, publishing them as the first ever annual 'Power Part Time' list.[5] They included chief executives, managing directors, finance directors and partners in professional services firms. Among the organizations employing them were Diageo, the multinational drinks group, the Bank of England, and the international law firm Norton Rose.

Many of them spoke about how the performance of the business had improved and about how productive and effective they were. 'Not only can it be done, but it is being done – not just in small local businesses but in some of the biggest and best-known brands in Britain,' Karen Mattison, founder of Timewise, told the *Financial Times*.[6]

These executives are doing extremely demanding roles, so they have to prioritize and manage their time well. Many of them emphasize communicating clearly and agreeing goals with their teams, and then trusting them to get on with the job.

Gender and generational shifts

In Chapter 4, we listed 'stronger management skills' among the intangible business gains associated with future work. Technical proficiency is not enough in the new world of work. More than ever, managers need strong people skills. Those who have these attributes, or who acquire them, should do well. Those who lack them will find their credibility and their position eroded. The organizations that make a successful transition to future work will be those that value such skills and encourage their growth.

INSEAD, the international business school, looked at ten 'critical components' of leadership and found that female executives received higher ratings than male executives in most of them. These ten components overlap with many of the attributes we believe managers need to succeed in the future world of work. They are: envisioning; empowering; energizing; designing and aligning; rewarding and feedback; team building; outside orientation; global mindset; tenacity; and emotional intelligence. Women were rated more highly than men by their bosses, peers and subordinates on all of these except envisioning, empowering and global mindset. On the latter two, neither men nor women stood out as being better.[7] These findings support the already substantial case for greater gender balance in top teams, since people who possess these leadership attributes will be particularly well-placed to manage and lead in the new world of work.

A separate study found a link between female leadership and trust. During the economic crisis, chief executives who protected jobs through creative approaches, such as flexible working and budget cuts, saw their trust scores rise, according to a survey of 5000 managers and employees by the UK's Institute of Leadership & Management, in collaboration with *Management Today* magazine. CEOs who instituted the most severe cutbacks, such as job losses and site closures, suffered a sharp drop in trust.

Women leaders scored more highly than their male counterparts on average. 'Our research indicates this is because female CEOs display a more pronounced interest in and concern for employees at all levels,' said David Pardey, the institute's head of research and policy. 'There is a lesson here for male CEOs to ponder – by demonstrating more interest in and awareness of the roles of the people they lead, they could enhance their levels of leadership trust.'[8]

There are interesting echoes here of the teachings of Mary Parker Follett, one of the early female management gurus, who wrote nearly 100 years ago about the importance of employee involvement and the exercise of 'power with' people instead of 'power over' them.

Beyond crisis management, leaders need to understand how work is changing, both in terms of technology and the physical environment and in terms of workforce attitudes. A report on twenty-first century leadership 'essentials' by The Conference Board, the global business membership and research organization, points to the changing nature of work and expectations of the workforce.[9] It says that leaders need to:

- recognize that individuals are more powerful than ever, with networks that transcend corporate boundaries
- understand employees' different motivations
- make flexibility a corporate value
- be comfortable with non-traditional career paths

The importance of such adaptability is recognized by Karen Newton, a managing director at Credit Suisse, the Swiss banking group, in London, who has promoted remote working in her team. 'Some managers say that it's more difficult to manage people that they can't see,' she says. 'I say to them: "Look around at our senior staff. Most of them have responsibility for people across different geographies. They can't see where their team is at any one time."'

Managers now regard the ability to manage people on a remote basis as 'an extra string to their bow', she says. 'People now talk about having remote workers on their team with a sense of pride and achievement. They say: "I'm preparing myself for a global role or for managing a geographically dispersed team."'

In our research for this book, we have found strong signs of a reaction against the pervasive notion that presence equals commitment. Younger leaders, in particular, appear to be less willing to play by the old rules. There is pent-up demand for greater autonomy, both for themselves and for their teams. Our survey of managers found that 58 percent want more freedom to let their teams work more flexibly, and over half also want more control over where, when and how they do their own jobs.

Younger managers appear less willing to sacrifice personal interests and responsibilities in the pursuit of leadership. They do not understand why this should be necessary. Indeed, some see it as their responsibility as leaders to demonstrate that a balanced life is possible and healthy.

This chapter shows how you, as a leader today or in the future, can benefit personally, and help your organization benefit, from future work. It tells how pioneering leaders from different sectors and countries have developed their individual work styles, and what lessons they have learned about managing teams and businesses successfully in the 24/7 world. They have these common features:

- They are strongly committed to their clients
- They value their personal lives
- They trust the people who work for them
- They want to change organizational life for the better

Finding the right 'fit': Slade Fester

Slade Fester, who was featured at the start of this chapter, is a leading figure in a 'People Force' initiative in his firm. 'Its aim is to empower people – staff and managers – to make BDO a better place to work,' he says. 'We realized that constant communication was essential in order to give equal attention to developing the business, managing resources and keeping people engaged. We have fortnightly teleconferences with staff from every level to solicit their thoughts about the mood of the office as well as topics relating to the business and resources. Employees voice their concerns and help to develop solutions to the issues raised.'

Like him, some employees live far from the office or have family responsibilities. He advises people on finding 'the right fit'. He also works with fellow partners who feel uncomfortable not having a manager or staff member physically present in the office all the time.

'In situations like these, it really just takes a tweak of the approach and an adjustment of attitude to make it work,' he says. 'It may be better coordination or communication when in the office. One of our star performers was grappling with his "long distance relationship" with work. To make his periodic visits to the office more meaningful and productive, he needed to cluster his meetings, make sure he was there for the key ones, and be more visible instead of spending all the time inside his own office. These were things that I found were helpful in my similar situation.'

Organizations that grant people autonomy are more likely to keep the talent they need, and he is a case in point. He took a circuitous career route to seniority – something we expect to become far more common as organizational structures change and working lives last longer.

After college and five years working for the accountancy firm then known as Coopers & Lybrand, he took a year's sabbatical to travel the world with his surfboard. When he returned home, friends who had moved to BDO lured him there with talk of its flexible culture. During his first years with the firm, he worked for six months of the year and spent the other six months surfing. Even after becoming a full-time employee in 1995, he took time out to build the house in the mountains, where he lives with his wife Reyna, a creative writer, and two children.

He points out that even the flexibility on offer here is not enough to keep every good employee. He gives the example of a high-achieving female colleague who had difficulties 'finding the right fit' after having her second child, struggling internally with her drive to do well at work and her growing family responsibilities. Having quit his own job to take a sabbatical in Mexico, where he met his future wife, he says he can relate to his colleague's decision. 'You have to be disciplined to get the work done, but there's almost more discipline to draw the line and *not* work, to spend the time with your kids, even with a deadline approaching, and not to let emails bother you.'

He sees his lifestyle as the only way to cope with the 'always on' world of work of the early twenty-first century. 'With technology, and with the world getting smaller and smaller, everyone's expected to get more and more done,' he says. '*How* you get it done is the question. I wouldn't still be doing a full-time corporate job if I wasn't able to release the pressure valves by going surfing or having these quality moments with my family. I'd make my own flexibility by doing my own thing as an entrepreneur.'

Change in an inflexible profession: Monica Burch

The City of London is hardly known as a hub of innovation when it comes to working patterns. Each day, hundreds of thousands of employees squeeze grimly into overcrowded underground trains and fight their way up escalators to their office blocks in the morning rush hour. Global competition and high rewards go hand in hand with old-fashioned, inflexible work practices and the pressure to be seen at your desk for long hours.

So Monica Burch's achievement in becoming the first woman to be senior partner and to chair Addleshaw Goddard, a leading commercial law firm with 1300 employees, is all the more remarkable. In 2010, Burch stood for election as head of the business and was chosen by her fellow equity partners. She made it clear in the election process that she would continue to work 90 percent, rather than 100 percent, of the year. This was what she had done since the arrival of her third child seven years earlier, and she was determined to keep space for her family as she took over the running of the firm. She was re-elected in 2012 on the same basis and started her second term as senior partner in May 2013.

Burch believes that setting a visible example is crucial to secure the talent on which the business depends for the future. When she joined the firm in 1988, women and men were already entering the legal profession in equal numbers.

'Now, 65 per cent of entry-level graduates are women. So there's a huge demographic issue,' she says. 'Thirty-three is the age when professional women tend to have children and it's traditionally the age when you look at becoming a partner. Women are either going before they start families, or they are saying: "I can't make this work" and are leaving later on.' Many of these women go to work in-house for corporate clients where the hours are a bit more predictable.

'Purely from a business perspective, you want to be able to pick the best people,' she says. 'It's not very good business practice if you cut off one large part of that talent.'[10]

Clients, especially those in the public sector, are demanding evidence of 'diversity' from law firms that work for them. Women represent 22 percent of Addleshaw Goddard's 169 partners. 'For our industry, that's on the good side of our peer group, and yet it's appalling when you think that lawyers all start the same way, with the same levels of qualifications, and the same training. It makes it more shocking when you look at the numbers, because partnerships are so broad. There are 12,000 partners in the UK's top 20 firms. It's not like trying to get onto a corporate board of directors where there are a far smaller number of seats.'

Her firm is unusual in treating flexible working as a smart business move, rather than a concession to employees. It has made a significant investment in IT, with BlackBerrys, laptops and electronic key fobs available to all staff who want them, so that people can log in securely while working away from the office. As well as formal flexible working arrangements, used by 16 percent of staff, most people have some informal autonomy over where they work. Working from home is 'pretty accepted and usual', she says.

The number of partners working flexibly is still fairly small – three men and six women – but Burch believes this is a good start. In 2012, women comprised the majority (60 percent) of internal promotions for the first time. In 2013, more than 40 percent of new internal partners were female.

Burch confesses that it is unusual for highly rewarded commercial lawyers 'to ever completely switch off'. Her own schedule is extremely demanding, even on a 90 percent contract. She typically works 11–12 hour days and usually has events with clients in the evenings. She uses the days she accumulates under her contract to take longer chunks of leave during school holidays or to have occasional days off during the term to attend sports days and children's concerts.

What will it take for the legal profession to move to a culture that judges people on results, not hours? As an advocate of change, she sees two major obstacles. One is the unpredictability of some of the work. Clients involved in corporate transactions such as mergers and acquisitions need their lawyers to work until the deal is done. This can mean several days non-stop without sleep.

The chief obstacle is the system of billing clients by the hour. 'The measure of productivity is the number of hours worked,' she says. 'The more you do, the better you are. In the traditional law firm model, the partner sits surrounded by their team, who feel they have to be in place, with their jackets on the chairs, until the partner leaves in the evening. Most law firms are grappling with this. There's a big debate about what's the best model for billing clients. If hourly billing is kicked into touch and you price by output, it will be easier to change the culture.'

Over the past five years, with leadership from the top, the firm has worked to shift attitudes and challenge assumptions. 'We have accepted flexible working as part of the culture and focused on performance, not hours worked,' says Burch. 'When we look at promotions to partner, the working pattern of the candidate simply doesn't come into it. That's a real change for us.'

Having to manage people working away from the office has been good for the business. 'If you don't have all your ducks in a row all the time, it makes people better managers. You have to think more broadly. It makes you more agile and better able to respond to clients because you are better able to cope with not having everyone lined up and waiting for the work.'

She believes attitudes are changing. 'There is a real rethink about how law firms deliver to clients, who does the work and how we bill for it in a way that I haven't seen in the profession before. It is just possible that this will kick the hourly rate into touch – the next five years will be critical – and I believe that will have a resounding impact on female progression.'

Burch puts today's practices into a historical perspective. 'Some law firms want 2500 charged and billed hours a year from their lawyers as a matter of course. I think people in the future will look back and say: "How did we put up with that?" in the same way that we look back now at the practice of sending children up chimneys and say: "How could people have put up with that?"'

Shared leadership: Carolyn Davidson and Tom Carter

The past 40 years have seen a dramatic rise in dual-earning couples. Women have become the majority of university graduates in many countries, and higher education has boosted their earning power. More than 20 percent of US wives today earn more than their husbands do, up from just 4 percent in 1970.[11]

These trends, while in many ways liberating, have created complications for couples and their employers with regard to international assignments. The main cause of failed assignments is partner dissatisfaction, and nearly half of people who turn down postings cite their partner's career as the reason, according to a survey of global relocation trends.[12]

In the British Foreign Office, as in diplomatic services around the world, promotion depends on readiness to take up foreign postings. So when one high-flying diplomatic couple, Carolyn Davidson and Tom Carter, were unable to find a ready-made way to combine their careers with bringing up their children, they invented one.

Neither wanted to stop working completely, so they came up with the idea of a novel job-share in which they would take it in turns to switch from the diplomatic to the home role every four months. After meeting some initial resistance, they were granted the post of Deputy Head of Mission in Slovakia in 2003. They achieved the balance they were seeking and their young sons took the arrangement in their stride. At work, the experiment proved so successful that in 2008 they were appointed joint British High Commissioner to Zambia – the world's first job-sharing heads of mission.

In a phone interview with them in Lusaka in 2010, their working relationship was immediately evident as they answered questions alternately and gave each other space to comment.[13] 'We take it in turns to lead, for four month stints,' explained Davidson. 'We work on the strategic stuff together, but the one "in the seat" at the time does the day-to-day implementation. We take special care in the run-up to handovers to brief the incomer on all live issues. We make a point of going round the High Commission and making ourselves known again, making it clear that there's been a change of sex! What people have commented on in our 360-degree feedback to managers is that it's a very seamless transition every four months.' Is this a future leadership model for couples working for the same organization? 'I think it is,' said Carter. 'You end up with a better set of decisions if there are two of you doing it. You get a much more comprehensive approach to an issue.' Indeed, they were told their joint problem-solving ability was notably better than one person's working alone.

There are other benefits for the organization. The Foreign Office has retained talent. 'If we hadn't done the job share and Tom had got another posting, I'd have been out of the office for seven years,' said Davidson. 'Experience dictates that people who are out for that long don't tend to come back.'

The arrangement generated mostly positive publicity for Britain's diplomatic service, depicting it as an innovative employer in the media and in the eyes of counterparts from countries such as Sweden, Russia and China. Another Foreign Office couple, Kathy Leach and Jonathan

Aves, has since replicated their job-sharing model as joint ambassador to Armenia. 'We spoke to them a lot before they took on the role, and are really pleased it's a model that works for others too,' says Davidson.

The main risk with any such arrangement would be if a couple's personal relationship broke down, and with it the job-share, she adds. However, marital splits can interfere with work and jeopardize overseas assignments, regardless of the working model.

The Foreign Office has two heads for the price of one, an advantage particularly when budgets are being squeezed. The financial aspect was the main drawback for Carter and Davidson, who traded their double incomes for a single one split between two. Back in London after their Zambia posting, the couple has reverted to a dual-income arrangement, both working full-time. They are clear that this is far from ideal, however. 'We miss the work-life balance that our job-share brought and find it more difficult to carve out that reflective time so necessary for getting strategy and decisions right.' They hope to revert to an overseas job-share at the end of their London posting.

Leading dispersed teams: Christel Verschaeren

Christel Verschaeren was in her first supervisory role at IBM when she received a call from the general manager for Belgium and Luxembourg inviting her to be his executive assistant. It was a highly desirable post, offering the chance to see the business from every angle, and a fast track to seniority. She wanted it, but she had seen that it involved being in the office from 7 a.m. to 8 p.m. every day. As a single mother, she decided she could not take on a job that meant she would not see her seven-year-old daughter during the week. She turned it down, thinking that was the end of her career prospects. No one had refused such an offer before.

A few weeks later, the general manager called her again. This time he asked her what she needed in order to do the job. 'I was speechless. I had never considered that question before,' says Verschaeren.[14] After reflecting, she said she needed to be able to take her daughter to school every day, and to leave the office early to pick her up. Then she could resume work later from home, and be contactable by cell phone – then still quite unusual at the company. The country manager agreed. From then on, all his executive assistants worked flexibly.

That was in 1999. Verschaeren has since risen to become chief information officer for IBM Europe, with global responsibility for change management within the internal CIO division. But she has never forgotten that her early boss, by being willing to contemplate a change in his own work routine, enabled her to stay with the company and flourish. The experience also opened her eyes to different ways of managing people.

'You don't have to be sitting in an office. You don't have to see your people working to be sure that they are working,' she says. 'I will never ask my people where they are or if they are doing A or B. I just ask them to do what they have to do by the time it has to be done. It does not make a difference if they do it at night or in the daytime, or if they do the laundry or go to the dentist during the "working day". We have video chats and phone calls and I never even wonder where they are. I may hear on the phone that they are in a car, but I don't ask. It has become automatic not to think about it.'

Managing people this way is not always easy, she concedes, especially when a deadline is looming. 'Intuitively you want to go back to controlling things because the deadline is tomorrow. You want to ask: "Where are we with this?" But I have taught myself to chat to my team in a supportive way, not in a policing way.'

As a female leader, Verschaeren has devoted much time to mentoring other women. She believes technology is good for women's progress because it enables them to manage competing demands on their time more effectively. Social media facilitate networking without having to go to the pub in the evening.

She argues that female characteristics (which are not exclusive to women) are useful for managing virtual and project-based teams. 'Some male managers who are used to working in a hierarchy find it difficult to do this. Women are more adept at making sure that everyone feels part of the team, independent of whether they report directly to them. With more and more work being done by teams who come together for a project and then disperse, the really good managers will be those who drive performance from people who don't report to them.'

Verschaeren believes that successful leaders in the new environment will:

- Demonstrate leadership from the front in a crisis but also emphasize flexibility and balance
- Be savvy with social media so they can work with and manage the 'digital natives' coming into the workforce
- Coach people to perform better, but not control them
- Respect and adapt to other cultures and languages
- Realize that no one, not even themselves, is irreplaceable

Finding balance as a high achiever: Mike Dean

Mike Dean is responsible for service delivery for Accenture Business Process Outsourcing in the UK, Ireland and Nordics, a division that employs 900 people and has annual sales of several hundred million dollars. Given his seniority, his email sign-off is striking. It says his typical working days are Tuesday, Wednesday and Thursday.

Dean is unusual for advertising his unconventional working pattern in this way. While a growing number of executives are reshaping their roles to be more manageable, many still prefer to keep quiet about it. He was one of the 50 senior people who spoke about their innovative work styles for the first 'Power Part Time' list[15].

Like many business leaders, he is an over-achiever. This caught up with him shortly before his 50th birthday. As a partner in BPO, he had been specializing in rescuing troubled contracts and had spent three years doing highly stressful work. 'I loved my job so much and I like to do everything pretty well,' he explains. 'I probably ignored some of the warning signs. I was meeting the finance director one lunchtime when I suddenly felt ill, went hot and cold, and started shaking. Then I lost consciousness and work up in hospital. I temporarily lost the use of one side of my body and was diagnosed with an adrenal imbalance.'

Switching to a reduced working week was part of his decision to rebalance his work and his other commitments, including his family and voluntary work with his church and young people. He believes it has made him a better leader, delivering more value to clients than other people do in five days a week.

The success factors are delegation, time management and putting people first, he says. 'This is a job with never-ending demands. You couldn't do it by yourself, even if you worked seven days a week. People often say to me: I've no idea how you get done what you do, let alone in three days. But it's just about being efficient and effective in making decisions, and ensuring that your team knows they can make decisions without always consulting you.'

On Mondays, he does the school run, gets some exercise, and spends a couple of hours planning the week ahead, using a grid to assign items as 'urgent' or 'important'. 'When assessing priorities, you have to have the guts to say: That one is a fire that needs to be put out, but it's going to have to burn a bit longer. You have to make sure you're only doing stuff that addresses the absolute priorities.'

On Fridays, he checks emails at the start and end of the day, but does not necessarily respond. 'If it's genuinely urgent, people in my team send me a text,' he says. 'They know I'm happy for them to make decisions.' Of his three working days, he typically spends two days meeting his teams at different locations around the UK, Ireland and Norway or at clients' premises, and one day at home. 'I don't have any fixed office and I just hot-desk wherever I need to be that day. I do tend to be truly mobile with just a small backpack as my "office", containing my PC, my mobile phone, my to-do list Time Manager and my day book.'

He stresses that new work styles should be visible. 'This was an aggressive, macho, bang-bang organization and there are still pockets where managers think that everyone has to be in the office seven days a week. It's typically a few men who have these views, and we have to change these attitudes. Someone will say to me: "This role has to be five days a week, and it has to be London-based", and I'll look at it and say: "I don't think it needs to be done that way". This has had a dramatic impact in helping to challenge the previous culture and embed much more flexible attitudes to work. And there are now more and more examples of where this flexibility has worked within Accenture and so success breeds success.'[16]

A wider pool of leaders: Isla Ramos Chaves

Isla Ramos Chaves has no doubt that the business world will change significantly as future work becomes more commonplace. 'It will take us to more diverse organizations in the widest sense,' says Ramos Chaves, executive director of business transformation and project management for Europe, Middle East and Africa for Lenovo, the Chinese-owned PC manufacturer.

'It's important for international businesses to have people in their leadership team who know about other markets and have a different way of thinking, rather than the old model of leadership where it was always the same people holding the same positions. It opens the door to so many possibilities.'[17]

Her own experience, as a woman and a Spaniard on the European board of the company, illustrates the point perfectly. An ex-IBMer, she moved to Lenovo when it was spun off from the US parent group in 2005. Having done various international assignments, she wanted to stay in Madrid to be close to her mother, who was unwell. The ability to do the job remotely, rather than to relocate to Lenovo's West European headquarters in Paris, was the deciding factor in accepting the job. She has since been promoted from director to executive level and taken on new roles.

'I wouldn't have taken the job if I'd had to move to Paris,' she says. 'The conditions of the job offer were important because it's really difficult for a Spanish person who doesn't want to move abroad permanently to get a senior position in a multinational company. These jobs are usually in the larger countries or big hubs.'

Leaders in international businesses today must have the skills to manage people scattered across different countries and time zones. 'It's not an optional model any more,' she says. 'If you're going to make the most of your global resources you don't have any alternative. Big fat headquarters are no longer affordable for many companies, and they're not very agile. Learning how to manage people remotely needs to be embedded in every management-training program: it takes a lot more work to lead remotely than on site.'

Ramos Chaves, 42, travels extensively but is still based in the Lenovo office in Madrid. She works with a virtual team of over 60 people, only two of whom are in Madrid. The others work in different European countries, some from home, and some from satellite offices, depending on the culture. Working from home is less common in Spain than, for example, in the UK.

The composition of her team changes according to the project on which she is working. 'I have a core of five very high-profile people and the rest are from all areas of the company and some external consultants, depending on the subject matter expertise I need for different projects. For example, I just finished a huge project where I led a team in Europe whose functional manager was actually in China.'

In her six-year experience of virtual teams, she has found it problematic if people work only from home and have little interaction with others. Getting the right balance is important. She encourages her team to spend time in their local office with colleagues. 'Some people go crazy if they're working on their own. There's a level of uncertainty that they can't handle. They may need constant reassurance, and you need to be very aware of that. When you're agreeing objectives, you need to see if it suits them.'

However, she says that giving people autonomy has had a positive impact on both men and women. They are much more productive when their work is judged on objectives and not on presence. 'It has empowered and developed the members of the team significantly. Many of them have developed incredible levels of autonomy and this has changed their approach to work completely, to being much more proactive and solution-oriented.' Having a mix of cultures, genders and perspectives in the team helps people to adapt more quickly to different ways of working and new roles because they are more open-minded.

She communicates with her team by phone, email, teleconferencing and videoconferencing, online chats and instant messages. She makes a point of sticking to scheduled call times.

'It's about them knowing where they stand in their communication with you. With a new person, I tell them that I don't always answer the phone because I'm very busy, but they should leave a message and I'll get back. Then they are not left with the anguish of not knowing where they stand. You have to create a virtual space with people: so you say, for example: "On Monday between 9 a.m. and 10 a.m. I'm all yours. Whatever happens, this is the time we spend together."'

She says future work practices will only be successful if:

- They are treated as a competitive advantage and embedded in the business strategy. 'It will be unsustainable if it isn't spread across the organization and seen as part of the way you do business.'

- The organization is set up to enable virtual and remote working. 'Being equipped with the right tools is essential. Even more important than the physical tools is having really good management systems. Without those, people are left on their own.'

- Communication with team members is made an absolute priority. 'It requires really high doses of discipline.'

In summary

The pioneers featured in this chapter offer many lessons for leadership in the new world of work. They share strong principles, a curiosity about how to get the best out of people, and an ability to learn and adapt. To be an innovative role model requires:

- Well-honed communication skills
- Delegating and trusting people
- Prioritizing tasks and meetings that matter
- Willingness to challenge the status quo
- Understanding that people are individuals
- Being disciplined about 'switching off'

In Chapters 8, 9 and 10, we give detailed guidance on these and other skills that managers and leaders need to develop or sharpen. In the next chapter, we investigate the changing role of location in work, and the implications this has for management and leadership.

CHAPTER 6

Changing workplaces

Just as eBay revolutionized the world of e-commerce ... we can now tap into this same idea to revolutionize the world of work. There are new ways to get work done, which eliminate the dependency on office buildings, commuting, and set work hours day in and day out.[1]

Maynard Webb, Silicon Valley veteran and author of Rebooting Work

Does the office have a future?

The entrance to the **Microsoft** building in Amsterdam, a huge reflective-glass box next to Schiphol airport, has the feel of an ultra-modern hotel lobby. People sit or stand around, chatting or waiting for appointments, bags and suitcases on the floor, laptops open on tables. Low sofas and coffee beckon from the hospitality corner.

There is no traditional reception desk with fixed phones. Black-suited receptionists emerge from behind a long white counter, greeting visitors, offering refreshments, and using hand-held messaging devices to alert hosts to their guests' arrival. Only the security barriers to the lifts and stairs signal that this is corporate territory.

The Netherlands office, designed for a world in which work is independent of time and location, was an experiment for Microsoft. Ever since opening in 2008, it has attracted about 45,000 visitors a year from around the world, eager to glimpse the physical embodiment of 'anytime anywhere' work. New Microsoft sites in Argentina, Australia, Belgium, France, India, Japan, Norway and Switzerland have adopted similar arrangements, though adapted to their local culture.

Theo Rinsema, vice-president for sales & marketing in West Europe and former Netherlands general manager, explains the concept behind the design. 'The office should be a meeting place, not a working place. We can work anywhere, so it is social cohesion that becomes the important factor in physical premises.'[2]

The first floor is the 'community' area. The atmosphere is purposeful but informal. The busy restaurant has three-sided booths, with low-hanging lights over the tables, and there is a popular café-bar. The meeting rooms have sofas, chairs and poufs but few tables, encouraging people to sink into whatever position they find most comfortable. Tiny red chambers are available for private phone calls, and there is a wall of lockers with individuals' names chalked, kindergarten-style, on the doors.

Every employee has a badge with a chip inside which gives them access to the building and to all corporate information stored digitally, apart from personnel files. 'Connectedness' is emphasized by the open view from the first floor down into the lobby and up to the quieter second floor, where there are internal meeting rooms, small enclosed workstations for concentrated work, and open plan desks that can be raised or lowered for comfort.

Sevil Peach, the architect who led the design of the Microsoft building, says the future is about 'empowering people to make decisions about how they want to work throughout a day'.[3]

With the growth of mobile working around the world, the purpose of the bricks-and-mortar office is under scrutiny. There is pressure on organizations to reduce their carbon footprint, and potentially large scope to do so while making cost savings on office space if employees are spending more time working away from their desks.

Employees' expectations are adding to that pressure. According to an international survey commissioned by Cisco Systems, the networking technology company, 60 percent of people believe they do not need to be in an office to be productive, a view that is strongest among employees in

India, China and Brazil. Based on these findings, Cisco asks: 'Is the office really necessary?'[4]

The answer is yes, but not in its conventional form. We do not expect, unlike some of the wilder predictions made back in the 1980s, that everyone will work from home and that offices will disappear any time soon. Even in the most technologically advanced companies like Microsoft, people are still social animals. Humans need to meet face-to-face, at least in early encounters, to develop fruitful relationships. Moreover, some people find solitary work difficult and stressful, while others thrive on it. What's important for most people is to have a healthy mix.

'People like the choice of working at home but they often go spare if they are there for more than a couple of days a week,' says Alexi Marmot, professor of environment and facility management at University College London. 'There aren't many jobs that even the most thoughtful people can work at for weeks on end without the company of others. You somehow get empowered by the presence of other people. Evolutionary biologists and psychologists say that mankind is generally equipped to live in social groups.'[5]

Online collaboration can be highly successful, but there are times when we have to be together in person to make things work. Advanced videoconferencing technology can simulate everyone being in the same room, even when they are dispersed around the globe, and it is becoming a good substitute for expensive and time-consuming business travel. But it cannot entirely replace the energy that people derive from each other's physical presence, or the more personal, thoughtful discussions that bond colleagues and collaborators and make people feel valued.

Offices will continue to be an important feature of the twenty-first century landscape. But the role of location in work is changing significantly, and with it the role of management.

In this chapter we examine some emerging workplace models, their benefits and limitations and the changes they require in management attitudes and behavior. We give examples from around the world including Macquarie and Commonwealth Bank of Australia, the US federal government in Washington DC, Unilever in Germany and Vodafone in the UK, starting with an in-depth look at how Microsoft's Dutch operation adapted its culture and management practices to the new world of work.

From workplace to meeting place

Employees of Microsoft in the Netherlands were used to working remotely, even before the move to the new building. But something was not right. People rated their work-life balance at just 5.3 on a scale of 1 to 10 because they found it so difficult to stop working. Things improved as a result of the new work styles, leadership styles and strong emphasis on communication, says Ineke Hoekman-van Hassel, human resources director for the Netherlands. The work-life balance score rose from 5.3 to over 8 and has since settled between 7.6 and 8, giving the Dutch operation one of the highest scores in Microsoft worldwide.[6]

Other benefits include a slight increase in productivity, as measured by a model developed by Erasmus University in Rotterdam, and a 30 percent reduction in CO_2 emissions through reduced car and air travel. Employee attrition is low, at 8–9 percent a year, which is a mixed blessing: it demonstrates people's attachment to the new environment but also holds back hiring new talent.

The Dutch business particularly wants to increase its female population. In the last few years, the female share of the workforce has risen from 17 percent to the Dutch IT industry average of 21 percent, but missed the 2012 target of 25 percent. A more challenging target of 30 percent has been set for 2015.

A number of people who were working part-time have switched to full-time, says Hoekman-van Hassel, who has done so herself. 'You can do a full-time job while still having the flexibility to pick up your kids,' she says. Less than 10 percent of employees, half of them men, work part-time – very low for the Netherlands where over 75 percent of women work part-time (see more on this in Chapter 7).

The 750 full-time employees, as well as 200 contractors and interim staff, work from home one day a week on average, and the rest of the time at customers' sites or the Schiphol building. Even people who have to be present in the building to do their jobs, such as the receptionists and caterers, have a degree of autonomy, as they are able to arrange their own schedules.

Central to the success of the transfer has been the leadership team's focus on changing culture and attitudes. 'When we moved to this building, we moved from control to trust,' says Rinsema. 'We manage by output rather than presence. I don't know an organization that has put so much emphasis on changing leadership styles as we have. We separated status from hierarchy. There was some resistance during the journey.'

He agrees that future work is about empowering people, making them more productive and helping their work-life balance or integration. 'It was perfectly clear to me that we had to further develop our leadership style in order to unleash employee empowerment. To be capable of leading based on trust, we as leaders realized that we had to look at our personal development, especially our personal drivers and control mechanisms.'

He used a coach and facilitator to develop his team, including himself. At the start of the sessions he asked what the program would be. The coach told him there was no program. This turned out to be the beginning of learning to let go.

'I gained a better insight into my personal control mechanisms and how much I depend on these,' he says. 'Fortunately I also gained insight into how I could loosen up a bit. I have the perception that I am much closer to the employees, with many more interactions through a variety of media. The balance between leading on the one hand and being a networked colleague on the other hand is, in this context, crucial. Regarding the anywhere anytime workforce, you have to support and coach people that you do not expect them to be "always on". You have to set the example as a leader.'

Responsibility for managing the boundaries between work and private life lies both with leaders and individual employees, says Hoekman-van Hassel. Around the time of the move, individuals and teams were offered the chance to assess their preferred work styles and stress profiles using the Myers-Briggs Type Indicator personality test, and this continues to be used for new hires. The insights into personal work style and other people's preferences are useful, for example in alerting employees and managers to stress-related problems and in making virtual team meetings more effective, she says.

One highly symbolic change is that there are no individual offices. This is culturally very different from Microsoft's vast US headquarters in Redmond, Washington, where enclosed individual offices generally still matter, and where the software giant has made huge investments in expanding its real estate portfolio on the campus and surrounding area in recent years.[7]

'Nobody has a dedicated office, not even me,' says Rinsema. 'You find the ideal workspace depending on what you are doing.'

It is no accident that this pioneering building is in the Netherlands. It is easier to make the shift to future working styles in some cultural contexts than others. In general, northern Europe is more open to this than southern Europe, says Gonnie Been, manager of corporate communications and social innovation at Microsoft Netherlands. But there is resistance in America too. 'In the US, it still matters how long you have been in service, so cultural patterns are preventing it from changing,' she says. 'Europeans were more traditional and we're moving faster now. We must not become complacent. I'm working on how we get that constant change so that we stay ahead.'

One of the hardest things is breaking the link between status and position in the hierarchy. In the Netherlands, they are trying to do this by redefining status as the individual's contribution and leadership skills. People are encouraged both to move across functions and to develop individual expertise.

'Status comes through leadership, if people want to work with you,' says Been. 'The whole approach to the new world of work is that you need to be a personal leader – you need to lead your own life rather than being controlled by the boss as in the past – and if you're able to do that you are able to lead others. My next step could be towards more of a specialist role.'

One breakthrough followed an agreement that people were no longer expected to be in the office for meetings. 'The most difficult situation previously was when you had a few people who were physically there for the meeting and others who were dialing in, because those present assumed the others hadn't bothered to get there,' says Rinsema.

Many meetings are now virtual, and communication takes place via web technology such as the company's Live Meeting service, using web cams and headsets. The use of internet phone lines, rather than landlines, has cut costs, increased efficiency and changed the way people communicate.

'Sixty-eight percent of phone calls used to end in voicemail,' he says. 'Now, we see if someone is available by starting a chat conversation through [Microsoft] Communicator, then we can move into a voice conversation if necessary and we can bring other people into the conversation and use web cams to replace physical meetings.'

More recently, the company has introduced Yammer, a private social network used by growing numbers of businesses around the world to encourage virtual collaboration.

Although employees already had flexibility, they felt uncomfortable about using the 'working day' to do something different like playing tennis, shopping or spending time with their children. The move to the new building has gone along with explicit permission to do these things.

'You disconnect time from work,' explains Been. 'Work is a series of activities to get results. You can meet or communicate smarter. You can save at least 20 percent of your time or energy to do other things. You finally do those things that you said: "If only I had time I would do that". There is no excuse any more.'

This does not mean that it is easy to change people's habits. Employees come and go throughout the day but arrivals in the office still spike around 9 a.m. and departures around 5.30 p.m. Attitudes have to be constantly challenged, both in wider society and in the company. 'It's an ongoing process,' says Hoekman-van Hassel. 'You need to keep on developing as an organization and finding ways to be more effective, productive and creative.'

Adapting to a world of work defined by trust, freedom and responsibility should in theory be easier for young people starting their careers, because they are not caught up in old habits. Yet this next generation, too, arrives with a set of assumptions.

When Microsoft invited a group of 16–20 year olds to visit the Schiphol building, their questions revealed both apprehension and excitement about the possibilities. 'Do people *work* here?' they asked incredulously. 'Is work fun?' 'Who is controlling you?' 'Where is your boss?'

Human and carbon footprints

While some organizations are eagerly grasping the opportunities afforded by technology, others are finding themselves forced into change. Two factors are pushing them to cut space and to encourage remote working, says Professor Marmot, who is a leading expert on the design, management and use of places for work and learning.

The more immediate one is the high level of office costs, especially where space is constrained. With average office occupancy rates at just over 50 percent during the working week, there is potential for 'huge savings' to be made, she says.

The West End of London is the most expensive place in the world, with occupiers having to pay $23,500 per workstation per annum in 2012, more than three times the global average, according to DTZ, a global property services company. In the US, occupancy costs per workstation fell in 2012 because of a decrease in the amount of space allocated to each worker, but the US is still the country offering the most space per employee on average.[8]

The second, longer-term, factor is environmental sustainability. Organizations are under growing pressure to cut greenhouse gas emissions from their buildings. The UK, for example, is making the transition to a low carbon economy with a legally binding reduction in emissions of at least 80 percent by 2050. Penalties will rise over time for organizations that fail to comply.

The cost savings and environmental gains to be made by those who invest in green buildings can be substantial. **Macquarie Group** in Australia is one financial services company to have adopted 'activity-based' working at its building in Shelley Street, Sydney, which was designed for collaboration and green benefits.

Everyone uses a laptop and the whole building is wireless, so people can choose the appropriate place for their changing needs during the day – from meeting rooms and themed 'breakout' areas to quiet zones, informal spaces for collaboration and cafés. Bookable glass-walled pods of different colors jut out over the central atrium.

Moving from Macquarie's previous office to Shelley Street led to a 52 percent reduction in paper use through printing and a 78 percent drop in paper storage space. The company says people also use elevators less, choosing to walk up and down the central staircase.

A culture change program accompanied the physical move, as Kate Strahorn, head of direct marketing for banking and financial services, told Australia's ABC National Radio. 'You're given a high degree of empowerment. But with that empowerment comes accountability, and with that accountability comes trust. So you really need to have those fundamentals with all of your people.'[9]

The **US federal government** is also promoting new ways of working as part of a drive to make its vast stock of real estate more efficient, cut costs and become a clean energy economy. The government is the largest property owner in the US, and in his first term President Obama directed federal agencies to generate savings of $8bn by eliminating excess building space and related spending.

Since then, the General Services Administration (GSA), the agency responsible for federal buildings, has pushed for more and more efficient use of office space. Federal agencies reported savings of $8.6bn by the end of 2012, and there is an ongoing 'freeze the footprint' policy to encourage consolidation of space and greater use of telework.[10]

While the agencies have telework policies, few employees had taken these up in the past because of management and cultural resistance and concerns about staff cover in the office. In 2008, less than 9 percent of the 1.2m eligible federal employees worked away from the office.[11]

Change appears to be on the way, albeit slowly. In 2010, Congress passed a bill to increase teleworking, which is defined as regularly working 'at home or other work sites geographically convenient to the residence of the employee'. Federal agencies are required to run training programs for employees and managers, to designate senior managers to promote the policy and to make it a core part of continuity planning. This could boost the number of teleworking employees to 1m, according to *Federal Times*, the online government news source.[12] A government report in mid-2012 said that 25 percent of eligible employees were now teleworking.[13]

The GSA had a major modernization project for its central office under way at the time of the telework legislation, and this provided the catalyst to explore how work gets done and to prepare for a new generation with different expectations and work styles. In 2011, it embarked on a pilot for new approaches to work and management after 1200 agency staff moved to interim offices while their long-term Washington DC headquarters was remodeled.

Three categories of employee began to emerge in the pilot: 'resident', or office-based, spending most of the day at their desk; 'roamers', who move around the floor or building but are rarely at their desks; and 'remote', working from home, traveling, on the move or at other sites, but rarely in the office.

GSA monitored occupancy in the pilot project and found that less than 50 percent of the workers were in the building at any one time. This is not unusual. Gensler, the international architecture and design firm which designed the new workplace, has been measuring occupancy in the US for some time and found similar results in the private sector.

Based on the pilot results, the agency redesigned its 100-year-old headquarters building to accommodate twice the number of employees that it did before, says Janet Pogue of Gensler.

'To achieve this, the building had to be redesigned to support the way that people work today,' she says. 'Instead of long corridors lined with closed doors, there are now low-paneled workstations punctuated with enclosed "huddle" or "focus" rooms where employees can work quietly or collaborate with others. An array of work settings is available for reservation by the hour or the day depending upon the worker's activities. There is also a mix of large and small team rooms and conference rooms for group work. The utilization of the building has not only increased, but the visibility and connectivity of employees has increased as well.'

The management implications have also been explored. GSA leaders began preparing managers for the return to headquarters when they first moved out. Mina Wright, director of the GSA's office of planning & design quality, says there were many training opportunities during the two-year modernization program to help leaders and managers adjust, although even more could be done in this area.[14] Daniel M. Tangherlini, head of the GSA, acknowledged in a *Washington Post* article that 'there is still resistance'.[15]

Experience from the private sector suggests that senior executives and young employees are better at adapting to the new world of virtual work, while middle managers may find it more difficult, says Pogue. 'Senior leaders have been mobile for years, traveling with their teams or traveling across their firm, but middle managers are used to seeing their staff face-to-face every day and they often have the greatest shift to make in managing people differently.'

However, managers have no choice but to adapt, Pogue believes. 'People in both the public and private sectors are realizing as they walk around their offices that most people are not at their desk any more. They are in meetings, traveling, with clients, working from home or from a coffee shop down the street. Work has clearly already shifted and it's time for the physical space to shift as well.'[16]

'In between' workspaces

As aging office buildings undergo refurbishment to make them more environmentally sustainable – known as 'green retrofitting' – a parallel trend is taking place with the rapid expansion of workspaces that offer mobile workers a halfway house between home and conventional offices.

These 'third spaces' cover a spectrum from formal serviced offices to private membership clubs to informal 'work hubs' and cafés that offer wireless internet access for the price of a cup of coffee. One example of a free third space is the **British Library** at St Pancras in London, which has become a popular drop-in place for focused work and meetings since it introduced Wi-Fi and comfortable seating with power sockets for laptops.

The growing range of such 'in between' spaces provides variety and essential infrastructure for mobile employees and self-employed professionals with no fixed work abode other than home. While serviced offices can be very impersonal, some third spaces, such as clubs and business lounges, are trying to give nomadic workers a sense of belonging.

Neardesk is a young business in the UK that gives workers access to a growing network of technology-enabled hubs where they can rent a desk by the day or hour using an access card. Founder Tom Ball says that working from home is not an option for everyone, yet many people want to be more productive and avoid long commutes. His goal is to get 1m people working near home one day per week, saving 100m commuting hours each year, leading to a more productive workforce and more vibrant communities.[17]

Meanwhile, entrepreneurs and freelancers are getting together to share space, ideas and leads in co-working spaces that are growing in popularity in both small and large metropolitan areas from Singapore and San Francisco to Berlin and London. One example of this is the area around the Old Street roundabout in London where start-up web businesses have grouped together to share space. Known as 'Silicon Roundabout', the area has attracted larger technology companies such as Microsoft and IBM wanting to join the wave of innovation. The district is home to the Google Campus, seven floors of flexible co-working space with free high-speed internet connections, aimed at small high-tech businesses. The importance of this area has been recognized by the UK government, which is investing £50m in a large indoor 'civic space', dedicated to start-ups and capable of supporting 10,000 students in coding and enterprise.

Commuting time is one of the biggest challenges around the world, as a report on the changing nature of work, *Agility @ Work*, underlines. 'In many developing economies, cities are becoming immobile – it can take hours to move around Beijing or Delhi,' say authors Mark Dixon, founder and chief executive of Regus, the leading provider of serviced offices, and Philip Ross, CEO of the Cordless Group, which specializes in the impact of technology on people, business and the built environment.

In Thailand, which has the world's longest commuting times, 37m hours are spent traveling to work every day, they say. 'In Bangkok, the average travel speed during the peak rush hour is now just seven miles per hour.'

Dixon and Ross believe there is a gap in the provision of places for people to work 'on the pause'. They predict a huge increase in third space, especially on the peripheries of cities, in transport hubs and in neighborhoods, which will help to reduce commuting and road congestion.

They also envisage corporate buildings having serviced offices or other spaces alongside them, run by external partners and providing additional meeting capacity, project areas and specialist technology such as video-conferencing when needed.

Technology is the catalyst and enabler of these future work trends, and management culture is the biggest hurdle, they say. 'But reducing the cost of real estate or "occupancy" will be seen to be a clear win-win, as new work styles change the cost base for doing business.'[18]

From office to virtual to 'creative hub'

When Mark Thomas set up **Word Association** as a marketing and PR agency, he took on staff and opened an office in Leicester, England. After a few years of growing the business, he decided to take a 'sabbatical' year and travel around Europe with his young family in a motor home. He kept in touch with the UK by phone and email so he could still be involved at a distance.

When he returned, he questioned why his employees needed to be in the office at all. If he could run the business from hundreds of miles away, why couldn't his people also be remotely located? So he closed the office down and everyone started working from home in 1998 – an early example of a virtual business. Over the following decade, turnover doubled, and overheads were kept low. 'We have had high levels of productivity and staff satisfaction and very low levels of absenteeism,' says Thomas.

The agency survived the tough recession and in 2013 decided to start recruiting again. With growth in mind, Thomas decided to rent space in the Atkins Building, a former hosiery factory in the Leicestershire town of Hinckley, which has been redeveloped and divided into serviced office space, studios, meeting rooms, an art gallery and a café.

New recruits will spend most of their time here while they learn the ropes. 'Some new members of staff in the past found it difficult to feel part of the team and learn their job in a home-working environment,' he explains.

Experienced staff will use the space for meetings and as a drop-in workplace. 'It's somewhere we can take clients back to, and being a creative hub it gives us a good opportunity to network with like-minded businesses.'[19]

The nature of creativity

For organizations investing in buildings that respond to new work priorities, an important question is whether changes in the physical environment can make people more collaborative and creative.

A striking feature of modern offices such as Microsoft's in Amsterdam and Macquarie's in Sydney is the emphasis on bright colors and light, airy spaces. Some companies in trend-conscious sectors such as technology and public relations go further, introducing as many unconventional features as possible in an effort to make work friendly, fun and collaborative.

Google, the world's leading internet company, is famous for the free meals, casual dress, pool tables and colorful deckchairs on display at its offices. The engineers can take time out of their main job to develop new business ideas, a freedom that has generated some of the search engine's biggest innovations. 'It's much less about top-down structure and processes than at a traditional organization,' says Matt Brittin, vice president for Google in northern and central Europe.[20]

In some respects, though, working practices are fairly conventional. Engineers and sales people sit in long rows in the open-plan London 'GooglePlex', absorbed in their PCs and Macs, or chatting in small groups. It's still a predominantly young workforce, with many employees in their mid-20s to early 30s. The perks and quirks – party balloons, rubber ducks stuck upside down on the ceiling, sweets, salads and drinks on tap – seem geared to keep people in the office, something that Brittin acknowledges. Google does not favor teleworking. 'Our business is built on collaboration,' he says. 'You can work flexibly and from home but it's not encouraged on a continuous basis.'

Interestingly, Brittin says he gets his best ideas while cycling to work through the peaceful surroundings of London's Richmond Park. 'It's just me and my bike and the occasional deer,' he said in a *Financial Times* interview.[21]

Can the physical look and feel of an office really make a difference to people's level of creativity? Professor Marmot of University College London is doubtful. 'We know that people say they are most creative and thoughtful when in natural environments with views of trees, mountains, lakes or seas. It's never at their desk at home or in the office,' she says. 'If you're interested in effective work in the knowledge economy, ideas generation and knowledge sharing, it cannot be fostered through space design, but through rewarding thought.

'Google for example has done lots of groovy things such as meetings in a rowing boat or in a bath or round a beehive, as if shaking up the physical environment might help do things better. I'm not sure we can say that's the case. The kooky thing doesn't make you creative, it just makes a statement that you're in the IT industry with a brand that's young and trendy. When you see how people actually work in those industries, it's not necessarily very different.'

Marmot argues that creativity can be hindered by dirty, uninspiring physical surroundings and by not having the right equipment in the right place. 'But you can't necessarily help creativity just by doing the office environment well.'

It seems that different personality types also need different types of space. An interesting paper by psychologist Nigel Oseland points out that extroverts prefer large, face-to-face groups, informal meetings, and stimulating spaces, while introverts prefer written communications, small groups, teleconferences, and quieter spaces. Since introverts often want to think things through before committing to ideas in public, the research proposes encouraging them to participate in collaborative work by providing more private spaces next to main meeting areas for follow-up conversations.[22]

Breaking down resistance

Collaboration is an important theme in the sparkling new **Unilever** offices in Hamburg's huge HafenCity development zone. The views over the River Elbe are a big break with the past for employees of the consumer goods company in the north German industrial city. The award-winning building, completed in 2009, is designed to be environmentally sustainable and transparent, with a café, grocery store and spa to attract the public and serve employees.

The move from an 18-storey building in another part of Hamburg was also motivated by the war for talent, says Harry Brouwer, the group's chairman for Germany, Austria and Switzerland. 'If you want top people you have to have top premises. The number of people who want to join Unilever increased significantly since we moved into the new building and actively updated the company culture.'[23]

The old Hamburg building had individual offices and long dark corridors and there was little interaction between people and departments. In the new Unilever Haus, people can work anywhere, including the roof terrace, with wireless connection to the local area network. The interior is entirely open plan, with no walled rooms and doors, even for the leadership team.

Two weeks after they moved in, a veteran employee told Brouwer that she had seen more of him in the short time in the new building than she had seen of the board of directors in the previous 20 years.

The exterior resembles an ocean liner, which is appropriate since the building is a flagship for Unilever's company-wide 'agile working' strategy. Personal offices, including those for senior leaders, are being consigned to history. New buildings and renovations are being designed for better communication and to accommodate 30–50 percent higher densities of people, enabling significant cost savings on real estate, the company says. They will be equipped with advanced teleconferencing facilities, 'free address' workstations that anyone can use, soft phones that make calls from a computer via the Internet rather than a fixed line, and 'thin client devices', which are mobile terminals that draw their computational power from central servers.

'Anytime anywhere', as practiced by Microsoft and many other technology companies, was an unfamiliar concept to most of Unilever's people in Hamburg. Not everyone yet has the tools to work remotely, and the 1100 managers and staff have to get used to performance measurement based on output not hours. 'We're starting the process,' says Brouwer.

To encourage greater autonomy and initiative, he has introduced what he calls the 'one-metre rule', which states that employees should deal with issues arising in their sphere of responsibility without asking permission of their manager. 'People appreciate this, but they are not used to it and still feel a bit insecure about it.'

There are ongoing discussions with the top 50 executives about managing people in the new environment. 'We talk about agile working, how to deal with the workforce, and leadership development. We talk openly about trust and coping with the fear of losing control of people. This is something you have to deal with. If someone isn't there, what does it mean? Does it mean loss of control, or better output?'

To help managers confront their fears, the leadership team invited a blind mountain-climber to come and talk about what it was like to experience every single move as a step into the unknown. 'We were saying to them: You too can move out of your zone of comfort.'

Like Theo Rinsema at Microsoft, Brouwer had to go through his own evolution 'from control to letting go', which he did in his previous role as head of the Benelux region of Unilever. In his current job, he works one day a week from his home office in Holland. Other members of the senior team telecommute, but still only occasionally.

'There is quite a lot of discussion and insecurity about working away from the office because people aren't used to it,' Brouwer says. 'The younger generation don't have a problem with it, but the challenge is to get the older generation to do this because they are used to working at specific desks.'

The transition is work in progress. But employee engagement, measured through Unilever's global 'pulse survey', has risen strongly since the move to the new building and the changes taking place in the internal culture.

Adapting as a leader

Redesigning the office layout and giving people the technology to work anywhere anytime are not enough to achieve a successful move to future work. As this chapter shows, it often requires a significant shift in organizational culture. To support and promote this shift, even the most open-minded leaders find they have to challenge their own assumptions and adapt their style.

Grahame Petersen is group executive for business and private banking at **Commonwealth Bank of Australia,** which introduced activity-based working at its new offices in Sydney's Darling Quarter in 2011 as part of a major culture change program. It has since adopted the new way of working in other buildings in Sydney and Perth. Petersen speaks frankly about the benefits and challenges for him and other leaders, as well as for employees.

The culture change was initiated in 2005 by then CEO Ralph Norris, he explains. Internally, the bank had a reputation for being hierarchical and operating in silos. Norris decided to prioritize collaboration, customer satisfaction and employee empowerment as ways to create long-term value for the business.

'A lot of our success has come from operating collaboratively, and this has encouraged us as the top leadership team to be very focused on developing a collaborative culture. This was a shift from a more "command & control" culture, so it has been quite a change but very worthwhile,' says Petersen. 'As I've learned to focus on empowerment rather than being directive, I've unleashed enormous potential in people. I've become much better at asking a person how they might achieve something, rather than telling them.'[24]

Activity-based working, which drew on examples such as Macquarie in Sydney and Microsoft in Amsterdam, has saved on office space and increased productivity at the bank. The new offices are fully Wi-Fi-enabled so that people can work in different locations, depending on whether they need quiet time, are involved in a team activity, or are liaising with a colleague or client. People do not have designated desks, but they have large 'home zones' designed to give them a sense of belonging to a team. The system is paperless, with employees relying on electronic files and with all paper scanned in centrally as it arrives.

The change was challenging, says Petersen. 'Some people really liked structure in their day, some are quieter or more introverted and wanted their own space, and some people find any type of change challenging. We've tried to understand their needs and work with them over time. Many people who were initially reluctant have found it terrific. Being much more empowered and engaged outweighs some of the more comfortable, traditional ways of doing things, such as having stacks of paper and personal belongings on the desk.'

Managers have had to learn to 'let go' of knowing where people are and watching them work, and to concentrate on output. 'This allows us to focus on flexibility, so that we can enable people to achieve what they need to do when it suits them, within reason. Technology of course really helps with this. As well as being mobile in the office, people can work from home or remote locations much more readily, and have better communication with colleagues. I've been surprised at how much more I've learned about the business and the people, as by walking around open areas good and bad news gets raised much faster than through traditional hierarchies. I also get to see the quiet achievers, not just those who are adept at managing up.'

Not everyone is comfortable with an empowering culture, and it takes continuing effort by leaders to make it stick, he adds. 'Some people prefer to "tell" or to be "told". Some are open to trying the new culture and are learning along the way, whilst others embrace it. I find that being consistent and trying to lead by example helps, as does talking frequently about the culture we aspire to and why it's important for the long-term success of the company.'

In summary

The conventional office is not well suited to a world in which a growing proportion of work can be done anywhere, at any time. Offices of the future, whether corporate buildings or 'third spaces' between office and home, will be primarily meeting places that also accommodate concentrated work, rather than the other way round.

Office layout and design can convey important messages about transparency, collaboration and individual responsibility, and can help people to realize their potential. Yet even a radical change in physical environment will not be enough without an accompanying shift in organizational culture and leadership style. To achieve this, leaders and managers need to:

- Confront their fears
- Move from control to trust
- Separate status from hierarchy
- Encourage initiative and accountability
- Make balance a priority

In Chapter 7, we explore culture. Based on our research findings, we discover what kind of organizational culture is needed to make a successful shift to future work. We also explore how countries and regions of the world differ in their openness to the changes that are under way.

CHAPTER 7

Culture is critical

> The entire knowledge economy is built on the trust that employees and
> their employers have in each other; there really is nothing else. It is only
> this relationship – the one between the employees and the organization –
> that keeps a company going.
>
> Vineet Nayar, co-founder, HCL Technologies[1]

We have talked about leadership and culture change as being essential
if organizations are to seize the competitive advantages offered by
new ways of working. The findings of our specially designed survey,
described below, reveal the type of organizational culture that
will adapt most easily to the forces transforming work. However,
the managers we questioned reported a big gap between current
organizational cultures and what they view as the ideal culture for the
new world of work.

National cultures also play an important part in determining how easily
future work styles will spread, an issue we address in the second part
of the chapter. Although there are big differences between regions and
countries, it would be a mistake to regard people's desire for greater choice
and control of their working lives as a concern only in Western economies.
Companies doing business around the globe need to understand how
attitudes and expectations are also changing in the growing markets from
which they will increasingly draw talent.

Part one: organizational cultures

What managers say

Organizations that have already implemented future work models have many common features. Their management style is often distinctly different from the traditional top-down, control-oriented corporate regimes that held sway during the twentieth century. But what exactly is it that makes the difference? Why do people feel more motivated and productive in some organizations than others? What are the links between successful management practices of the twenty-first century and innovative ways of working?

To answer these questions, we turned to the people who face these issues daily – managers from around the world. With the help of two business schools, Cass and Henley, we obtained responses from 366 managers to an in-depth survey about them and the organizations for which they work.

About half our respondents were based in the UK. The rest represented 38 nationalities working in 40 countries. As well as the alumni of Cass and Henley, about 120 responses came from managers around the world through our various networks.

Key survey findings

- Two-thirds of managers believe there will be a revolution in working practices in the next decade

- Most feel their organizations are not adapting quickly enough to new ways of working

- Nearly 90 percent believe people are more productive given autonomy over their working patterns

- Over 80 percent think new ways of working would benefit the business and nearly 60 percent want more freedom to let people work flexibly

- Women put a higher priority than men do on giving people freedom to achieve results in their own way

- Organizations that encourage new work styles, such as remote working, are much more likely than others to value creativity, to trust employees and to assume they are self-motivated

■ These types of organization are much closer to what managers say is their ideal culture

Actual versus ideal cultures

We asked a series of questions about the values, management style, processes and decision-making they experience in their current organization and then asked them what they would like to see in an ideal situation. We expected some differences between reality and the ideal, but were surprised to find the size of gap that emerged.

Underlying every organization there is a set of values. In some, these values are expressed openly, clearly set out in mission statements and repeated in public proclamations. In others they are not explicitly stated and have to be deduced from management behavior.

In many cases, values expressed publicly at the top are at odds with the actual behavior in the organization. Senior managers set the tone. If they work extreme hours, they send a message that success is associated with complete dedication to the job, at the expense of personal life. They may say they support flexible working, but their behavior is what will be believed. They may say that they reward people for results, but if in practice they are seen to favor people who are visibly putting in lots of time in the office or on late night emails, then that becomes the cultural norm.

We, therefore, set out to discover what managers currently experience and how this compares with what they believe the culture should be like. We asked them to rate their organization on a scale between two opposite statements, A and B, where A represented a traditional approach and B represented the characteristics we believed were conducive to future work.

We use 'Type A' and 'Type B' as shorthand for two distinct types of organizational culture. In common with Douglas McGregor's 'Theory X' and 'Theory Y', the management practices are based on opposite assumptions. Type A organizations have a 'command and control' style of management, monitoring people closely because they cannot be trusted to work on their own. Type B organizations, on the other hand, give responsibility to employees, empowering them to make decisions for themselves and trusting them to get on with the job.

In total, we asked questions about 25 pairs of opposite management styles to cover a broad range of elements of organizational culture. These are listed in **Table 7.1**. We asked managers to answer the same 25 questions about their current organization and then about their

Table 7.1   Type A and Type B cultures

TYPE A	TYPE B
Organizational values	
People seen as a disposable resource	People seen as a long-term investment
People status conscious, hierarchical	All people are equal
People are closely monitored	People take responsibility
Keep personal life separate	Work and personal life intertwined
Work is serious	Work is fun
People need to be directed	People are self-motivated
Management style	
Bureaucratic, formal	Casual, informal
'Do what I tell you'	'Do the right thing'
Competitive (between employees)	Collaborative teamwork
Cut back on cost	Improve effectiveness/productivity
Short-term focus	Long-term focus
Low trust in employees	High trust in employees
Rigid	Flexible
Management processes	
Manager-only appraisal	360-degree appraisal
Individual performance pay	Team/Organization-based pay
Multi-level hierarchy	Flat structure
Necessary information only	Open communications
Command and control	Enable and empower
Reward time/attendance	Reward outcomes/targets
Keep work in-house	Outsource where possible
Decision-making	
Top-down decisions	Everyone has a vote
Managers decide	Teams decide
Follow precedent	Be creative
Multi-level sign-off	Freedom to act
Follow the rules	Question the rules

ideal one. The difference between the two answers showed us how well employers were meeting the hopes and expectations of their managers.

We found that for every one of the 25 factors, managers rated their current organization closer to A than they would like it to be. Top of the list, with the highest gap between the actual and ideal culture was 'A = Multi-level sign-off' and 'B = Freedom to act'. In this case, two-thirds of respondents described their current organization as A, while only a quarter chose B. However, when asked what they believed was the most effective approach to management, only 15 percent chose A, while over 70 percent opted for B.

So, based on this answer, about half of the managers in the survey are currently working in a Type A culture but would prefer a Type B. They see their current organization as keeping decision-making power at too high a level and not delegating authority or freedom to get on with the job.

This is also evident in the second most misaligned factor: 'A = Follow the rules' versus 'B = Question the rules'. It appears that many organizations expect people to do what they are told blindly, and not to use their initiative. Yet managers know that this is not the best way of engaging their employees.

When asked about 'A = Follow Precedent' versus 'B = Be Creative', almost half of managers put their organization in A but only 7 percent thought this was ideal. It appears that the way to get on in those cultures is to keep a low profile and not come up with new ideas. Yet managers clearly believe that the best way to run an enterprise is to tap into the creativity of their people.

Similar numbers say that their current organizations work on 'necessary information only' while they would overwhelmingly prefer 'open communications'. They strongly believe that employers should focus on individual effectiveness and productivity, as opposed to cutting costs, yet in practice only half do so. Two-thirds work in a status-conscious culture, yet the same proportion believe all people should be treated equally.

Tackling inertia

These results show that there is a major mismatch between what is actually happening and what managers would prefer. But if these are the managers who are running teams and operations in those businesses, why are they not practicing what they believe? What is stopping them from managing in a more effective and empowering way? We think that inertia is standing in the way of change. The attitude often seems to be that, unless there is a serious crisis, there is no need to change the existing way of getting things done.

Many senior managers have built their careers and credibility on a lifetime of working in a particular way. If it was good enough to get them to the top, then it's good enough for the next generation, they say. This was underlined by the answer to a question in the second part of our survey.

We asked respondents to agree or disagree with the following statement: 'Senior managers think that the way they have always worked is the right one'. Half of them agreed, or strongly agreed with the statement, while 34 percent disagreed or strongly disagreed.

As we have seen from the examples throughout this book, support from the top is essential to success. In some innovative companies like W. L. Gore, or Semco in Brazil, the founders set the tone, while in others, such as BDO or Gap or Microsoft Netherlands, leaders with vision have set about changing the culture and ways of working. Shifting management habits in a large organization is almost impossible without a champion for the cause who has the influence to make the change happen.

However, as the bottom line benefits become increasingly obvious, resistance is harder to maintain. Future work is no longer confined to a small handful of interesting companies, but is becoming more widely accepted as a sensible way of getting the best return from an employer's most important asset. This view seems to be shared by the managers who responded to our survey. Their reaction to the statement 'There will be a revolution in working practices in the next decade' was emphatic. Two-thirds agreed and only 16 percent disagreed.

Linking culture to future work

How exactly does organizational culture relate to the adoption of future work practices? We wanted to see if there was any link between these practices and Type A versus Type B cultures. We asked survey respondents about the flexible working practices in their businesses. We then divided the responses into those from 'High' Type B organizations (those displaying more than 10 of the 25 factors categorized as B) versus the rest.

We found that cultures that were predominantly Type B were much more likely to have people working from home. About half of them had home-based workers compared to only a third of other employers. They were also more likely to have mobile workers, term time-only workers, part-time working, compressed hours and hot-desking.

So, the findings bore out our observations about cultures that support flexible working. To check this further, we looked at respondents' answers to the statement: 'My organization encourages new ways of working'. We split them into those who agreed, or strongly agreed, with this statement ('pro' organizations) and those who disagreed, or strongly disagreed ('anti' organizations).

Not surprisingly, only 26 percent of the 'anti' employers were rated as flexible, versus 73 percent of the 'pro' ones. More importantly, we found that employers that encourage new ways of working are three times more likely to enable and empower their people generally than 'anti' ones. They are also much more likely to value creativity, trust employees, assume they are self-motivated and allow them to 'do the right thing'. As many as 84 percent of the 'pro' organizations reward outcomes and targets rather than time and attendance, compared with only 44 percent of the 'anti' ones.

It is clear from our survey, as well as our observations of leading organizations, that there is a type of culture that is associated with future work. This Type B culture is much more open to implementing new working practices because its existing values and processes will support the necessary changes.

Looked at another way, those organizations that have adopted new working practices are most likely to have a culture of trust and empowerment. To erase any doubt about the importance of empowerment, a massive 95 percent of the managers in our survey agreed with the statement that 'Good leadership is about empowering people'. This brings us firmly to the conclusion that the adoption of future work practices is a strong indicator of good leadership and a progressive organizational culture.

Gender and leadership styles

Type B cultures are more people-oriented than Type As. They consider people to be a long-term investment rather than a disposable asset. They expect them to work collaboratively in an environment of open communication. They give people freedom to act on their own initiative. This contrasts with the traditional command and control, hierarchical structures that were designed and built for an era when the vast majority of the workforce, and all of those at the top, were male.

Type B cultures contain characteristics often associated with a more 'female' style of leadership and management – one that motivates people, builds effective teams, fosters trust and respect and takes into account the wider world. Research studies have identified such characteristics as important leadership attributes for the twenty-first century, as well as ones in which women do particularly well.[2]

Interest in gender-balanced leadership has been heightened by the financial and economic crisis. As the book *Why Women Mean Business* puts it:

'The need for countries and companies to make best use of women's potential in addressing the challenges of the 21st century is even more urgent today. It is only through the leadership of women *and* men, working as partners, that we can build a saner, safer and more sustainable model of capitalism.'[3]

In our survey, we had responses from 225 men and 141 women, giving us a reasonable sample to analyze further. On average, the women rated their current organizations as slightly less Type A and more Type B than the men. The fact that their environment is already more B could be due to their direct influence on the management style or it could be that they chose to work in this type of culture. Slightly more women than men agreed that their organization encouraged new ways of working and that it did its best to improve the work-life balance of its people. Just over half the men and 69 percent of the women said they worked in a high-trust environment.

Gender differences were more pronounced in the ratings for the ideal organization. Women showed a stronger belief in 360-degree appraisal, open communications, improved effectiveness and collaborative team-work. Eighty percent of women opted to question the rules rather than follow them, compared with 68 percent of the men. Ninety-one percent said they would like their people to be creative and not just follow precedent, compared with 81 percent of the men.

So the women in our survey feel more strongly than the men about creating an environment in which individuals have freedom to work in their own way to achieve results. They were also nearly ten percent more inclined than men to want people to do the right thing rather than do what they were told.

Interestingly, the women who responded to the survey were happier with their own personal flexibility than the men. Only 49 percent said they would like more control over where, when and how they do their job, compared with 59 percent of the men. This may reflect the fact that men often face greater resistance – and more perceived career damage – when asking their employer for greater choice and control over their working arrangements than women do. This is something that companies need to rectify. If they base their talent management strategies on the assumption that women are the only ones who want flexibility, they are seriously out of date.

Organizations that want to promote gender diversity in their top ranks need to understand what is happening to a growing proportion of the men in their workforce. Instead of focusing all their gender initiatives on women, companies would do better to take account of the other sex. Enabling men to play their full role as fathers is good not only for children and families but also for women's progress in the workplace and for developing more rounded leaders of both genders.

Part two: national cultures

Future work around the world

Work cultures vary widely around the world. Social attitudes and expectations, communications infrastructure, legislation and public policy can all affect a country's openness to new work styles. Executives we interviewed for this book stressed the need for cultural sensitivity when implementing a future work program.

Working from home is a case in point. While increasingly common in countries like the US and UK, it is far from being globally practical. Thomson Reuters, the information group, collected interesting data about country differences regarding flexible working in its content, technology and operations division, now called the Unified Platform Group. The group employs about 5500 people, roughly one third of whom work in development centers in China, India, Thailand and Poland, and one third each in the US and UK.

It found that working from home is an option in most places, but can be a challenge in some parts of Asia where internet connections are unreliable, slow and expensive, there are sometimes power outages and many employees live with their families around them. Richard Cleverly, global head of HR for the division, says job-sharing can be an issue in countries where local employment laws and regulations do not recognize the status of such workers, and there are also cultural barriers as sharing a role is an unfamiliar concept. In Asia, the group found that people value salary, career advancement, competitive benefits and convenient work locations more highly than flexible work, he adds.[4]

A useful guide to the global cultural maze, *Balancing Work and Family*,[5] looks at the availability and use of a wide range of approaches, including flexible hours, flexible location and flexible careers. In Kenya and Nigeria, for example, human resources managers view telecommuting and alternative work schedules with suspicion and mistrust, and poor infrastructure and lack of access to technology are barriers to new ways of working.

In Latin America, the book says, young people moving into management roles in the next decade are seen as catalysts for change. They have a different attitude to work, 'having seen their parents and other lifetime employees suddenly become unemployed because of mergers or restructuring'.

Professor Nuria Chinchilla, co-editor of the book and director of the International Center for Work and Family at IESE Business School in Barcelona, says relationships at work, in the family and in society are changing everywhere, especially with the mass entry of women into the labor market. 'Companies doing business around the world must respond to pressure to create fairer, more human working environments which are also more productive and competitive,' she says.

The cost of office space in major cities around the world is a common factor driving change, but the speed and extent of that change will be influenced by the local culture. In Singapore, the move into a new office building was the catalyst for Group M, the media investment arm of the WPP global advertising and marketing group, to introduce agile working. Group M consists of four companies who share support services such as finance and are located in the same building. Each had a slightly different implementation plan. One with 150 people went for 100 percent agile working while the others started more slowly. According to Mike Jackson, MD of one of the companies, MEC Access, 'We have a mixture of expats and local employees, some with local clients and others covering all of Asia, so we needed to be flexible in our approach. As senior managers, we are setting an example but giving managers discretion in how to implement the policy.'[6]

South Korea – broadband leads the way

In some countries, it is the fast pace of technological development that is forcing a rethink of how and where work is done. South Korea is a prime example of this. In 2010, the government announced an ambitious 'smart work initiative' to have 30 percent of employees working from home, on the move or from specially equipped 'smart work' centers by 2015, using laptops, mobile internet devices and videoconferencing.[7] The capital, Seoul, is a world leader in high-speed broadband connections.

The policy, designed to improve productivity and cut congestion and carbon emissions, represented a dramatic shift from a work culture heavily reliant on face-time in the office. South Korea has some of the longest working hours of OECD countries, although these have been falling, and relatively low labor productivity levels.[8]

If public officials use their local smart work center for a day or two per week, rather than traveling to central government facilities in Seoul, this will cut emission trading and transport costs by about $310 per telecommuter per year and reduce commuting time by up to 90 minutes a day, says the government.[9]

Employers' and employees' willingness to change will be a decisive factor. BT, the UK communications group, has advised the South Korean government and other organizations on the initiative. 'It has been much slower to take off than anticipated,' says Dave Dunbar, head of BT flexible working services.[10] 'There isn't a hunger for full-time home working, but there is more occasional home-working starting to happen and attitudes are changing. People will increasingly work from a variety of places including home.'

If ultimately successful, the strategy could boost low female participation in the labor force and the extremely low birth rate of 1.2, enabling more women to combine career and family by working from, or near, their homes. Research shows that countries that make it easier for parents to continue working tend to see higher birth rates and higher growth through greater female participation in the labor force.[11]

Among Western economies, the UK is furthest ahead in its range of work flexibility, according to Caroline Waters, former director of people and policy at BT. 'America has made significant advances but I don't think they have such a sophisticated model,' she says. 'In Germany, the tax legislation is prohibitive, although lately more examples are emerging. Works councils have some concerns but continue to be a part of the debate.'

'France hasn't had great take-up nationally but again there are pockets of good practice. In France, the unions have tended to focus on the length of the working week rather than when and how people want to work. Again, the good news is that this is changing, as the possibilities presented by greater flexibility become more widely understood. In countries such as Italy and the Czech Republic, BT's flexible workers are seen as "trend-setters".'[12]

As Europe grapples with aging populations and low birth rates, there is a strong focus in many countries on reconciling careers and family life. Working patterns and hours vary widely across the region, from an average of nearly 49 hours per week in Turkey to below 31 hours in the Netherlands.[13] Part-time work also differs significantly by country from almost half the working population in the Netherlands and a quarter in countries such as the UK and Germany down to 10 percent or less in eastern and southern Europe.[14]

The Netherlands is a particularly striking example of how attitudes to working hours and location are changing, with the rise of dual-income couples and greater sharing of family responsibilities between women and men.

Rise of the Dutch 'daddy day'

The Dutch are 'world champions' of part-time work, says Professor Paul Schnabel, director of The Netherlands Institute for Social Research. Over three-quarters of Dutch women work reduced hours, compared with a European Union average of 32 percent. In recent years, however, there has been a big rise in the number of men working a four-day week, or working from home once a week, to look after the children, an arrangement known as *papadag* ('daddy day').

Over a third of Dutch men now work a shorter week, according to the institute. Of these, 25 percent have part-time jobs, against an EU average of just 8 percent. The rest fit a full-time job into four long days, or spend short days at work and make up the shortfall during evenings and weekends.

Employers generally accept this. 'I'm an employer myself and it's quite a normal thing,' says Professor Schnabel. 'If people apply for a job, we ask them whether they would like to do four days or five days. I'm not in favor of people working long hours because you become less productive if you work nine or ten hours.'[15]

For employers, it is a way to attract and keep good people. 'Once the recession is over, the job market is going to be very tight,' says Ronald van de Krol, editor of the Saturday edition of *Het Financieele Dagblad*, the leading daily financial newspaper, who works in the office four days a week and spends one 'daddy day' at home. 'Younger managers in their 30s and 40s have grown up with people around them working four days. So it's not strange for a man to say "I'll take the job, and I want to work four days or work a day from home".'[16]

Employees have to be flexible, however. 'For the employer, it works really well because the employee tends to do the same amount of work for less money,' says van de Krol. 'You continue to work, even when you're not *at* work. It requires a level of trust by the employer. But people say they get a lot more done at home if they have to write a report, for example, because there are fewer interruptions.'

The trend aligns with the Dutch government's drive to encourage people to work more frequently from home to reduce road congestion and costly office space. It also reflects national attitudes. 'If you ask a Dutch person whether they want more time or more money, they almost always go for more time,' he says.

Legislation introduced in 2000 gives all employees the right to reduced hours, as in Belgium, France and Germany, unless the employer can show a serious business or safety reason why this is not possible.[17] The extensive use of reduced hours is also due to primary schools being closed on Wednesday afternoons, and to Dutch society frowning on parents who put their children in childcare for five days a week. Half of all women work fewer than 25 hours a week.[18] The traditional female part-time model has been coming under pressure, however, with a government taskforce calling for women to increase their hours to at least 25 a week to ease labor shortages.

Although arguably progressive, the Dutch approach is still largely a variation on the traditional work model. People work a set number of hours and days, rather than being measured and rewarded purely on output.

Common ground

In our survey of managers around the world, the UK respondents rated both their actual and ideal organizations as being closer to Type B than respondents from other countries. Most notably, almost half the UK managers classified their actual organization as encouraging creativity, compared with only a third of respondents from the rest of the world.

However, all the respondents agreed that their current organizations should ideally be significantly more Type B than they are. Since most were alumni of two UK-based business schools, this uniformity is perhaps not surprising.

Asked what would be most effective, over 80 percent of all the managers opted for creativity over compliance. Two-thirds of non-UK managers, and 77 percent of UK managers, also opted for 'question the rules' versus 'follow the rules' for their ideal organization.

Overall our conclusion is that the UK is marginally more inclined toward Type B organizational cultures, but there is a highly consistent view around the world about the desire to shift from Type A to Type B.

Another indication of common ground comes from a survey of employee engagement by BlessingWhite, an international consulting firm, covering North America, Europe, Australia and New Zealand, South East Asia, India and China. Covering 11,000 employees, it asked people to choose the item that would most improve their job satisfaction.

'Career development opportunities and training' and 'More opportunities to do what I do best' were the first two in every region, except in SE Asia where 'More flexible job conditions (e.g. control over how my work gets done, flex time, etc)' came second. Flexible conditions came third in Europe, North America and Australia, fourth in China and fifth in India. So greater control over how work is done has a universal appeal. In all cases it beat 'Improved cooperation among my co-workers' and 'A better relationship with my manager'.[19]

Talent in the global economy: India

Multinational companies competing for talent around the world can gain by innovating in this area. Here we look at two examples in India, where the need to attract and retain able, skilled people is forcing a review of traditional work and career models.

HSBC, one of the world's largest banking groups, started to introduce flexible work options in India in 2008 in response to an employee survey showing that work-life balance was a concern. Vikram Tandon, head of human resources for HSBC Bank India, says it was the first foreign bank in the country to do so.

Flexible work, once only available in the IT sector in India, is now becoming more widely accepted by multinationals as a way to attract and keep diverse talent. 'People are looking to have greater control and a more balanced life,' he says. 'In the past, these things were not so important to employees. But Indian society has changed and so have people's expectations. For the newer generations in the workforce, Gen X and Gen Y, flexibility has become a priority.'[20]

Many HSBC employees in India have formally opted for the program, most of them varying their start and finish times where previously they had to get to the office by 8.30 a.m. every day. This has cut hours of commuting and given people more room to respond to personal needs.

It takes time to break old habits and address managerial concerns, says Tandon. But the culture is becoming more flexible, and managers are getting better at encouraging people to find the right option for themselves. The aim is that people should be measured on outcomes, not hours. 'We're working towards a results-only environment. We position this as a better way to do business because it enhances your productivity at work. We're not completely there, but the mindset is changing.'

The bank has invested significantly in technology to enable most people to work from home with secure electronic access to the office. In a successful teleworking pilot, one of the bank's sales teams increased productivity and exceeded its sales targets while working remotely from the office in other locations.

'Regular teleworking is being institutionalized in roles and teams where there is no risk and no dependency on systems which need the individual to be in a designated workplace, and where the banking regulator permits,' says Tandon.

Stuart P Milne, chief executive of HSBC India, and his top management team have demonstrated their support by teleworking at least twice a month and encouraging their teams to do the same. As a result, more and more teams and managers are doing so, says Tandon.

Chief operating officer Deveshwar Mathur says: 'In an increasingly virtual world, spending hours on the road appears completely unnecessary. We are significantly more efficient when telecommuting. As COO, I've taken a conscious decision to introduce "hot desks" at most of our facilities and to encourage staff to opt to work from their most convenient location. This has worked wonders for both morale and productivity.'

Another company trying to address the changing attitudes of employees in India is **Deloitte**, the professional services firm, which has introduced a tool to help them define their own 'career–life fit'. The tool, known as Mass Career Customization (MCC), was first applied to Deloitte's US practice. It describes careers in terms of a corporate 'lattice', rather than a corporate ladder, offering employees options to change the pace of their job, workload, location and schedule, and type of role at different stages in their working lives.

The firm decided to introduce MCC in India to attract talent, give young people in particular a new reason to stay, and inspire performance, says Bob Chapman, managing partner of Deloitte's India operation. In growing numbers of Indian families, both spouses have careers and are equally involved in raising children. 'We also wanted our US and India professionals working as a single integrated team.'[21]

The approach is still work in progress. Only about one percent of more than 15,000 employees in Hyderabad, Mumbai, Delhi and Bengaluru have so far been approved to accelerate or decelerate their career. The concept is relatively new to the Indian workforce and 'we are continuously educating our people and raising awareness on MCC and career-life fit', says Chapman. The goal is not to 'sell' formal flexibility but to help provide staff with options as their needs change, he adds.

In summary

Managers are increasingly recognizing that although they have inherited a command and control (Type A) culture they need to move to a trust and empower (Type B) one. But there is resistance and inertia in many organizations.

They nevertheless see a revolution in working practices as imminent. The speed of change and the form it takes is heavily dependent on national cultures and local working norms, but there is a worldwide movement towards working practices that engage employees and improve results.

The successful introduction of future work practices often depends on a change in organizational culture. Managers will almost certainly need help with this process, as much as with the practicalities of implementing new work styles. In the most compelling examples we have seen, senior leaders recognize the need to change their own behavior and introduce programs to address managerial resistance and inertia and to improve key skills such as open and consistent communication with employees.

In Chapters 8, 9 and 10, we offer a guide to making this culture change happen, demonstrating how businesses large and small are learning in practical terms how to adapt and thrive in the new world of work.

CHAPTER 8

Strategies for change

Laura Terheyden is a 30-year-old professional who works in San Francisco's technology sector. Like many of her peers in Generation Y – young people entering, or already in, the workforce – she places a high value on anything an employer can do to make life easier as she focuses on building her career. Being able to decide where and when she works is a big part of that.

She has worked for traditional companies as well as Internet firms, and is now involved in recruitment at Airbnb, a marketplace where people can list and book accommodation around the world online or from a mobile phone. It is part of the so-called 'sharing economy', which uses information technology to distribute, share and reuse spare capacity, from office space to private homes and car and bicycle pools.

Laura relishes the freedom to work outside the confines of specified time and place. She says that Airbnb has a 'very flexible work culture' where people are encouraged to move and sit with different teams according to the project they are working on.

In a previous role at McKesson, the US healthcare company, she noted that her own work style was worlds apart from that of peers. 'Some of my friends are amazed when they hear about the flexibility I have,' she told a conference. 'A lot of my friends work in places where they feel like they are clocking in and clocking out even as salaried employees. That's a struggle for them.'

One friend in a finance function felt under pressure to stay in her cubicle and had her movements watched by an older member of staff. 'The older co-worker, to whom she does not report, expects my friend to be physically present on a routine schedule that matches her own, even though my friend may be working after hours at home or on weekends unbeknownst to her colleague,' Laura explained.

Laura's experience was very different. 'Instead of working 9–5 in an office or designated cube, I may work from home, a coffee shop, a park with Wi-Fi, or have a cube-share with another employee. I work the amount of hours needed to get the job done by the deadline instead of doing the job between certain hours on certain days. It's just a different way of looking at time.[1]

The main difference between the work experiences of Laura and her friend is the presence or absence of a trusting culture. It is not difficult to see which of these environments is more likely to encourage initiative, creativity and a willingness to put in extra effort, rather than simply counting down the hours to going-home time. Nor is it difficult to see which environment is more likely to attract and keep good employees. Laura lists the benefits of having a trusting manager and working in a progressive company. 'There is flexibility that allows you to work in *your* most productive way,' she says. 'You may work better late at night or be working with business partners in another time zone. In my experience, more work gets done in a flexible workspace environment because I can take care of things like getting my car registered. I can work hours at home when I would normally be traveling to and from work. I can do focused work without the distractions that come with sitting at my cube, and I can be completely accessible for tasks that can be handled over email.'

In the first half of this book, we set out the consequences of freeing people to work in the way that suits them. We have shown compelling evidence that it delivers better results for business, individuals and the environment. Given this evidence, why are companies not adapting faster to the new world of work? Why do many of them cling to unproductive, morale-sapping habits, such as requiring people's presence at their desks in a fixed location for long and often unsociable hours, when technology enables many tasks to be done more efficiently at a place and time of their choice? What will it take to break these old habits?

Barriers to change

It is useful first to examine the obstacles that must be overcome if employers are to compete with their most fleet-footed rivals and keep pace with the accelerating opportunities afforded by new technology.

The first is this crucial matter of **trust**. Managers are the key to success in making the shift to future work. They can also be the biggest barrier. Some managers fall for their own PR, believing that they represent the clever elite whose role is to exercise power and keep the rest of the workforce under constant surveillance. This may be a façade, however, beneath which anxiety and insecurity lurk.

Managers are more likely to give their team a free rein if they are confident of their own skills and value to the organization. However, managers who want to do this may come up against the barrier of **corporate culture**. A manager may be enthusiastic about giving her people greater flexibility but feel crushed by the prevailing expectations that presence and long hours equal commitment. This is perpetuated by **leadership resistance** to new ways of working. One senior executive who experienced this at a multinational technology company told us: 'The view here is that we only hire "go-go" people. If people start talking about wanting balance and flexibility, they are no longer seen as "go-go" people.'

Such attitudes are often entrenched in organizations that are still wedded to **hierarchy**. Hierarchy thrives in many large organizations and the 'alpha' personalities who rise to the top are often driven by a desire for status based on their rank in the structure. For them, the trappings of power are alluring. There are still bloody battles for the corner office, even in some of today's supposedly flatter, 'matrix'-type companies. To managers naturally disposed to hierarchy, a radical change in the way people work poses a threat. Giving people the power to control their own work feels to some managers like a loss of face, as well as a loss of face time.

Then there is the barrier of **inertia**. What's the point of trying to change the system, the argument goes. Okay, people aren't exactly happy round here, but the company is still functioning fine, and besides, this is the way we've always worked. It's too hard to change.

Guy Laurence, head of **Vodafone**, the mobile technology operator, in the UK, spends a lot of time talking to senior executives from other companies about the benefits of future work. 'The biggest problem is getting companies to believe they can do it for *their* company,' he says. 'The chief executive wants to change but doesn't want to be the first in the sector. Organizations are scared of change and they think it's extremely complicated to move from the old style to the new style. They don't realize the technologies needed to support this are freely available in the marketplace and are often present in their company but just not used in a coordinated way.'[2]

Laurence insists there is no business that technology-enabled future work cannot improve. 'Even if it's a production line, a third of the company will be non-production line, back-office, staff who could be using technology to work this way.'

There are many **myths**, too, that stand in the way of progress to future work. Flexible working arrangements, although a boon to many individual employees, have helped to perpetuate these myths. Governments have pressed employers to adopt flexible working practices as a way to 'help' employees in particular circumstances, working parents and caregivers being the main beneficiaries. As a result, flexible work programs are seen as a measure to accommodate certain employees' needs, rather than a strategy to drive business results. This results in a stigma being attached to those who ask for flexibility. Organizations often end up with great policies on paper but very little take-up in practice.

'Employers think it's costly and disruptive,' says Caroline Waters, former director of people and policy at **BT**, the UK communications group, and a pioneer of new working practices. 'They also think that employees won't work if they are given flexibility. Managers think they'll lose control – the fact is they never really had control just because they were co-located. There's often a failure to see it as anything other than home-based working – and many managers will write it off if they think it means people will be working from home all the time.'

Flawed attempts at introducing flexible working policies have made things worse, she says. 'Employers try to prescribe flexibility, which can't be done. Some say: "We've introduced a policy of people going home at 5 p.m. on Fridays". But that blanket approach doesn't work for everyone, and it doesn't represent true flexibility. The flexible working legislation in the UK stipulates that hours are agreed in perpetuity. This was put in to protect people from unscrupulous employers, but it puts many organizations off. Business changes every six months. Why put something in "forever" which in itself becomes a barrier to business flexibility?'[3]

Another myth we have encountered results from confusion over fairness. Managers sometimes argue that because certain operations have to be done in a fixed place or at a fixed time it would be unfair to give anyone else greater choice about where and when to do their work. But employees are not fools. If their work is restricted to a certain location because they serve customers in a store or operate a metal-pressing machine, they will not expect the same latitude as a knowledge worker in the same company. What matters is that they are granted as much autonomy and choice as possible within the logical and reasonable constraints of the job.

Moving to the new world of work takes courage. As we showed in Chapters 5 and 6, some pioneering leaders have already taken the plunge. In some cases, they have had to 'unlearn' their default mode of wanting to control people and situations. They have also had to work hard at management skills such as communicating clearly and consistently.

Being a manager and a leader is not about standing still. If competition, globalization and new market opportunities require you to be adaptable and good at 'managing uncertainty', why should the same not apply to the vital task of managing people?

Five TRUST principles for progress

We have drawn up five principles for organizations that want to make a successful transition from the old to the new world of work. These are based on the business and socio-economic case for change, the large body of research on motivation and the effective approaches we have encountered in our research. They are designed to be global guidelines. We call them the 'TRUST' principles (**Table 8.1**).

Table 8.1   TRUST principles

PRINCIPLES
1. **T**rust your people
2. **R**eward results
3. **U**nderstand the business case
4. **S**tart at the top
5. **T**reat people as individuals

You may wonder why technology does not figure in this list of principles. Clearly, people need the right infrastructure and equipment if they are to be able to work 'anytime anywhere'. Technology is an essential tool, or enabler, for the new world of work. Without any concomitant change in the *rules* of work, however, technology enslaves rather than liberates people.

'Anytime anywhere' easily becomes 'always on'. People are expected to be at their desks during regular working hours and then to be available on their smartphone or email outside these hours. As individuals, we must get better at pressing the 'off' switch. But we cannot do this if the culture of the organization continues to expect and reward people's physical (or virtual) presence round the clock.

Technology offers us a wonderful opportunity to 'free' time. First, it can end the tyranny of clocking up fixed hours in a fixed workplace by enabling work to be done regardless of time and place. This can then free up time for people to combine their work with the other things they want, or need, to do in their lives. This freedom, in turn, can motivate them to contribute their ideas and expertise freely, over and above their contracted hours, because they are treated as adults and trusted to get the job done.

It is not technology but the approach taken by management that enables this opportunity to be seized – or prevents it. Putting the technology in place is relatively easy. What is harder is to gain cultural acceptance of the need for a change in working practices. Managers may have to challenge and change their own assumptions about their role if they are to free people to be most effective in the new world of work.

1. Trust your people

Time and again in our discussions with business leaders and managers, trust emerges as the essential ingredient when people are liberated to do their best work. Trust is a two-way process, requiring open-mindedness and adaptability on both sides. In the first three chapters of this book, we investigated the high level of disillusionment and disengagement in today's workforce and the evidence that people are more likely to produce outstanding results if they are self-directed rather than micro-managed. We saw how money is only one of a range of motivations for work, and how fulfillment and engagement come from other aspects of work such as flexibility and choice over how it is done, recognition and new challenges.

In chapters 5 and 6, we demonstrated trust-based leadership through the eyes of senior executives who understand its importance. Another of these is Sir Richard Branson, founder of **Virgin Group**, who emphasized the centrality of trust in his blog in February 2013. 'To successfully work with other people, you have to trust each other,' he wrote. 'A big part of this is trusting people to get their work done wherever they are, without supervision. It is the art of delegation, which has served Virgin and many other companies well over the years.'

Swiss Re, the global reinsurance company, embarked on new ways of working in 2012 (see case study in Chapter 10). 'We want to move away from a leadership philosophy that's ultimately based on command and control to a leadership philosophy based on trust, freedom and shared objectives,' explained David Cole, chief risk officer.[4]

For some leaders, trust will come naturally, but many others have to learn it through experience and deliberately challenging their own assumptions.

2. Reward results, not hours

To break free of the old model requires a radical change in the way work is rewarded. Future work will only fully succeed if the number of hours worked is decoupled from 'success'.

Under the prevailing model in many organizations, even salaried employees are expected to put in their minimum contracted hours – and to work considerably more to be seen as 'dedicated', 'loyal' and 'conscientious'. This is a deeply ingrained belief that can only be overturned through a well-orchestrated change program, driven from the top.

Ending the long-hours culture is a critical step on the path to future work. The argument for this change is very simple. People who work efficiently get the job done in less time than those who are less efficient. People who take a long time to do their work are probably wasting time and are certainly not as productive per hour. People who are paid by results have every incentive to think up smarter ways of getting the work done. Their reward is more 'spare' time for them to use as leisure or to generate more income.

Managers have historically been bad at defining and measuring the output from work because the Industrial Age model judges and rewards people for their time. They have described work as a series of tasks – the job description – instead of approaching work in terms of goals and outcomes.

In future work it is results that count. Work is about the purpose, and the focus of management is on achieving that purpose. What is achieved is important; how many hours it takes the individual to achieve it matters less.

As a leader who believes in managing by output, **Vodafone UK** CEO Guy Laurence has the five 'big-ticket' objectives of each of his 100 top managers captured in a single electronic chart. Managers have to negotiate with each other to ensure that departments and resources are lined up to achieve the objectives, which are reviewed and revised every 12 weeks.

Laurence says managing by results means trusting people to manage themselves and use common sense. It does not mean the culture is soft or lacks discipline. If anyone abuses the freedom, 'we'll have a quiet conversation with them, and if they continue to abuse it we let them go', he says. This does not happen often, and peer pressure usually takes care of any problems. 'If you move to team-based objectives and measure on output, it's mostly self-regulating. If one person lets the side down, someone else picks them up on it.'[5]

Setting targets and outcomes will vary between sectors and roles. In many jobs, it is not just about achieving the numbers. Indeed, a pure focus on hitting numerical targets can be harmful. Wider outcomes such as excellent customer service, or ensuring patients are treated compassionately, or creating an environment where diverse talent can flourish, are equally if not more important.

3. Understand the business case

In every case where we have found organizations whole-heartedly embracing new working practices, the reason is a business one. It may be that the company is losing talented people (see Gap case study later in this chapter). It may be that there are risks to business continuity, whether from severe weather, pandemics or terrorist attacks. It may be that the company has a technological advantage and wants to translate this into more efficient ways of working, as in the case of Microsoft in the Netherlands in Chapter 6. Or it may be a combination of factors.

Each organization has to establish its own business case for moving to future work. This can be a challenge. As with any big change, the case has to be made, often in the teeth of resistance. 'The pain is upfront in proving the case,' says Caroline Waters. However, the many business benefits highlighted in Chapter 3 will help you understand the potential gains for your organization. The important thing to remember is that this is about doing better business, not just about being nice to people.

In his book *Employees First, Customers Second*, Vineet Nayar explains how he turned management orthodoxy on its head at **HCL Technologies**, the Indian IT company, by making managers accountable to employees. We would agree that creating a culture of trust and a sense of common ownership is crucial to enable employees to give their best. 'Putting the customer first' should never be at the expense of the employee or it will backfire, since employee satisfaction is intimately linked to good customer service. We also believe the transition to future work should be underpinned by business goals. Offering alternative work patterns simply to suit individual employees is unlikely to bring about the fundamental changes in the work model that will benefit the business – and other employees. Unless it is business-driven, any improvements in 'flexibility' will be subject to the whim of individual managers and may be short-lived.

Manufacturing is not an obvious place to encounter a 'give-and-take' relationship between management and staff. But Stuart Fell, owner of **Metal Assemblies**, a medium-sized engineering firm in the West Midlands, the traditional heart of England's manufacturing industry, believes in two-way flexibility based on trust. Employees at the company, which makes pressed metal components for car manufacturers such as Nissan and BMW, must be flexible in responding to sudden changes in customer demand, and managers must be flexible in responding to employees' 'real world' responsibilities.

Most of the work has to be done in shifts round the clock at the fixed location of the metal presses. Even so, within the 100-strong workforce there are about 50 different working arrangements, which fluctuate over time as their needs, and those of the business, change.

Fell describes it as a symbiotic relationship. 'The needs of the business can frequently be met better by people who also are having their needs met,' he says. 'I could name employees who would not work for us were it not for the flexibility we offer. I also know there is business we have won because we have been able to respond quickly to a customer demand … The organizations that don't adapt will end up the dinosaurs. They won't be able to move fast enough or recruit people to work for them.'[6]

4. Start at the top

As with any major change program, leadership needs to come from the top, even if pressure starts from below. To shift to a new work model, senior leaders must not only encourage other people to change, but also change themselves. Otherwise, attempts to adapt and thrive in the new world will remain confined to small pockets within an organization and risk being snuffed out by a dominant culture that is inclined to stick to 'the old ways'. A strategy that produces strong results for the business and for individuals should not have to rely on the lone efforts of a single pioneer manager or department.

The CEO may be an early champion of change who instinctively grasps the business case. The stimulus may come from outside, such as an imminent threat to business continuity, or an urgent need to cut costs while maintaining productivity. Or the chief executive may have to be persuaded by an influential colleague or a successful trial in a business unit. However it happens, the leadership team must be convinced, in order to convince others. The best way to do this is to demonstrate that the change applies to them too.

This is very different from the adoption of flexible work policies, which in large organizations are introduced and implemented by the HR department, and in small firms tend to be offered on an *ad hoc* basis. These policies are add-on programs rather than a whole new way of working.

Leaders and managers have to learn how to let go of control, rather than hanging onto it. 'Don't dictate, delegate' is a useful maxim. This will be harder in some national cultures than others.

Openness and adaptability should be attributes of today's leaders and should be integrated into leadership development. Unconscious biases (which we all have) can act as a barrier to the acceptance of different leadership styles and help to perpetuate a monoculture in the upper echelons of business. One of these biases is that 'presence equals commitment'. Many of today's leaders grew up in a 'face time' culture and can find it hard to see that this is not the only way to be effective. Surfacing and addressing these hidden biases is an increasingly important part of leadership development in progressive companies.

It is also part of the leader's role to demonstrate the importance of maintaining a healthy balance, and we address the need to manage technology-induced overwork later in this chapter and Chapter 9.

Grahame Petersen, who heads the business and private banking division of **Commonwealth Bank of Australia**, used not to tell colleagues that he was flexing his work schedule to spend time with his young children.

'I'm a private person, but then it occurred to me that I actually needed to lead by example, so now I talk a lot about how I've built flexibility into my working life,' he says. 'I always point out that I didn't need to seek approval, I just manage my day sensibly so that I meet my obligations to my clients, my colleagues and my family. I redistribute my work so that most evenings after my children are asleep I write speeches and catch up on emails, reading and other things that don't require face-time.

'I stress that it is different for everyone, but I do encourage people to talk about how it might apply to them and their colleagues. I've been amazed at the "long shadow" of leadership. Each week someone will come up to me who's heard me speak on this point and say that they've had the confidence to make minor changes to their week – coach a child's team, do a school pick-up, spend time with a parent or a charity. It's often a relatively minor change in their "scheduled" hours, and yet they feel so much happier, and by association, more loyal to the organization.'

5. Treat people as individuals

To be successful in the new world of work, you have to treat people as the individuals they are. This is the essence of good people management and it is put to the test when people are working remotely or are part of a team dispersed across different regions or time zones.

Prescription and uniform solutions do not work. To produce their best, people need to be able to work in the way that suits them. Some are temperamentally suited to long spells of solitary work, making them ideal remote or home workers. But most people need regular contact with colleagues, and at least some of this must be face-to-face. Nor is everyone able or willing to work from home, even for some of the time. Home may be a place to escape from, rather than to.

Some people are highly self-driven, while others need deadlines, even artificial ones, imposed from outside to get down to the task in hand. Being in an office surrounded by other people working, or at least appearing to work, can be the motivation they need. People also work to different rhythms: some are early birds, others night owls.

Managers, therefore, need to be highly adaptable and sensitive to these differences among the individuals who make up their teams. In the next section, we look at these and other skills that managers need to develop if they are to survive and thrive in the new world of work.

Lessons from Agile Working at Unilever

Unilever has been introducing radically new ways of working to its operations around the world, from Dublin to Durban, Barcelona to Bogota, and Schaffhausen in Switzerland to Shanghai, over the past few years.

Its Agile Working program was launched at the end of 2009 as a strategy to help the consumer goods multinational achieve its goal of doubling turnover from €40bn without increasing its carbon footprint, and to attract and retain talent, particularly among women and Generation Y.

Senior business and HR leaders endorsed the following five principles:

- All employees may work anytime and anywhere as long as business needs are fully met
- Leaders must lead by example, working in an agile way themselves
- Performance is determined by results, not time and attendance – every employee has a personal work plan identifying desired results and how they will be measured
- Travel is to be avoided whenever possible
- Managers are assessed annually on how well they support agile workers and this feeds into the variable element of their pay

Implementing the strategy across the company, which employs over 170,000 people in 170 countries, is the responsibility of a cross-functional team comprising the heads of HR, finance, and enterprise and technology solutions (which includes IT). The communications team plays a crucial role in making it part of the culture, with slogans such as 'Ideas can fly without a plane' and 'Impact results, not the environment'.

The strategy is linked to Unilever's continuing drive to increase women's representation in senior leadership. By 2015, it aims to raise the proportion of female managers from 40 percent at the start of 2011 to 55 percent, and of female directors, the next level up from managers, from 30 percent to 50 percent.

Senior leaders are required to be role models by adopting 'Agile Working' principles, technology and facilities themselves. Around 20 percent of jobs in senior management and above are 'location-free', meaning that the executive may be based anywhere in the world. The company has invested in training people in the business benefits, in how to work and collaborate remotely, and in managing and being part of virtual teams.

With over 40 'agile' workspace projects completed or underway around the world, Unilever has tracked a number of business gains, including:

Cost and environmental savings:

- New workplaces are typically 30 percent more cost-effective and 40 percent more energy-efficient
- A 50 percent increase in virtual meetings between 2011 and 2012, and a rise in cost savings from travel avoidance to €95m (from €39.5m)

Business continuity:

- Critical projects were not disrupted by events such as the 2012 London Olympics or Hurricane Sandy, which forced the closure of Unilever's US headquarters for several days. Staff worked from home or offices nearby using technology powered by portable generators

Employee productivity:

- Eighty percent say their new workplace aids productivity, compared with 67 percent saying this before the move

Employer reputation:

- Unilever was named fifth most in-demand employer globally on LinkedIn, after Google, Microsoft, Apple and Facebook. 'We know that Agile Working is a key part of our employee value proposition in many countries,' says Laird.

New performance targets, focused on results, have been critical to the success of the program, she says. Everyone has three business goals a year, plus one personal developmental goal. Previously, individuals' bonuses were determined by how well their part of the business did, regardless of their personal performance. The bonus pool available for distribution now depends on the company's overall performance, but individuals' personal bonus is based on how well they meet their four goals. 'The change in performance management has helped managers become more comfortable with Agile Working, by having robust performance targets and success measured by output, not by being seen in the office,' Laird says.

Shifting large companies to future work inevitably takes time. Over the past four years, Unilever has encountered three main challenges:

1. Getting the technology and infrastructure right:

'We've made a huge investment in collaborative technology to support Agile Working and enable teams to communicate effectively across borders and time zones,' she says. 'But there are still not enough people who are all on the same communications platform. It's also a question of learning to use the technology. Using "virtual presence" technology, any employee can see the availability of any global colleague from their desktop thanks to red, yellow and green "presence indicators". It's part of our skills training that if you want to have an informal or spontaneous conversation with a remote colleague, you can see if they are available (green) and send them a quick chat message. This replicates those coffee machine conversations.'

There can be noise distractions in virtual communication. 'Some leaders say they need people to come into the office because they can't hear them on teleconferences – someone is calling from a hotel, someone else is on a mobile – and these little annoyances create a situation where the leader says "It doesn't work." We tell them that if they learn little skills around facilitating great virtual meetings, like people muting their phones, or ensuring the people joining remotely are equally included, the annoyances go away.'

2. Boundaries:

'Part of the new etiquette is about the boundaries between work and people's own lives,' Laird explains. 'We've had to educate people that "anytime anywhere" does not mean "all the time everywhere". Some teams have started rotating the time of calls so that no one time zone suffers all the time. Others arrange teleconferences so that team members in one time zone join for the start and then drop off the call, with a subsequent debrief, while those in the other time zone join towards the end.'

3. Changing culture and attitudes:

'We've learned that culture is tough to change and old habits die hard,' she says. 'We've created some great enthusiasm for Agile Working and the vast majority of the organization embraces it fully, but there are still pockets of people and some executives who don't fully understand the business case. The last bit of the journey is probably more difficult than the first part.'

Individuals have far more choices than they did before. 'Most people want to take advantage of both working from home and working in the office. But some people need a structured environment in which to work and find the freedom of Agile Working daunting, while others have developed a sense of entitlement about having a fixed day working from home. You have to teach people to find the responsible middle ground.'

As for leaders, an annual employee survey includes an assessment of each manager's perspective on Agile Working. It shows that a few remain skeptical. 'We talk to the leadership about the business case and ask them what frustrations they are having with agility. We're also helping each team to develop an Agile Working manifesto that facilitates a team conversation around the challenges and what they're doing to address these in terms of technology, behavior and problem-solving.'

Unilever's Colombia operation adopted Agile Working in 2010 – the first in Latin America to do so. Since then it has seen an increase in annual underlying sales growth from 5.7 percent to 7 percent in 2013, directly linked to the new work style, says Fabricio Kaplan, vice president for human resources for Middle Americas. It has also proved an important differentiator in attracting new recruits.

The most important lesson is that everyone is responsible for making it work, he says. 'It should be promoted from top to bottom. You have to keep reinforcing the key messages and every leader has to be committed to applying it in their work team to keep the Agile Working culture alive every day.'[7]

What skills do managers need?

I do think there's a gap. Lots of managers don't understand that a critical aspect of the role they now have is to share what the business needs, to lay it out for people, and make sure they have the right skills and tools, and that people are then ever so sensible and bright about how to manage it themselves.

Caroline Waters, former director of people and policy, BT[8]

Fortunately, managing in a future work environment does not mean learning a completely new set of skills. Some managers will adapt fairly quickly, because they simply need to extend the strong people skills they already possess. Others will need more help and support to develop the necessary skills. Even the most experienced senior leaders, however, admit they need to make some changes to their personal assumptions and management style, as we have shown in previous chapters.

The Future Work Forum at Henley Business School carried out research over ten years into the management of new working practices. It interviewed managers and HR directors and surveyed employees to establish what skills were required to run remote teams. It concluded that there was common agreement that managers have to work harder with such teams. Priorities may have to change, but they do not require radically different skills.

In a further study, it found that managers felt ill-equipped to deal with the day-to-day reality of managing remote teams. 'Almost half of respondents said that managers were unprepared for supervising flexible teams, and only a quarter had undergone specific training for managing remotely. In particular, anxiety around communication skills had been singled out and more support identified for developing better ways of binding teams together.'[9]

This finding is similar to that in the survey we conducted for this book, in which 60 percent of managers said they had never been trained to manage remote or flexible employees. At the same time, most of our respondents felt they had the right skills to do so.

What's needed is a fine balance between being more hands-off and more hands-on. This is not about piling even more work onto the individual manager's already overloaded agenda. In many ways, it should be less onerous. Setting goals, and leaving it up to people how they achieve them, avoids the burdens of micro-management, such as checking time sheets and monitoring employees' every move. By freeing people to schedule their own work, individually or in teams, managers can save a lot of time and effort.

Instead, the focus is on the more interesting aspects of management – communicating, inspiring and motivating. These are leadership skills. In these areas, managers have to be more hands-on, in terms of organizing, planning and, crucially, communicating via many different media. They have to oversee the new rules of the game, such as ensuring that people know how to press the 'off' switch or dealing swiftly with any abuses of trust. This can be demanding, but extremely effective if done well.

Table 8.2   TRUST principles and management skills

Principles	Skills
1. **T**rust your people	■ Openness to change ■ Delegation ■ Relationship-building ■ Prioritizing ■ Challenging status quo
2. **R**eward results	■ Planning ahead ■ Clear objective-setting ■ Inspiring and motivating ■ Sensitivity to changing needs ■ Decisiveness and consistency
3. **U**nderstand the business case	■ Awareness of big trends ■ Stakeholder orientation ■ Technological competence ■ Influencing ■ Resilience
4. **S**tart at the top	■ Willingness to change ■ Ability to give up 'control' ■ Leadership by example ■ Time management ■ Tenacity
5. **T**reat people as individuals	■ Appreciation of difference ■ Responsiveness ■ Adaptability ■ Reliability ■ Team-building

We have grouped the skills needed alongside each of the five TRUST principles (**Table 8.2**).

1. **Trusting your people** requires managers to be open to change, confident enough in their own competence and position to be able to delegate, enthusiastic about people's potential and willing to believe they will use their autonomy responsibly. Managers need to be good at building relationships, between themselves and their team and also between team members. They must be able to prioritize the things that really matter, because future work does not allow for micro-management.

They should be constantly questioning and challenging of the 'way we do things', for example meetings for meetings' sake.

2. **Rewarding results**, rather than input, requires strong planning and organization. It needs an ability to negotiate, set and communicate clear objectives so that people know exactly what is expected of them. Managers should be good at inspiring and motivating people, even if they do not see them on a regular basis. They should be adaptable to the changing needs of the business, and able to communicate these quickly, and also sensitive to the changing needs of their team members. They must be decisive and consistent in tackling breaches of trust or poor performance to protect the benefits of future work and reassure everyone else that being responsible and accountable is valued.

3. **Understanding the business case** requires awareness of the big trends affecting business, work and society beyond the confines of the organization. Managers need to be alive to the changing expectations of internal and external stakeholders – employees, customers, suppliers, investors and regulators. They need to keep abreast of technological advances (though this does not necessitate becoming a geek). The important thing is to understand how technology can enable new ways of working, what is available, what investment will be required and what the payback will be. They need to be able to influence decision-makers and employees, and to be resilient in the face of resistance or inertia.

4. **Starting at the top** means leaders taking the initiative to move to future work. Since this will probably involve a change of culture, leaders need to be aware of their own style and what messages it sends to people. They have to be open to questioning their own assumptions about people and about established norms of work and careers. They need to be able to let go and allow people to manage themselves, which may feel like taking a risk and stepping outside their comfort zone. They must represent the culture change visibly in their own behavior, whether that means dispensing with a private office, working from home once or twice a week or delegating more consistently. They will need to be highly efficient with their own time and work methods. In maintaining the new culture, they will require considerable tenacity.

5. **Treating people as individuals** demands sensitivity to differences between people, and an ability to turn these into strengths, both for the team and the wider business. This is particularly important when

managing teams across different cultures, often working virtually, but it applies to superficially homogenous teams working mainly from a single location too. Managers need to be quick in dealing with issues that arise, and prompt in responding to phone calls or messages from individuals working remotely. They have to be adaptable and good at building cohesive teams. Being a dependable communicator who makes time for each team member is essential.

'Three-year competitive advantage' for Gap

Gap, the global apparel brand, has begun to break free of the old model with a bold shift to results-only work in core parts of its North America business. High staff turnover prompted it to begin a radical overhaul of working practices at its Outlet division in California in 2008. A year earlier, the division had started buying product from Asia via online auctions. The time zone difference meant that US production staff were often online working at 1 a.m., but still expected to be at their desks in the office at 8 a.m.

These employees, most of them women in their 30s, tend to have long commutes to work because the high cost of real estate means many cannot afford to live near the office. Combined with the difficult hours, they were finding it impossible to balance their jobs with other personal commitments. 'Our staff turnover rate was 30–40 percent in key areas and it was killing us,' says Eric Severson, senior vice-president of Human Resources for Gap Inc., in an interview in San Francisco.[10]

Traditional flexible work arrangements had failed to staunch the outflow. So Gap opted for an approach called 'Results-Only Work Environment' (ROWE), designed by consultants Cali Ressler and Jody Thompson. This approach measures and rewards people for output, not hours, leaving it to individuals to decide where, when and how to carry out their work.

'It's like being back in college,' says Severson. 'People are held accountable for what they achieve rather than how much time they spend on a project or where they do the work. As in school, it doesn't matter how long or where you study – only if you pass the test. Ironically, employees love the freedom of ROWE so much that they are protective of the program, and put peer pressure on slackers to straighten up.'

Right from the first trial, the HR team measured the business impact in order to have a sound basis for pressing ahead or dropping the experiment. After six months, it recorded a halving in the attrition rate of staff in the production and technical design department, which supplies Gap's global Outlet and Banana Republic Factory stores. The apparel sourcing organization in Asia, with whom they work, reported an increase in responsiveness and productivity in the US team.

Senior leadership at Gap wanted more proof before agreeing to roll it out across the division, says Severson. Another pilot, this time across functions from merchandising to store support, produced similar results. 'Employees, managers and internal customers all reported better service quality, timeliness and productivity, and staff turnover went down.'

After a third successful six-month pilot, the scheme went live across the division's head office in 2009. 'It has given us at least a three-year advantage over our competitors,' he says. 'Retail is very old school and we knew our competitors would be incredibly reticent to do this. But control over time is more precious to talent in this market than having more money, which they can get somewhere else.'

In 2011, the scheme was expanded to employees at Gap North America and Banana Republic global headquarters as well as a number of Gap corporate functions such as HR and Legal. In each instance, staff retention and engagement statistics improved, and recruiters noted a marked increase in the number of desirable job candidates interested in joining the company because of ROWE.

Employers' resistance to giving people autonomy is often based on fear that they will desert their desks, abuse their freedom and be impossible to contact. Such fears proved unfounded at Gap, where there has been no wholesale desertion from the office. The main change, says Severson, is that people arrive and leave at different times, often before or after the rush hour, and that most of them now work at home once a week.

Another objection raised was that people would be unavailable in the event of a 'fire drill', the term used for crises requiring all employees to be on site. This also proved to be an unwarranted fear. 'It's a principle of ROWE that there are no fire drills,' says Severson. 'This causes you to challenge your mentality. A fire drill isn't necessary most of the time. It's often the result of someone failing to plan ahead. We actually saw more responsiveness and flexibility to urgent business needs with ROWE, not less. The idea that being in the office makes one more responsive is a myth.'

The Gap Inc. head office employs only a fraction of the company's workforce of about 135,000 employees globally. Introducing a version of ROWE in the stores, where 90 percent of employees work, would be much harder, but Severson does not rule it out. 'This is where the heart of the business resides, and *that* would be the revolution.'

One issue with ROWE is that it does not necessarily reduce the number of hours people work, but just enables them to distribute those hours in a way that suits them better, he says. Gap has found that people work *more* hours, partly because many are now at home one day a week, making productive use of time they would otherwise spend commuting.

Giving people the freedom to work anywhere, anytime, is not always enough, he says. It needs to be combined with more effective work techniques to avoid the overload that many workers experience.

Nevertheless, he describes ROWE as 'the perfect marriage of employee and business needs, with neither getting sold short'. He sums up the lessons from Gap's experience so far:

- Change will not happen without the backing of the CEO and the leadership team
- Pilot, pilot and pilot again
- Managers need to brush up on their communication and planning skills
- Rules are important, for example making sure people put their cell phone numbers on the shared calendar so everyone can keep in touch

In summary

In this chapter, we have set out the five TRUST principles to guide organizations in making a successful transition to future work, and illustrated them with case studies of Unilever and Gap. We have also listed the skills that leaders and managers need, including relationship-building, clear objective-setting, resilience, adaptability and appreciation of difference.

In Chapter 9, we give detailed advice on how to apply these skills in practice. Using more illustrations, we explain how to manage different individuals working remotely, how to build cohesion in virtual teams, and how to address common concerns about the switch to future work.

Chapter 9

Making it happen as an organization

> We like to give people the freedom to work where they want, safe in the knowledge that they have the drive and expertise to perform excellently, whether they are at their desk or in their kitchen. Yours truly has never worked out of an office, and never will.[1]
>
> Sir Richard Branson, founder of Virgin Group

We have shown the wide-ranging benefits of future work practices. The most successful examples grow from the values of the business founders or from strong leadership. For a manager lucky enough to work in such an environment, introducing a new work model will be relatively straightforward. For others it will be more of a challenge, pushing back against deeply ingrained habits. Based on our experience of working with, and talking to, hundreds of managers in organizations undergoing such change, this chapter sets out the practical steps to implement and sustain effective twenty-first century work.

First, it is good to know why you are doing it. Alternative work patterns, generally in the form of 'flexible working arrangements', are often introduced by HR departments as a policy that managers must follow, without a clear business case. They may be driven by legislation, employee requests, union pressure or 'diversity' goals, or they could be the result of a rationalization of space designed to save costs.

This is not enough. They need to be presented as a full-blown strategy to boost the bottom line. Only this way can future work produce the greatest benefits in terms of productivity, creativity and loyalty. It requires a change of culture from 'do what you are told' to 'do it the way that works best'. If implemented properly, it can make a huge difference to the lives of almost everyone in the enterprise. This chapter is about how to implement it, what works best and how to overcome resistance, using the TRUST framework introduced in Chapter 8.

The Way We Work program

Hertfordshire County Council, in the southeast of England, set about rationalizing its office portfolio in 2005, reducing it from 62 buildings to just four, saving revenue costs and releasing capital to invest elsewhere. But the council soon realized it needed a broader approach to gain the full benefits. 'What started out as a relocation program turned into a massive cultural change,' says David Robinson, program director of 'The Way We Work'.

The council asked employees what was preventing them from being more efficient and were told 'Give us IT that works.' It made a major investment in providing technology that allowed people to perform their jobs effectively, an investment that was easily covered by the large savings in occupancy costs.

The relocation program was used as a catalyst to introduce new ways of working. For some employees the extra traveling time was an incentive to try working from home, but for many it was an opportunity to review their personal work pattern and try something different. By the end of the five-year program, 47 percent of the staff had changed the time and/or place they worked.

The initiative had full support from senior management, with the program director reporting directly to the chief executive and the leader of the council. Directors and heads of service set an example by sitting in open-plan office space with their staff. Champions were appointed in each department to sell the ideas to managers and staff. But not all managers were keen to change.

According to Robinson, 'we had some old-fashioned managers who would only trust their people if they were in the office at 9 a.m. But the role of a manager in 2010 is very different from that in 2005. We've provided help, training, advice, guidance, but eventually for those that were unable to adapt we provided a speedy exit route.'

It took five years, with carefully planned steps along the way, and has continued to improve the use of office space since 2010. The transformation has attracted huge interest. Robinson has hosted over 70 other local authorities. Many visitors have said they would love to introduce a similar scheme but their chief executive and senior officers would not support the changes.

Other councils have attempted smaller change programs with less success. They have tried rationalizing their office space, sharing services with other authorities or offering flexible working, without treating it as a major cultural change. 'The secret to it all is having one overall program,' says Robinson.[2]

1. Trusting your people in practice

The key to the successful implementation of future work is an under-standing of when and how a job can be performed. One of the first steps is to analyze the constraints and see what tasks can be performed outside conventional hours and away from the normal workplace. If a job involves face-to-face contact with customers, it might have limited flexibility in terms of location but still allow a choice of hours for employees. In retail, for example, demand for extended hours of service creates a need for people to cover early and late shifts.

In many sectors, it's useful to start with the counter-intuitive assumption that the work can be done whenever an employee chooses and then only restrict the scope based on logical constraints. It is also helpful to assume that work can be split up into units that do not have to be full-time jobs.

So, instead of designing jobs by listing a series of tasks, the future work manager begins with the outcomes and describes what needs to be achieved. This way she can come up with creative ways of getting work done and not just repeat old working patterns.

Managers often struggle with the idea that a job can be done outside the office, simply because it has never been tried. They assume that, because the whole job cannot be performed remotely, none of it can be. Yet most organizations that introduce future work practices end up with hybrid arrangements. Some work is performed in the office during normal working hours, some may be done at the same desk outside conventional hours and some may be done remotely, both inside and outside normal hours.

Where managers have fully implemented future work, they may have as many different patterns of work as they have employees. While this sounds like a recipe for chaos, it manages itself well – provided the manager is prepared to trust people to get on with it.

What happens in practice is that people get together to work out how to achieve their business goals at the same time as meeting their personal requirements. If they do this as a team, with the support of their manager, they take ownership of the solution and make sure it works. If someone has to make a change to the new arrangement, he or she will first agree it with a colleague and then tell their manager. They present an answer, not a problem, since they have been handed the responsibility and have a vested interest in making things work. This contrasts with the convention of managers deciding a rota and being left with a problem if an individual falls sick or needs to make a change.

This is empowerment in action. It gives people more control over the time and place that they carry out their job, on the assumption that they will act responsibly and not abuse it. It is based on trust – and it works.

Sainsbury's, the UK food retail chain, has found that self-scheduling works best in small teams of 10–15 people. It has piloted this on food counters, such as bakery departments, and filling stations. 'We've said to them: "Put together schedules you think will work and try them for a month,"' says Rhona Caldwell, human resources manager for Sainsbury's in northwest England. 'In 99 per cent of cases it has worked, with a few tweaks. The teams manage issues better themselves. People work for people, not for organizations, which they see as a bit faceless. Small teams will spot if somebody is not very happy. When people get support, they want to come to work.'

In the new world, managers who feel the need to control their minions' every move will have difficulty. Those who see themselves as catalysts for people to perform at their best will adapt quickly.

Social media: enemy or friend of the corporation?

The way companies respond to the use of social media is a good reflection of their attitudes to trust. Many make the assumption that if they allow people access at work they will spend hours tweeting to their friends or gossiping with colleagues. Worse still, they may spread malicious rumors about their managers or criticize the company. But what does this say about the attitude toward the people they hired to work for them? Obviously employees 'can't be trusted' to use these tools sensibly, so banning them is the easiest option to avoid putting temptation in their way.

According to Gartner, the IT research company, 50 percent of large organizations were blocking employee access to social media in 2010 but this is dropping by about ten percent a year and by 2014 will be less than 30 percent.[3] So perhaps this is a sign that employers are trusting their staff more, or maybe they have simply found it impractical to maintain the ban.

Many organizations that have embraced social media have found that they can create significant business advantage. Employees use information technology to improve communications with their colleagues and do not spend all their time socializing with their friends. If they are being judged by their output, they know that it is in their own interest not to get distracted. They also know that if they are trusted to use social media sensibly, they work for an organization that treats them like adults, and they live up to this.

BT is reaping the benefits of social media at work. 'With a flexible working culture and infrastructure already in place, BT was able to experiment with and encourage social media at an early stage.' says Dave Dunbar, head of BT flexible working services. 'All sorts of blogs, podcasts and wikis have sprung up across the organization, generated by employees and not moderated by BT. In all its forms, social media is helping us tap into the knowledge, talent and skills of our people to an extent that was not previously possible.'

He adds: 'We get tremendous benefits from people giving us fresh ideas and innovation. As for security, the policing of it is covered by the same regulations as would cover any employee saying unacceptable things in the normal office, except that with social media there is an audit trail.'

With more and more people bringing their own devices to work, organizations will find they are introducing flexibility by default, he says. 'At that point they need to decide whether they really do trust their people or not. If they do, they may as well enshrine that trust in doctrine.'[4]

2. Rewarding results in practice

Once people are working 'out of sight', whether at home, on the road or in a virtual team scattered across different countries, managers are forced to focus on results. Instead of measuring the hours that someone puts into the job, they have to measure the outcomes.

Goals have to be set that allow people to work without constant supervision. The manager and employee must have a clear understanding of what outcome is required. By expressing the goal in terms of a tangible product, both parties can be sure that they are aiming for the same result and there are no nasty surprises when the work is submitted. The goal should specify quality as well as quantity. There is no point in an employee beavering away for a month and producing the right number of outputs only to find that they are not of the quality expected.

It is critical that the work is not just expressed as a job description but as a series of targets that are understood and agreed by the employee. Once this has been established, it is much easier for the manager to let the individual get on with it because she no longer has to look for proof of effort. She has the results to show that the work has been done.

At first, deadlines for goals can be quite short term. Daily or weekly checks on output may be needed, but these can stretch to monthly or longer deadlines as confidence grows between manager and employee. This will be an individual arrangement. Two employees doing similar jobs might have different deadlines or report-back times based on their experience and competence.

At the start, some employees will welcome tight deadlines as a way to maintain their own concentration on the job. People used to working under supervision can find themselves distracted when working at home or varying their working time. Some people need to learn new ways of managing themselves.

We have shown how workers who are given autonomy generally report big improvements in productivity. Good managers see the benefits of this and stop rewarding long hours and insisting on people being present when it's not strictly necessary. Instead of having to put in additional hours in the workplace to demonstrate 'dedication' to the job and the company, the objective is to complete a quality job in the shortest time.

3. Understanding the business case in practice

Organizations need a clear plan for the transition to future work, outlining the business objectives as well as the stages of implementation. Managers will embrace the move to future work more willingly if they understand that it has clear business goals. If they see it as another piece of bureaucracy to stop them getting on with their jobs, they will greet it at best with apathetic acceptance and at worst with downright antagonism.

This is as important as introducing a brand new product line, taking over another company, launching additional services, relocating the business or selling off a division. It is a major step in the development of the business and should be treated as such.

It should be discussed, understood and agreed by the board. This is not easy. Board meetings often consist of facts, figures and tangible data. Here we are talking about the way we work, the atmosphere in the organization, the relationship we have with our people and what we are doing to their lives. It is about HOW we manage, not just WHAT we manage. Because some of this can be seen as soft and intangible, it is vital to have as many data to hand on the business benefits as possible (see Chapter 4 for the full panoply of benefits). Otherwise the issue risks being ignored and the culture remaining stubbornly unchanged.

Collect clear, measurable results from other companies and, preferably, from inside your own business, and link them to broader business goals. **BT** used peer group pressure to bring about change. 'Find people who really make it work,' says Caroline Waters, former head of people and policy. 'We found people's opposite numbers who were doing it and had all the right performance metrics. We held them up, gave them a platform, and brought them together in groups and at conferences. It changes the role of HR: the line managers do it, and you [HR] help them. One converted line manager is worth ten suits from HR. They're much more influential with their peer group than we could ever be.'[5]

Identify and cost the resources involved in making the change and clearly lay out timescales. Include the cost of additional information technology and any up-front investment. Offset this against the cost savings in real estate and the expected benefits from increased productivity. Translate this into increased output from existing staff, or a reduction in headcount while maintaining current levels of output.

For most organizations, the transition represents a major change program and it needs to be planned and executed as such. Resources need to be allocated to the program and money set aside for management development. A realistic investment of leadership time is essential. A project team should be set up with representatives from operational management as well as specialists such as HR, IT and real estate. A senior project manager should be appointed with access to the leadership team and the authority to push the program forward when it comes up against the inevitable resistance from entrenched individuals.

Measure the impact of the changes from the start. Don't just measure employee engagement or satisfaction scores. Look too at productivity, customer service, cost savings on business travel and real estate, speed of entry to new markets, staff turnover, knowledge retention and the health of the workforce.

4. Starting at the top in practice

Selling the concept of future work has to top the list from the start. This is much more than a change in operational practices or the addition of a few more policies and procedures. It is a change of culture.

It will not happen if senior managers set themselves apart. In many organizations that offer flexible working policies, the implicit message from top management is: 'Yes, we allow our employees to work flexibly but managers need to be working full-on all the time.' Work-life balance is for the troops, not for the officers. In the most macho work environments, people brag about the long hours they work, just as heavy drinkers boast about how much alcohol they downed on a Friday night.

To be effective, a future work strategy needs visible support and momentum from a senior champion, or champions, preferably at board level. Getting top management backing is essential and the program manager will need to be politically astute to win over the skeptics.

Ideally the chief executive should be heading the initiative, not just paying lip service but demonstrating behavior that can be mirrored by managers throughout the company. The worst examples of so-called flexible workspaces have junior employees crammed together in poorly run hot-desking areas while senior managers maintain separate fiefdoms, luxuriating in their thick-carpeted personal offices. The best examples have the CEO and directors sitting in open-plan areas, symbolizing the abolition of traditional hierarchies.

'The first and most important step is leadership support and accountability,' says Marcee Harris Schwartz of **BDO USA**, the accounting firm. 'We spent a lot of time at the very beginning of the strategy design with the very top-level leaders at the firm, having them take real ownership of what the strategy was and how it was communicated. It wasn't an HR program or benefit. It really was a business strategy.'

A key differentiator for BDO USA has been the commitment of successive CEOs. 'I have been a champion of the BDO Flex Strategy from its inception,' says Wayne Berson, who succeeded Jack Weisbaum, a vocal advocate, in 2012. 'Since I was elected CEO, I have become an even bigger proponent of BDO Flex. In addition to my extensive domestic travel as the CEO of a national accounting firm, I also travel a great deal internationally as a member of BDO International's Policy Board. Given these responsibilities, when I am home I try to maximize my personal time with my family and community by working at home as often as possible.'[6]

Future work practices must not rely on the enlightened leadership of a single manager, or they risk being reversed when that manager moves on or when the company merges with another organization that is culturally very different. These practices need to be part of the way the whole organization works. This is why they require the commitment of the entire leadership team, and a thorough understanding of the business case by middle managers, so there is no going back.

A US business had made big strides in enabling people to work from home some or all of the time, reducing office space and equipping workers with mobile technology. One team worked with colleagues around the world, and their hours extended well beyond the local business day, so this gave them much needed flexibility in the daytime. This manageable new model was broken by the arrival of a boss who decreed that everyone should be at an office desk during the business day. As a former employee explained, their jobs did not change, so this meant they were effectively forced to work day and night. It was a recipe for burnout, plummeting productivity and rock-bottom morale. 'The goal was for us to play as a team, but our team was not local, so sitting in an empty office had no rationale.'

Introducing future work is an opportunity to revisit the values of the organization and see how working practices align with them. Do the values reflect a respect for people and a belief that they will respond responsibly to being trusted? The implementation plan should be explicit about the values that lie behind the new practices. Employees can then test managers' behavior against the espoused values and point out where they do not live up to their public statements. This puts meat on the bones of statements such as 'our people are our most important asset' and 'we believe in equality and fairness'.

A useful tool for breaking down barriers to future work is 'reverse' mentoring of senior executives by Gen Y employees. The idea is that the young employees explain the uses and benefits of the latest technology and social media to top managers. Having this responsibility, and the ear of senior executives, is motivating for the junior employees, while their seniors gain useful insights into how the next generation thinks and communicates. An alternative version of this is reciprocal mentoring, where senior executives in turn give career advice to younger staff.

5. Treating people as individuals in practice

Traditionally, good managers have motivated employees by being seen, walking about and saying 'well done'. They have spent time getting to know people and have been available for a chat when needed.

As work becomes increasingly dispersed and virtual, they can no longer literally stand over people to see what is happening. Not all employees are self-starters. Some may need more encouragement and handholding during the early days of the new work patterns. If they are used to being given directions, they may take a while to feel comfortable about making decisions for themselves and getting out of old habits. It is important for managers to understand what motivates each individual and to adapt accordingly.

Treating people as individuals is an important aspect of future work. Because everyone is different, and employers need to get the best out of each person, working arrangements will vary. Managers often raise concerns about the potential for unfair treatment of employees if they do not all have the same work pattern. After many years of being told not to discriminate, they fear 'breaking the rules'. But this is to confuse fairness with equality. Future work is about treating people fairly without needing identical work arrangements for everyone. This presents a challenge to managers who prefer simply to follow a set of rules, as it requires them to use some judgment and actually manage.

In its management training, **Sainsbury's** has recently put the emphasis on individual judgment, says Rhona Caldwell. 'People in our organization can become too rule-bound,' she says. 'It's important to listen to colleagues and to treat them as individuals. The rules are just a framework. None of it is rigid. We say to them: What would you do if it were a member of your family?'

As with any big change program, employees need to know well in advance what is happening and how it will impact them. Managers should sit down with individuals and teams and discuss plans and options.

Where people have to be in face-to-face contact with customers, there is less scope for autonomous working, but where they mostly use telephones there is greater opportunity for change. Many jobs have an element of report writing, form filling or answering emails that can be done anywhere and anytime, provided the technology is available. These tasks are often performed more quickly and efficiently in the quiet of a remote location than in the middle of a noisy office. It may suit one individual to work from home one day a week to perform these 'solo' tasks and spend the rest of the time in the office interacting with colleagues. However, another person doing the same job may find home totally unsuitable for quiet concentration.

Addressing managers' concerns

Not surprisingly, many leaders and managers used to the conventional work model initially have misgivings about making the transition to the new world of work. In this section, we address the questions and concerns that commonly arise.

Q. How will I know they are working?

This is the biggest worry for managers faced with the prospect of people working remotely. They are concerned that individuals will spend all day watching television, talking to the neighbors or shopping or otherwise 'wasting time'.

'Will I have to phone them every morning to check they are out of bed and getting on with the job?' 'Do I need software that tracks their activities on their computer?' The answer is straightforward. If your people get the work done, then you will know that they have been doing the job. Moreover, if it is the kind of work that does not have to be done between fixed hours, checking when they are working is irrelevant. The only real test here is the quality, quantity and timeliness of the work output.

One company ran workshops for managers and employees to prepare them for a more flexible work culture. Some of the managers expressed concern that they would lose control, that productivity might fall and that it would not be possible to have the entire team present for 8.30 a.m. meetings in the office. The facilitators asked the managers: 'Why is it so important to see the person?' 'Why does it matter as long as they are responding to you?' 'Would *you* not have worked if you were working from home?'

Managers can be so absorbed in being supervisors that they can take a rigid view of how, where and when employees should work. Ask yourself how you can be sure that employees are working when they are in the office? Just because they are at their workstations, or tapping away at their keyboards, there is no guarantee that they are producing worthwhile results.

Q. Won't this open the floodgates?

Why would it matter if it did? Ideally, your strategy will be to create a wholesale shift in work styles, enabling everyone to have a greater degree of autonomy over where and when they work, as this will benefit the business and themselves.

Where the job or sector allows only limited choice over time or location, however, you should share around what flexibility is available. Think in terms of desired outcomes, not tasks (see **Trusting your people in practice** earlier in this chapter). Explain the business objectives to the team and ask them to find more efficient ways of achieving them.

There is no need to limit the variations in work patterns, provided business objectives are met. All individuals are different, so it is unlikely that any two work patterns will be identical. Some people like to start work early, while others are late risers. Some want to work longer days but shorter weeks, while others will prefer to take some work home to complete in the evenings. Provided customer needs are met, these variations do not need to be supervised. Experiment and see what works.

One route that organizations take is to use pilots and trial periods before making more permanent changes. Managers often fear that once they have agreed to something they cannot look back. But until it is tried out, neither party will really know if it is working. Once the benefits, such as greater productivity, extended customer service coverage or real estate savings, become evident, everyone will be more comfortable about taking the plunge.

If things do not work out at first, make adjustments and try again. Keep an open mind. Investigate whether the problem is really to do with the new working practices or is actually a specific performance issue, which needs to be dealt with separately.

Q. What happens to relationships and team spirit?

A common concern about new work styles is that team spirit will suffer. In a conventional workplace, people sit together and exchange ideas. They have coffee and lunch breaks together. They spend the first 20 minutes of the day chatting about traffic problems or last night's soccer match or soap opera. By virtue of sitting together, a team spirit is born. A good manager will nurture this and encourage people to collaborate.

In the new world of work, this teambuilding is at risk. How will people get a chance to build the informal relationships that tie the team together? Managers need to recognize the importance of informal communications between team members. If all contacts are about work, people will take a long time to get to know their colleagues. The few minutes each day sharing personal experiences that are unrelated to work are critical to maintaining team relationships.

For people who now see their colleagues once a week instead of once a day, this is no great problem. But there is an increasing chance that remote working, shifted hours and virtual teamwork across time zones mean that some people rarely see the rest of the team. Managers discover that there is hardly ever a time when all their people are together, whether virtually or in a physical office.

This is when it makes sense to build back some of the lost 'team time'. Team meetings can be arranged, perhaps monthly, to communicate the latest business information and get people to discuss their ideas. But it is equally important to compensate for the loss of casual chats about non-work topics. Arranging for people to take a coffee break during the meeting and encouraging everyone to go to the staff restaurant together for lunch is probably sufficient. However, more formal teambuilding exercises have their place and can reap real rewards in terms of improved collaboration, especially if people are dispersed across different countries and only meet rarely.

Q. Don't we still need our meetings?

While face-to-face meetings are important for individuals and teams who spend most of their time working remotely, the conventional office meeting culture needs to be challenged. For a start, if more people are working anywhere anytime, a whole-day meeting will be difficult to arrange.

This is a great stimulus to question the purpose and value of routine meetings. Does the weekly update meeting on a Monday morning really need to happen at all? Can the information be communicated by email, voicemail or as part of a discussion forum on the intranet? If it requires feedback from participants, can this be given in a text form rather than verbally in a meeting room? What is the purpose of the meeting anyway? Is it just for sharing information or is it for making decisions? Can it be held by audio or video link so it is still live but people do not have to be in the same place?

In many conventional cultures, having a diary full of meetings and being seen as overloaded, to the point of being stressed, is a sign of importance. Not so in the world of future work. People are judged by their output, not the number of meetings they attend.

There are many technologies available to achieve the desired results without taking up people's time and energy getting to a meeting room, from simple text solutions such as Instant Messaging to sophisticated Virtual Presence conferencing systems. It can take terrible events like the 9/11 attacks or the 2011 Japanese earthquake and tsunami to make people stop and think about alternatives to the overflowing schedule of back-to-back meetings. We hope the benefits of future work will be realized without such disasters and tragedies in future.

This is not to say that all face-to-face meetings should be abolished. There are times when getting people in the same room to hear and discuss issues is the most effective way of achieving an objective. It is essential for relationship-building and consideration of sensitive and personal issues, such as leadership development. But the cost savings, and the environmental and human benefits, of reducing travel to physical meetings are powerful reasons to use alternatives such as videoconferencing wherever possible.

The global HR team at **Unilever** holds half of its seven to eight meetings a year via Telepresence, for example. 'It forces great discipline,' says Fiona Laird, co-head of the company's Agile Working program. 'We meet for less time and focus on priority items. If people fly a long way, they tend to make sure the meeting lasts two to three days to justify the journey.'

Collaborating in a virtual team

How can teams work effectively when they are dispersed? The question was hotly debated in the wake of Yahoo's ban on remote working in 2013.

Christel Verschaeren, chief information officer for **IBM** Europe, has a 12-strong leadership team mostly working across Europe, with two in the US. 'I've never met one of my colleagues in the US, though I've worked with her for three years, but I've met all the others at least once.' Face-to-face team meetings happen only when they need to spend a few days together on implementing a major project or when there is a particular problem to discuss, and meals are a good way to bond.

Verschaeren argues that working virtually is *more* effective than face-to-face, at least in terms of productivity. 'It takes 30 minutes before you really get going when you're meeting face-to-face, and it's less focused. When I go to the Brussels office, it's great to meet people and talk to them, we drink coffee together, but you lose a lot of productive time. It is useful but you need to find the right balance.'

How does collaboration happen in her dispersed team? 'I have many calls with my team on different topics and we have "sharing" calls where everybody just talks about what issues they have or what's on top of their mind and we see how we can help. We use Instant messaging software and Connections, which is our internal social collaboration platform. It's not yet as fast as I'd like, and it requires a change in behavior, but we progress step by step. I can post a question and I don't have to sit and wait until someone answers. I can go back and see what people have replied later. You have a discussion in a disconnected way.'

In a face-to-face meeting, it's easier to tell if someone is not happy through body language. What about spotting hidden problems in a virtual team? Verschaeren says she generally knows if something is not right during an Internet chat or a phone call. 'I don't know if it's another sense that you develop, but I think I have developed that. I say: "What's up?" And there's always something behind it.'

Having the freedom to work the way you want is appealing, even ideal, for many people. For some, however, it becomes an accelerating treadmill from which there is no escape. Verschaeren once had to tell an employee that he could no longer work from home and had to come into the office every day — not because he was being lazy, but because he could not stop working.

'I saw him going into burnout. He was mad at me because it was a difficult commute for him and I had intruded on his way of working. A few months

> later, he said: "This is the best thing you could have done." He didn't see what was happening to him. Coming back to the office taught him that there's a beginning and an end to the working day. When implementing any such program, I would pay much more attention to this than we did years ago.'

Q. Won't our clients object?

A common concern is that introducing future work will reduce the quality of customer service because employees will not be available when needed by clients. It turns out that the opposite is often the case. One of the advantages cited by organizations implementing agile working is that they can provide services to clients over extended hours by having people working outside the normal 'nine to five'.

Nobody can be at work 24/7, so most customers understand that they cannot insist on an individual being available all the time. They can expect a level of service that relies on reasonable availability of a specific person plus appropriate cover when that person is busy doing something else.

Many clients are keen to move to more agile working themselves, and appreciate the opportunity to learn more about it. Mike Dean of Accenture, featured in Chapter 5, says he has met no objections to his work style from clients, contrary to what many managers fear. 'I think it's nonsense that the client wouldn't like it. Often it's a business opportunity. When you talk to the client, they say: "We see Accenture as being very advanced in this area. Could you come and talk to us about what you do?" They often realize that they can become more balanced about their demands without it harming the contract. They appreciate the benefits of a more enlightened culture. It just takes guts.'[7]

Q. What happens to employment contracts?

Future work questions the need for a contractual employment relationship in the traditional sense. If it is possible to get the work done through a results-based arrangement, then employing someone by the hour or month makes no sense. It could simply be a service, purchased from a supplier as with any subcontracted relationship. An individual engaged under this relationship could be self-employed or might have an employment contract with an agency.

If an individual is working for an organization on a long-term basis, they will expect to have a more permanent arrangement than just a contract for their next piece of work. Employment legislation in most countries will insist that they have certain rights such as a minimum period of notice and paid vacation time. So employees will still have contracts setting out their rights and responsibilities but these are becoming more flexible as work patterns change. They may still have to specify a time and place of work but can often be varied by mutual agreement between employee and employer.

In some instances, labor laws have not caught up with the latest working practices and might prevent an arrangement that suits the employer and employee. It is beyond the scope of this book to look into the details of contractual legislation everywhere, but it is clear from the numerous examples of future work across the world that major employers are devising working solutions that are legal. Since the flexibility of the labor market is a key factor in economic success, it is likely that legislators will be motivated to remove any serious roadblocks to prevent work from moving offshore to more flexible jurisdictions.

Q. What's in it for me?

The benefits of future work may be obvious to the project champion and the senior team leading the change, but the individual manager can see it as an unwelcome disruption. To overcome this, many organizations run management workshops to explain the benefits and reduce the fears. These provide practical information on how to manage flexible, remote and virtual teams and they give participants the confidence to experiment.

The idea of loosening control and empowering employees can be very threatening to a manager, particularly one who is insecure in his position. Future work can be seen as undermining his authority and hindering his ability to get the job done. It is important, therefore, that managers can see past the initial barriers and appreciate the benefits that will follow on.

Workshops can introduce the experiences of other organizations that have already gone through the change process and can be used to share experiences across the enterprise. If one department or business unit has successfully implemented new working practices, this story can be used to help others follow suit. Assembling a core of convinced managers will help to spread the word. Using them in the workshop and elsewhere will contribute to wider success.

Future work involves genuine autonomy for employees. This probably means the need for fewer middle managers. If employees are managing themselves and are trusted to work without close supervision, management resources are freed up. It should be possible for more people to be reporting to any one manager without any detrimental effects.

The manager's role also changes. Instead of being a taskmaster or micromanager, she needs to be a skilled leader of people, a coach and a guide. The job is, therefore, both more exciting and more challenging. For those managers who want to retain control over people, the transition will be difficult or impossible. For those who can see the benefits of change and who relish the chance to motivate individuals and teams to produce the best results by treating them as adults, the future looks good.

Managing across borders and cultures

Three-quarters of managers at **IBM**, the IT, software and consulting services giant, have people in their teams who work remotely, and whom they do not see on a daily basis. About 40 percent of the more than 400,000 employees are classified as mobile, with no fixed work base. Employees, other than those working in client contact or delivery centers, where uninterrupted service is necessary, have flexibility about where and when they work.

Gary Kildare, a global vice-president for human resources at IBM, stresses the importance of people skills in managing mobile employees and teams dispersed across the world, who collaborate virtually rather than face-to-face. 'You can be wonderful technically, but you also have to focus on people or it will hold you back as a leader,' he says. 'Technology can also help us to focus on people. For example, through online tools a team can collaborate in real-time on a project. With virtual offices and working spaces, you can see and interact with your colleagues, and you can quickly identify the expert(s) you need in a particular area or specialty from anywhere across the whole company through an app on your smartphone.'

Two things are really important: relationships and sensitivity. 'It can take longer to build trusting relationships because you don't always have that face-face contact with people. Leaders and managers must take time to understand how individuals are performing if they don't get to observe them directly every day in an office setting. It's about setting very clear goals and objectives and expectations and measuring the outcome.'

Communication is at the heart of it. 'I tend to use a lot of conference calls with my own team. This means setting a schedule one quarter (three months) in advance so people know when things are going to happen. I try to avoid missing or cancelling calls unless it's inevitable. People like to see regular patterns and feel included.'

As for sensitivity, this is especially important in relation to cultural differences. 'There can be misunderstandings. When people send emails, there can be multiple or different interpretations. As a leader you mustn't make assumptions about anyone or anything. You can't speak 20 languages but you can respect everyone's culture. In some cultures, people are quiet, in others they are not. Some are very outspoken, some are less so. It's about treating and respecting everyone as an individual.

'You have to set standards and insist on team collaboration and involvement. You have to be quite tough if you feel someone has overstepped the boundary. We have a very intellectual, highly skilled workforce. Our people are graduates, double-degree holders, doctorates and extremely able. When we use email and instant messaging, people use different styles and sometimes they can be quite direct. It's important to think about what we write, just as much as what we say – adding a smiley face doesn't make a tough message any easier.'

Given the profile of the workforce, it is far more likely to contain committed 24/7 workers than people who are work-shy. How can managers act to stop people feeling that they have to be 'always available', given that the technology makes that possible?

'Managers will help if they see people who are online too much,' Kildare says. 'Managers are expected to help balance workload across teams and, if someone is struggling to meet a deadline, to make sure they're getting help and assistance needed. In team-oriented work environments, it's important for people to be staying in touch with colleagues. Often it's colleagues who tell you that you're doing a little too much.'[8]

In summary: principles, skills and practices

In **Table 9.1**, we summarize the key principles and management skills again, together with the practices set out in this chapter to help you manage successfully in the new world of work.

Principles	Skills	Practices
Trust your people	■ Openness to change ■ Delegation ■ Relationship-building ■ Prioritizing ■ Challenging status quo	■ Start from the assumption that all jobs have some potential for future work ■ Discuss job with the employee and agree constraints to flexibility ■ Give people as much freedom as possible to work the way that suits them best ■ Don't insist that people work at specific times unless the job demands it ■ Allow people to use social media appropriately ■ Encourage people to work as a team even if they are not sitting together ■ Challenge the need for meetings ■ Don't keep work to yourself if it can be done by other people
Reward results	■ Planning ahead ■ Clear objective-setting ■ Inspiring and motivating ■ Sensitivity to changing needs ■ Decisiveness and consistency	■ Set clear outcomes and measure results ■ Hold regular reviews, particularly at first ■ Give plenty of feedback, with a personal touch ■ Don't micro-manage, but do check people aren't working 24/7 ■ Act quickly on poor performance or abuse of trust ■ Give people challenging work to develop them
Understand the business case	■ Awareness of big trends ■ Stakeholder orientation ■ Technological competence ■ Influencing ■ Resilience	■ Keep in touch with demographic, social and environmental trends, as well as business trends ■ Identify potential for reduced costs and increased productivity ■ Invest in technology to increase output ■ Monitor and measure the impact on business outcomes ■ Build results into business plans ■ Share successes across the business
Start at the top	■ Willingness to change ■ Ability to give up 'control' ■ Leadership by example ■ Time management ■ Tenacity	■ Get senior management to support this as a major business and culture change program ■ Set an example by doing it yourself ■ Communicate the message that this applies at all levels ■ Use technology effectively to control your own workload ■ See it through as you would any change program that benefits the business
Treat people as individuals	■ Appreciation of diffference ■ Responsiveness ■ Adaptability ■ Reliability ■ Team-building	■ Understand what motivates individual employees ■ Don't try and fit people into a fixed work pattern ■ Keep in touch with remote workers when you say you will ■ Use judgment and don't just follow rules ■ Help people to integrate work into the rest of their lives ■ Hold face-to-face meetings for dispersed and virtual teams

Following the guidance in this chapter will help you to move into the exciting world of future work. If you are a manager, you now have plenty of examples for your organization to follow. In the next chapter, Chapter 10, we provide case studies and practical suggestions for individuals – employees, managers and leaders – to seize the opportunities and address the challenges of this move for themselves.

Making it happen yourself

> *The younger generation has greater expectations around flexibility and the ability to choose how they work. A job for life isn't their mindset. They want to work in an environment and an industry that motivates them. Being rigid about working patterns is likely to be counter-intuitive to them.*[1]

> Emma FitzGerald, CEO of Gas Distribution, National Grid

Future work represents a significant change in working practices for many organizations. In previous chapters we have given the business arguments for implementing future work as a strategic initiative. In this chapter we provide practical advice for individual managers and employees in bringing future work to their jobs and teams.

Ideally, as we have explained, new working practices should be part of the business planning process and not a disconnected 'flexible working' initiative. But we recognize that in many organizations it will be an individual – whether an employee, a team supervisor, or a functional leader – who initiates the conversation. Change is best driven from the top down and the bottom up, but individual courage and initiative at any level can start to create the momentum for change, which can then gain support through well-placed sponsors.

In this chapter we give you ways to address the inevitable resistance to change that you will encounter. We also give you tips to avoid the ever-present danger of overwork in the 'anytime anywhere' era. This chapter shows you, through both individual and business case studies, how to shift your own and other people's thinking and to develop new guidelines that will help you and your organization thrive in the new world of work.

As a framework for thinking about the practical issues, we use the TRUST principles which underpin future work.

Trust your people

Probably the biggest challenge is creating trust in a culture based on distrust. Traditional 'rules', 'policies' and 'procedures' in organizations are put in place to restrict the discretion of employees. They typically tell you what you are *not* allowed to do. They assume that, left to your own devices, you are likely to go astray or simply avoid working where possible. Yet the overwhelming evidence is that, given freedom and managed properly, people flourish and work much more effectively. The aim of a future work culture is to minimize constraints and maximize autonomy so that individuals can perform at their best.

As a manager, you may not have the option to 'disobey' the rules in your organization but you have some discretion on how they are interpreted. New work styles can be agreed locally between manager and worker without having to fit into a formal scheme. In our survey, 55 percent of managers agreed or strongly agreed with the statement 'People often work flexibly without any formal agreement in my organization'.

As an individual employee, you will be able to progress faster by being personally accountable for making the change work, not assuming that all the responsibility lies with your manager. It's worth starting with a temporary arrangement to see how it works. Letting go of control, and trusting that the freedom will not be abused, can feel like a brave step in a highly controlling culture. Both parties can review progress after the first few weeks and then fine-tune the working pattern.

In the wake of the financial crisis of 2008 many banks needed to revisit their working cultures as well as their customer relationships. Recognizing this, the **Royal Bank of Scotland (RBS)** developed a group-wide agile working initiative, RBS Choice. Getting managers on board is crucial, according to Tim Yendell, Head of RBS Choice. 'One of our key workstreams for managers is "Culture and capability". We shouldn't expect managers just to "get" this and be able to do it. They need to be provided with support and guidance to help them become comfortable with all aspects of agile working, especially the element of trust required. Equally, those people who want to work flexibly need to be clear about their responsibilities, and make sure that they are playing their part. There can be a tendency to see this as the manager's responsibility to make it work but I believe that most of the responsibility sits with the individual.'

Trust also has to exist between team members. It is important for people to see that alternative working arrangements are beneficial, not detrimental, to everyone else in the team.

Swiss Re's 'Own the Way You Work'™ initiative

Swiss Re, a global reinsurance company founded in the nineteenth century, has made a big shift in recognizing that traditional working patterns were not suited for the twenty-first century. When a new approach was first proposed in 2011, and again when implementation began in 2012, it met resistance.

Crucially, however, it won the backing of the group executive committee and other key executives. David Cole, chief risk officer, willingly stepped into the role as primary sponsor of the initiative. In 2013, 'Own The Way You Work™: Living team spirit' had been rolled out in parts of the Zurich headquarters, across the Americas, and in other locations including London, Munich, Bratislava, Sydney and Tokyo.

Cole said Swiss Re wanted to move away from the idea that 'face time' and presence in the office were more important than results. There were clear business reasons for doing so, including the changing expectations of the workforce and the need for operations to keep going in the face of natural disasters like Japan's 2011 Tohoku earthquake and tsunami and Hurricane Sandy on the US east coast in 2012.

'We want to open up our company and our leadership to different working styles to allow us to have access to all the talent that is available in the organization and be an attractive employer for talent to join the organization', he told a Swiss Re-hosted seminar in November 2012. 'We have to focus on relationship building, delegating, planning ahead, prioritizing, and continuously challenging the status quo. We have to be role models, to be more flexible.' This chimes with two of our TRUST principles – Understand the business case and Start at the top – as well as some of the key skills for managers set out in Chapter 8.

The trigger for the initiative was a request in 2010 from the then group chief underwriting officer for a toolkit for flexible working hours to attract and keep more women. Like most large companies, Swiss Re had flexible working policies, but individuals' access to these depended entirely on having a manager who was open to them.

Nia Joynson-Romanzina, head of global diversity & inclusion, argued for a more fundamental rethink of work practices and how this could serve business priorities. She tapped into senior executives who supported the idea. Collaborating with the chief underwriting officer and three group management board members, she drew up principles for a new working model. These were distilled into four 'building blocks' for managers and employees:

1. One size does not fit all: Embrace flexibility and support non-traditional work models
2. Work smarter not longer: YES to managing by results; NO to face-time
3. Focus on the team rather than the individual: Discover how you and your team perform best
4. Reinforce trust, respect and open dialogue: Between you, your manager and your team

These building blocks are in line with our other core principles of Trusting your people, Treating people as individuals, and Rewarding results.

Trust emerged as fundamental during the year that it took to prepare the ground for the first pilots. 'The importance of the trust issue became quickly very apparent, and was clearly linked to transparency, along with safe and open dialogue in teams', says Joynson-Romanzina. 'When trust and open dialogue are nurtured in teams and there is transparency around different working preferences, you can see the positive impact. Then it becomes ok.'[2]

Reward results

In principle, many managers buy into the concept of paying for results. In practice, most are defeated by their company compensation schemes before they even start. An employee is paid a fixed salary each month depending on the level of job he or she holds, and only in a few cases is there an extra bonus based on performance. The employment contract is invariably based on time. A full-time employee is paid more than a part-timer regardless of results. People are expected to turn up on time, or even if they have the luxury of flexi-time, to put in the required number of hours. Extra effort and hard work are seen as virtues.

Joynson-Romanzina of Swiss Re explains why switching to managing by results was a challenge in parts of the business. 'In the US, it was a problem of guilt. For example, people felt guilty leaving at 3 p.m., even though they had come in at 7 a.m., because nobody knew they were in so early and everybody else was working until at least 5 p.m. In Zurich, it was people just sitting at their desks for eight or nine hours to show commitment, even if there wasn't work to do. There was competition about overtime, which was seen almost as a badge of honor.'

To promote the initiative in each location, they appointed a group of 'ambassadors', consisting of managing directors and middle managers. To tackle resistance, the company employed actors to play out different scenarios and invite managers to role-play. Scenarios are also used in an internal online training program for managers, enabling them to think about how and why they would react to a particular situation, and how other parties might feel about it. One such scenario shows a male employee leaving work early to take his daughter to ballet class, while co-workers comment negatively on his commitment to the company.

Workshops at Swiss Re revealed that, while senior executives assumed flexibility was normal and employees keenly wanted it, middle managers had no idea what it meant or how to handle it. 'We are giving them a hand to hold to take them through it', says Joynson-Romanzina.

Managers may not have much control over the pay rates for their people but they do have the hours of work under their direct supervision. If they agree the outcomes required, then they should be congratulating the person who works most effectively to get the results, not the one working the longest hours. The employee who achieves good results quickest should be rewarded with more personal time and not just given extra tasks to fill the 'spare' work time. So, as an employee, you can have a discussion with your managers about how they know you are getting the job done. Agree the goals and make sure you have good evidence of what you have achieved.

Lessons in leading by trust and results

Emma FitzGerald spent 20 years rising up the ranks at Shell International before being headhunted in 2013 to be CEO of the four UK gas distribution businesses owned by **National Grid**.

She describes her leadership style as transparent and transformational, with an emphasis on trust and empowerment, and her experience demonstrates how individual managers can develop this style provided they are open to challenge. Making the switch from being a sole contributor to her first line management job in 2001, in charge of a team of marketers, she was shocked to receive negative feedback in her 360-degree assessment.

'They said I was too directive about how things should be done. I didn't spend enough time helping them think through issues, or worse, I'd take something off them and do it myself. It was like a slap in the face. So I sat down with each of them and spent time asking them "How do you want me to support you?" It was the first time I recognized that everyone is different and that you've got to understand their motivations and needs.'

She put these lessons to good effect when achieving a major business turn-around in China in 2006. 'I had to connect with and motivate an incredibly young and inexperienced team who were dispersed across many locations', she says. 'I found that if you follow your instincts and delegate deeply, people will achieve the most extraordinary things. Not enough leaders are prepared to do that. On my departure from China, the employees presented me with a scroll with the letters "Dare to win". They were thanking me for giving them the confidence to dare to believe it was possible.'

Managing by results is central to her leadership philosophy. At Shell, she agreed outcomes and how these were going to be tracked with her team members at the beginning of the year. 'The conversations we had were about what help they needed from me, what the blockers were, and how they could use me as a resource to help them deliver. They were not about reporting back on how they were doing the work.'

She believes it is up to her team to take responsibility to meet their goals in the way that works best for them, and she acknowledges that people have different preferences. 'Some people prefer a shorter, more structured biweekly interaction, and more interactions by email or phone. Others love having the autonomy and are happy with just a monthly catch-up.'

The nature of her role at National Grid involves spending more time in person with her team than she did at Shell, but she says she is encouraging a greater focus on results and empowerment. Setting an example, she runs the business from her home on days when it is possible to do so.

'My ground rule is that you structure your own time', she says. 'But it's up to you to make sure that if you work strange hours your people understand why there's no expectation that they do the same. You have to be explicit and consistent.'[3]

Rewarding results is a fundamental principle for **Netflix**, the film and TV streaming company. Its culture is summarized in a presentation available on SlideShare which includes a slide with the title 'Hard Work – Not Relevant'.[4] It states that it does not measure people by how many hours they work or how much they are in the office. It does, however, care about accomplishing great work. If someone gets 'A for effort' but gives a B-level performance they are rewarded with a generous severance package. But 'Sustained A-level performance, despite minimal effort, is rewarded with more responsibility and great pay'.

Until 2004 Netflix had the standard vacation policy with a set number of days per year. Interestingly, it was an individual employee who pointed out that they did not track hours worked per day or per week, so why were they tracking days of vacation per year? This led managers to conclude that they should focus on what people get done, not how many days are worked. So the policy now is that 'there is no policy or tracking'. They make clear that no vacation policy does not mean 'no vacation'. They say that Netflix leaders 'set good examples by taking big vacations – and coming back inspired to find big ideas'.

Netflix is not alone. An article in the *Washington Post* pointed out other employers taking the same approach.[5] It quotes J. D. Sherman, chief operating officer of Hubspot, a marketing software firm, referring to their policy as 'two weeks to infinity' to make clear that employees are expected to take at least two weeks off but may take as much as they wish. It also cites Evernote, another software company, which gives a $1000 bonus to anyone who takes an entire week off to encourage vacations.

Understand the business case

Future work is a business-driven approach aimed at improving output from the workforce. As a manager you should be taking the initiative and including new work practices in your business planning, quantifying where possible the anticipated benefits.

These benefits come in many forms, covered in detail in Chapter 4. The Agile Future Forum, launched by 22 leading UK organizations in 2013, cited 'significant and tangible economic benefits for their businesses' including real estate cost savings (Citi), retaining talent (BP), better patient satisfaction (BUPA), improved quality (Ford) and increased productivity (Eversheds).[6]

In many jobs it is difficult to measure precise numerical output. Outside strict, production-line environments, it is quality as much as quantity that is expected. If you are a manager in this situation, you might find the 'increased productivity' argument difficult to prove when introducing future work. But you can make sure that there is mutual understanding of the results or outcomes that are expected, and there should at least be clear agreement with employees that work output will not suffer. It may feel like an act of faith going into this new territory, but all the evidence shows that it is highly likely to benefit the organization as well as the individual.

If you are an individual seeking greater autonomy in a resistant work culture, you will have to take the initiative yourself. First, think about the wider implications. You may want to change your work style because you feel you have a right to ask, perhaps backed by legislation or what company policies say on paper, or because you have family caring responsibilities. However, if you put the onus on your manager to figure out the consequences, and these involve a disruption to established routines, you may well meet resistance.

Think through how an alternative working pattern might impact customers and colleagues, both positively and negatively. If there will be times when you are unavailable, will someone else have to cover? Maybe you can now cover for another person on a different day of the week, or even extend 'opening hours' for customers.

Some tasks can be done more effectively at a time and place that you choose, maybe at home, especially if that is where you are best able to concentrate without interruptions. Other work may require detailed collaboration with colleagues and be best performed in a shared workspace.

Organizing work to suit your personal preferences is quite likely to improve your output, so there is a business case to be made for higher productivity. Don't think about yourself in isolation, however. Think about the rest of your team and be prepared to discuss the impact with them and with your customers.

Start at the top

Future work should ideally come from the very top of an organization with senior leaders setting an example. Reality is often different. There may be lip service from directors who say that flexibility is good for the organization but who work excessive hours and expect others around them to do so. Employees may have to share desks while senior managers still retain a personal office, even though it is empty half of the time.

Despite such gaps between rhetoric and reality, individual managers can implement future work from the top down within their own department. If you are in this situation, don't wait for your employees to ask but get them together to discuss what can be done to improve their work-life balance while still meeting the business goals. Find out about the corporate approach to agile working and use whatever resources are available from HR and other support departments.

In the RBS Choice program, each of the separate businesses has its own tailored agile working solution, but the overall message from the top is consistent. 'We recognized that this type of change doesn't happen without executive support', says Tim Yendell. 'We engaged our non-executive directors, who are also non-execs for other companies, recognized that they have a forward-looking view of the world and were interested in the external context. We also talked with our chairman about the future of work and about what this could do for the organization.' For large implementations of RBS Choice, help is provided by nominated champions who support around 100 employees each. Their role is to disseminate information about the cultural change management process, explain how the project is going to be delivered and what the benefits are, and help to break down myths. People selected for this role are respected in their own part of the business and are positive about the change. They go through workshops that cover the psychology of change and allow them to pose all the questions that they think might be thrown at them. Once agile working has been implemented and the workspace redesigned, they remain available to help to maintain the new environment and prevent people slipping back into old habits.

Treat people as individuals

Everyone is different. Some people are 'larks' and at their best in the early morning and some are 'owls' and most productive at night. If you are a manager, your role is to enable your people to maximize their contribution. You can do this by freeing them to work in their most productive way.

'If you provide the right technology to keep in touch, maintain regular communication and get the right balance between remote and office working, people will be motivated to work responsibly, quickly and with high quality', says Sir Richard Branson of Virgin in his blog.[7]

There is a common misconception that it is unfair to treat people differently and allow freedom to one employee and not to another. Some jobs have to be done at an employer's premises. However, to then say that nobody can work from home because that would be 'unfair' is poor judgment. Employees are not stupid. They understand that some jobs lend themselves to greater autonomy and choice than others. As long as the reasoning behind the decision is fair and transparent, it will be accepted. Good managers treat people 'fairly'; poor managers constrain freedom under the guise of treating people 'equally'.

Encouraging other viewpoints

With a fast-growing team spread across several countries, Marc Decorte, head of customer value technology at **Shell International**, puts a premium on good communication. He has an hour-long phone call with the whole team every Monday, which he describes as a 'virtual coffee chat'. There is no agenda, and the emphasis is on bonding as much as on business.[8]

Decorte, who is also president of Shell in Belgium, says he makes his electronic diary available to the team, so that people can put in appointments at a time that suits them. When a new recruit joins in another country, he arranges for them to work in a nearby company office for their first year, so they get to know the people and the culture. He has bi-weekly calls with new recruits reporting directly to him and encourages his leadership team to do the same.

He says he strives to ensure that everyone has a chance to speak in meetings. 'I also say to my team: "Go to lunch with someone you don't know and listen to them ... This is important in your career because it builds networks."'

With his dispersed team, he already inhabits the new world of work into which the next generation will arrive. He encourages his people to work where and when it suits them. He works from home about 30 percent of the time, and says that his most productive time is late at night. He prefers to work into the early hours and typically gets up around 8 a.m.

He stresses the importance of being explicit about his expectations of his team. If he chooses to send an email at 1 a.m., he states clearly in the message that he does not expect the recipient to respond until it is convenient.

He often does a couple of teleconferences at home before setting out, after the rush hour, to start his 'office' day at 11 a.m. 'This is much more efficient in terms of time usage', he says. 'Work is something I do, it is not a place I go to.'

New rules for the new world of work

If implementing future work is all about hands-off management, rules might seem out of place. In fact, the new world of work needs new guidelines to help people to break out of old habits. These are unlikely to look or sound much like the old rules, although how they are expressed will depend on the type of organization you work for.

Our own 'rule for new rules' is that they should not be imposed by management – that smacks of old-style command and control. Instead, new guidelines should stress mutual respect, trust and accountability. Ideally, they should come from employees or, at the very least, be agreed in collaboration between managers and employees.

Each company will develop its own guidelines and etiquette. Here are two examples to get you thinking about what your own approach might be:

The atmosphere at **Vodafone's** UK offices, on a purpose-built campus near Newbury, west of London, is informal, with most of the 4500 staff wearing casual gear. There are no individual offices and all meetings of six or fewer people take place in the ground-floor café area, so 'we can grab people as they walk past', says Guy Laurence, UK CEO.

He says he expects people to use common sense. But there are strict rules about how the space is used:

- Open-plan means just that. If anyone moves filing cabinets around their desk to create some privacy, 'they get a phone call from me saying "I suggest you don't do that"'.

- No one, including the CEO, has more than a single drawer in a filing cabinet to keep their possessions.

- When people move desk or building they have to carry their own belongings. This is to prevent clutter and paper files. 'Everything is electronically archived'.

- There are £50 fines for talking in the three glass-enclosed rooms available for silent, concentrated work. These 'libraries' are shared, spacious rooms. Previously, they had tried small booths for concentrated work but abandoned them 'because people turned them into private offices'.

- New recruits have to travel to meet colleagues face-to-face when they first join. Once accomplished, they are discouraged from traveling, and have to communicate electronically instead. This has cut business miles and business flights by more than a quarter.

Microsoft Netherlands has rules for behavior in the 'anytime anywhere' world of work:

- To make meetings more productive, every team agrees a 'physical minimum' – how much it needs to meet in person in order to be able to collaborate virtually in the most effective way. The Netherlands management team meets in person for a day and a half every quarter but holds its monthly three-hour meetings virtually, with people logging in from different fixed locations (calling from a car is not allowed).

- There are also generic rules for meetings. 'You have to read the documents beforehand, and there are no exceptions,' says Gonnie Been, manager of corporate communications and social innovation. 'If you want something on the agenda, it has to be there 48 hours beforehand, including all documents for preparation. At one meeting, nobody put any items on the agenda, so the meeting was cancelled.'

Dealing with technology overload

Leaving people to their own devices can have the opposite effect to demotivation. Some people have difficulty switching off from work and the blurring of the boundaries between home and work exacerbates this problem. 'With this new 365 x 24 x 7 work shift, and technology allowing easy and quick access to networks and information, the danger of becoming "workaholic" or "connectaholic" is a reality', says Yves Veulliet, a diversity and inclusion leader at IBM. 'When you're in a global role having to connect with people located around the world, the logic would be to start working early, stop in the afternoon and start again in late evening. But in reality more and more people, because of these different time zones, do remain connected all day long. When I started working remotely more than ten years ago, connecting to networks required cables, and patience due to the slow response time, and so you'd connect only if this was crucial on top of your regular work schedule. But today, it is so easy to connect using so many different tools that the temptation is big to "have a quick look".'[9]

Some organizations have countered the danger of overworking by disconnecting people from their emails outside of 'working hours'. Under an agreement with the works council, Volkswagen stopped its BlackBerry servers sending emails to some employees in Germany outside their shifts.[10] However, this solution implies that work can only be done in a fixed way and removes some of the benefits of flexibility as well as the dangers. A better solution is to educate employees in time management and help them to learn how to turn off from intrusive technology. Managers also need to respect the personal time of their people and not assume that they are instantly available day and night wherever they are.

As an individual it is easy to become addicted to technology that allows us to be connected all the time. Some people choose to live their lives on Twitter and Facebook and are never parted from their smartphone, suffering withdrawal symptoms if it is ever lost or broken. If you are one of these people then you should try to exercise some self-discipline to help both your work performance and your ability to relax outside of work. There are many ways to relieve the stress of constant work interruptions and most of them involve finding some quiet time for contemplation, away from constant bombardment by email or instant messages.

Thierry Breton, chief executive of Atos, an international information technology services company employing 80,000 people, has gone one stage further. He has set a goal to ban all internal email by 2014. As a former chief executive of France Telecom and France's minister of economy, finance and industry for two years, he is no Luddite. He has studied the situation carefully and realized that his employees were receiving over 100 emails a day, of which only 15 percent were useful. They were spending 15 to 20 hours per week just checking and answering internal emails. He also noticed that young recruits had abandoned email and were using instant messaging and social media. So Atos is piloting new tools that will replace email and offer an approach more appropriate for an information technology company.[11]

Eric Severson of Gap also has some practical advice, such as turning off incoming emails to avoid distractions. Multitasking is less productive than working on one task after another, he says. 'I was responding to emails all day long. When I started dealing with them in bunches, three times a day, I became more productive. I find if I let them accumulate and prioritize what I have to do, other people solve the problems they could have solved on their own from the beginning.' He also offers a time trick – keep meetings to 45 minutes and minimize the use of slides. Start meetings at 15 minutes past the hour and finish on the hour.[12]

Have we gone too far, or not far enough?

The announcement by Yahoo in 2013, pulling home workers back into the office, triggered a debate on whether we have gone too far in implementing new ways of working. Does the pendulum need to swing back a bit to find a middle ground? Have some organizations allowed people to become too disconnected from the organization and lose their sense of purpose? If people are just measured on results and left to devise their own work patterns, are they likely to lose their motivation?

One perspective comes from Vodafone's Guy Laurence, who does not agree with the principle of people working from home three days a week, or on fixed days of the week, although 'the odd day working from home is fine'. This might seem at odds with the company's informal and mobile work styles, but Laurence says that 'team dynamics are most productive in an environment that promotes regular interfacing with colleagues including physical gatherings ... The problem of structured home working is that it reduces the scope for these gatherings and can ultimately fracture team dynamics.'

He argues, however, that it is not a black and white issue, and that it will differ between companies and sectors, as well as depending on whether the business is under pressure or expanding.[13]

We believe there has to be a balance between 'physical gatherings' and remote working. There is inevitably give-and-take. From an individual employee's viewpoint, it may be easiest to have a regular pattern of work to fit around personal commitments because essential support services such as childcare or eldercare often lack flexibility. Knowing which day of the week you normally work from home or what time you leave the office each day will be crucial. Leaving it completely open week by week makes life complicated, if not impossible. However, if there is a good business reason for a regular pattern of meetings, such as the weekly update or monthly progress report, then new work styles will need to accommodate them.

From the manager's viewpoint, it is better to have meetings scheduled well in advance. If people are working from home or having days off on a fixed pattern, it should be straightforward to organize meetings around these schedules. But there will also be emergencies and reasons why people have to get together at short notice. As long as managers do not abuse this, most employees are prepared to be flexible and respond to the need.

Future work is all about giving autonomy to employees and reaping the benefits of an engaged workforce. The minute that employees stop being able to manage their own work patterns, the rot sets in. If people think they are being called into the office to attend meetings that could have been held remotely they will not be happy about it.

Ad hoc, informal 'corridor' encounters can suffer if people are working remotely. To compensate for this, good managers deliberately build in social time for their teams. If there is a face-to-face meeting finishing at lunchtime, get everyone to eat and chat together over lunch instead of rushing off to catch up on emails. If yours is a virtual team, build in video meetings or teleconferences with no fixed agenda so that people can stay connected as human beings, not just workers.

In summary

Implementing future work requires open discussions between managers and employees, not imposing a one-size-fits-all fixed solution. It has to work for individuals and for the organization and may need to be adapted with experience. It is important to measure outcomes and focus on tangible benefits, in order to make this way of working 'business as usual'.

There are dangers in introducing new working patterns and not managing them effectively. Teamwork can suffer. At one extreme of poor management, people can become disaffected and cut off from the organization. At the other, they can overwork and burn themselves out. The solution to these challenges is not to give up and revert to outdated working practices but for management and employees to work through them together. As we will show in the final chapter, the world of work is changing fast and there is no turning back.

11

Looking over the horizon

When Larry Smith joined IBM in the UK in the late 1980s, he used to make sure he walked past his manager's office after 6.30 p.m. so his presence was noted. It was almost an unwritten rule.

Twenty-six years later, he is still working for the company, but in a radically different way. He is a contractor, supplying his services via Persistent, one of IBM's preferred suppliers in India. He has done this for over three years without ever coming face-to-face with the people who manage him.

'I have never met my manager or any of his management chain, yet I lead his business development efforts which represent several million dollars of business', he says. Asked where his boss is based, he has to check. It turns out to be Connecticut – though it could have been anywhere in the same time zone.

Larry's experience will seem alien, though possibly quite appealing, to legions of office workers around the world. He is an example of how the future of work has already arrived for individuals and organizations at the leading edge. He works closely with teams in India and China, talking to them weekly by phone and chatting online by IBM's in-house messenger service every day, but he has never met any of them. Most of his colleagues are based in the US and China, while he works from home in Britain.

He is also working on an IBM product area where the leadership is in the UK, the project team is in the US and the development team is in China.

He has met the UK leader once for a coffee, but has not met anyone else in the team that he works with on a daily basis. 'You have to be very self-motivated to work this way', he says. 'I'm a self-starter and I'm good at planning my day. I have to be structured and organized. I don't work at weekends and normally not after 7 p.m. on Fridays. But during the week my life and work are intertwined.'

If you work like this, you also have to be firm about drawing boundaries, or the job will take over your life. 'For example, on Wednesday night at 11 p.m. I presented to 20 people in Sydney. At 9 p.m. that night I was having a conference call with people in Austin, Texas, on a business proposal, which I presented at 7.30 this morning to people in Finland. On Tuesday night they wanted me to join some important conference calls but I was going down to the pub with my son to watch Tottenham [football club] play, so I refused to attend. I said: "Sorry, but I have a life. My family are important to me."'

As someone who works online, it was natural for Larry to use the Internet in his social life as well. He met his wife, Sharon Boyse-Smith, a senior executive with Sony/ATV Music, through an online dating service. 'She's in a totally different industry and we would never have met without profiling on the Internet.'

He says he has a far better quality of life in this virtual environment than spending time traveling to meet people. His manager completely trusts him to get the job done. 'He doesn't start work until many hours after me so he can't monitor what I am doing. If I want to take the dog for a long walk this afternoon, I just will.'

Larry believes all organizations will have to have this kind of relationship with their people in the future. 'Empowering professionals who are task-driven has to be the way forward. It's been pioneered in the IT industry but eventually everyone will offer it.'[1]

How soon will this be? In our survey for this book, two-thirds of managers agreed there would be a revolution in working practices in the next decade.

Cloud cover

Forecasting is a hazardous business, especially as the technology that opens the way to these far-reaching changes is advancing so rapidly. IDC, the global market intelligence provider, has described the rate of internet innovation as 'breakneck'. The number of internet users worldwide doubled to an estimated 2.7bn between 2007 and 2013, according to the International Telecommunication Union.[2] That is nearly 40 percent of the world's population. With the numbers growing fast in China, India and Africa, there are predictions of a surge to 4bn users worldwide by 2020.[3]

One thing that can be certain is that technology will have an increasing influence on all our lives, particularly our working lives. Already it is difficult to remember what we did before the Internet existed. How did we cope before Google pointed us to the answers? In ten years' time we will look back on today's tools and think of them as clunky or quaint. We will also take for granted that connectivity is available wherever we are at speeds unimaginable today.

One development that will influence our work over the next few years is the growth of cloud computing. Instead of having ever more powerful desktop or laptop machines, the computing power is provided over the Internet and is available on demand like any other utility. While it's not a new idea, the latest portable communication devices combined with ubiquitous, secure networks and high-speed connections make its implementation a practical reality. Large organizations can hold their data and applications centrally but accessible from anywhere. This allows them to free up employees to access information however they wish. For smaller businesses, a whole new raft of internet-based services is emerging to replace their aging technology.

Wi-Fi hotspots are popping up all over the place and we now have 4G mobile services giving fast internet access to people working on the move. In the same way that individuals in the past chose their favorite pen and paper to take notes, they will decide their preferred way of accessing the cloud, whether it's an Apple iPad, or a Windows netbook, and use these for work. Leading employers have already decided not to issue and maintain a fleet of corporate laptops for employees to lug around. Instead they have a 'Bring your own device' policy, leaving the choice to the individual.

Cloud computing is already providing people with their office in their hand, enabling them to work where and when they want. 'Cloud removes location from the equation,' says Guy Laurence, Vodafone UK CEO.[4]

'You don't have to go to the office or be at home. It's wherever there's connectivity. People work best where there isn't a location requirement.'

As an example of working independently of a fixed location, he points to 7 causes, a Dutch marketing consultancy run and staffed by women that has its office in a converted bus equipped with mobile broadband. The consultants take the office to the client, working on the way, and avoid wasted travel time.

We are now in the era of superfast, fiber-based broadband, extensive social media and mobile apps for every imaginable need. What impact will these advances, and continuing globalization, have on work? There are enough trends already under way to be able to predict the likely shape of things to come. These are some of the key ones to watch:

Growth of the 'contingent' workforce

Work will become more of a tradable commodity, rather than a job. There will be more independent contractors and freelancers. More than a quarter of the average organization's workforce is already 'contingent' or contract-based, according to one study.[5] In the US, nearly 18m Americans identified themselves as independent workers in 2013, up 10 percent on 2011, and this number could grow to 24m by 2018, another study predicts.[6]

Contractors and consultants will increasingly bid for work online and will be paid for results. This is an emerging form of what has been termed 'crowdsourcing' – using the power of the Internet to allocate tasks to people anywhere in the world by issuing a request for work. Initially, this was largely associated with finding volunteers to contribute their expertise for free. The whole free, open-source software movement is based on this model and there are high-profile examples such as Wikipedia, the free encyclopedia.

However, there is now a growing market for paid work via the Internet. Elance and oDesk, both launched in the US in the mid-2000s, are two of the better-known online marketplaces where businesses can find freelance professionals to carry out work on demand. US spending on online staffing will rise from $1bn in 2012 to $5bn in 2018, predicts the consultancy Staffing Industry Analysts.[7]

There are other examples. Since 2005, Amazon has run its Mechanical Turk as a marketplace for work that allows requesters to pose 'Human Intelligence Tasks' and pay people to perform them. These are typically simple repetitive tasks, such as searching for information on the Web, paid a few cents for each successful result. At the other end of the scale is Innocentive where cash awards of up to a million dollars are given for successful solutions to research problems.

These markets cut across established employment patterns. Workers are paid for results but have no employment rights or benefits. There is no question of paying a minimum wage, expressed as a rate per hour, since this is results-based work and time is irrelevant. It's a very attractive model for businesses able to allocate work across the Internet as they can choose suppliers who will perform tasks for a fraction of the cost of employees. In fact it is quite possible to get the work done at no cost if there are enthusiastic contributors willing to donate their effort for free.

Alongside these developments is the growth of 'homeshoring' or 'homesourcing', where all kinds of jobs are being contracted out to people working from their homes. LiveOps is one such example – a virtual call center business that uses 20,000 independent agents across the US. Maynard Webb, former CEO of LiveOps and now chairman of Yahoo, expects these new models to run alongside traditional ways of working, rather than replace them.

'Some individuals will still prefer a traditional building in a corporate business park where they go 9–5 every day,' he says. 'I think that is great but I just believe there is so much more we can do as far as defining our work and personal life, and why not consider it? Frankly, that sense of "entrepreneurship", or working on your own terms, is what is behind the start of so many small businesses, great consultants, and the birthplace of even some of the most reputable large businesses. What is assuring to see is that individuals have more options and can choose to contract if they wish.'[8]

As with the use of a contingent workforce by large companies, these new models contain a mix of potential disadvantages and benefits.

On the negative side, the business that uses an agent workforce may offer little if any employment security to the individual. Workers may not be covered by employment legislation designed to protect people against exploitation. They will miss out on the employee benefits and job security that go with conventional employment. This is recognized as an issue by the European Union in the Agency Workers Directive, which attempts to close the gap. The EU uses the term 'flexicurity' to denote labor market flexibility combined with worker protection.

There is an important debate to be had about what safety nets will be available to the growing numbers of workers outside traditional employment. One idea is for workers to have portable rights to training and other benefits, says Denis Pennel, managing director of the International Confederation of Private Employment Agencies (CIETT). 'We need to reorganize so that whatever your status or your job, you can still keep your rights – not lose them when you change employer,' he said in a *Financial Times* interview.[9] 'Portability of work is the future, with rights attached to an individual, not their employment.'

On the plus side, these models provide great flexibility for both employers and workers. For the business or the intermediary broker, it is a lower-cost operating model, using contractors only as needed without having to pay salaries or office overheads. Corporate clients get access to skills when they require them without having to employ them directly.

Deployment – providing skills and services where they are needed – is starting to replace employment, according to Caroline Waters, former director of people and policy at BT, the UK communications group. Some groups of professionals have been working this way for a while. 'Deployment is particularly prevalent in skill areas such as software development.'

The combination of an employed and a contingent workforce provides more options, Waters says. 'You turn the dial up if you need a bit more, be it space or people, and in a downturn you are able to reduce the cost of resource but still retain key skills by giving people access to options such as sabbaticals.'

A socio-economic benefit of online businesses is that they can provide work opportunities for people who would otherwise be excluded from the workforce, for example if they are confined to their homes by disability or by caring for an elderly or sick relative.

Depending on their income and location constraints, individuals can work at a time and place of their choosing, and for as little or as much time as they want or need. This is effectively self-employment, but with the expectation of a flow of work from the intermediary.

Trading the relative security of employment for the freedom of self-employment is likely to attract growing numbers of people who want a different deal from work and who now have the technology at their fingertips to achieve it. It is a trade-off that will inevitably work best for individuals who have the higher skills that are in constant demand, because they will not have to sacrifice earning power.

Given the increasing choice of employment types, we believe that companies keen to attract the best talent will in future have to replicate as many of the benefits of self-employment as possible, while continuing to provide the safety of the employment contract. If they do not, they risk seeing that talent go elsewhere, or go solo.

Careers change shape

It follows from the trends described above that individuals will have to take greater responsibility for keeping their skills up to date and adapting quickly to shifting demand. Online learning will play an increasing role in people's career moves and planning, as will keeping an up-to-date online profile.

Individuals, especially those doing demanding global roles, will also have to take responsibility for determining their own boundaries between work and personal life. We see this as a two-way responsibility, since it is also a core duty of managers to ensure that people in their teams are not overworking.

With the rise of women, the arrival of Gen Y and longer working lives, careers are becoming more fluid and less linear, or ladder-shaped. People will have more jobs during their careers, and more careers during their working lives. They may move in and out of formal employment, with spells in self-employment or in hybrid models, such as partial paid employment combined with self-employment or business start-up. There will be a further decline in lifelong loyalty to a single employer, and individuals will rely more heavily on marketing their unique skills, reputation and 'personal brand'.

'Few people will start on a course and stay there throughout their working lives,' Maynard Webb told us. 'People will take detours, take time off to raise families, or to learn new skills. I believe that workers will become more well-rounded and multi-faceted as a result of this shift.'

Virtual working and measurement by results will enable more diverse styles of leadership to flourish, by removing the anachronism of rewards for long hours spent in the workplace. Online collaboration with teams around the world will create more opportunities for people to gain experience of working with different cultures without necessarily having to relocate.

There will be more women in senior executive roles and on corporate boards, and more senior men and women working in non-traditional patterns, like those we featured in Chapter 5.

Sarah Jackson, chief executive of the UK charity Working Families, expects flexibility to be much more 'embedded' as a normal way of working a decade from now, for men as well as women. 'The quality of leadership will be more clearly recognized as vital to achieving all of this,' she adds. 'We'll be putting plenty of investment into leadership skills.'[10]

The digital generation will drive important changes in communication, work and the rhythm of life, according to Damien O'Brien, head of Egon Zehnder International, the executive search firm. 'Rigid 8 a.m. to 5 p.m. hours were partly predicated on people needing face-time,' he says. 'This new generation is going to have a different view. That's going to play well to women. A lot of large companies are locked in to tracking employee time, where they're sitting, and what they're doing. That's the old world. I'm confident that in 20 years' time that's going to look very out of date to the vast majority of the world.'[11]

Forging a hybrid career path

Gail Sulkes, former global head of organizational development at Thomson Reuters, has been developing her own hybrid career model over the past five years. She still works two to three days a week for the information group, focusing mainly on executive development, and spends the rest of her time on her own consulting business.

'It's nice to be independent but affiliated with a team in an organization,' says Sulkes, 47. 'I had decided I didn't want to be a lifer at one company and I didn't want another big corporate job. But I still wanted to contribute, and felt able to contribute, at the highest level of the organization.'

The arrangement has evolved. 'To begin with, while I was testing the waters as a sole trader, I was on the payroll of Thomson Reuters. Once I launched my own company, it seemed more appropriate to stop being an employee and start being a contractor. Their flexibility and open mindedness enable us to have an ongoing dialogue about what works to our mutual benefit.'

She sees hybrid career paths becoming more common. Although her age puts her in the 'Generation X' category, she says her personality is more 'Generation Y'. 'There's nothing about the way I work that relates to the Industrial Age model of work,' she laughs. 'I have a lot of flexibility. I don't have to go to the same building every day, I can work remotely very effectively, and it gives me greater balance most of the time.'[12]

Status and hierarchy

Work status will change. From being defined by job, organization and place in the hierarchy, it will increasingly be about a person's skills, reputation and ability to contribute and build networks. As work becomes more dispersed and less dependent on location, this shift in the source of status will apply both to the contingent workforce and to employees inside organizations.

Dave Aron, vice president and research fellow at Gartner, the IT research and advisory company, predicts a big increase in work carried out by what he calls 'clusters' – self-managed units of independent specialists who are hired and paid by organizations for long periods.

'A cluster can be considered a real asset of the business, just as high-performing staff members are today,' he says.[13] 'Businesses will need to work hard at managing and leading them well, just as they have always done for their emerging talent assets.' Elite military teams, medical units and film crews are current equivalents of the clusters he envisages spreading through the working world.

The death of corporate hierarchies has often been predicted, yet many of today's so-called 'flat' organizations still contain hierarchical thinking. However, in organizational cultures that learn how to separate status from hierarchy, the gap between top management and workers, in terms of pay, benefits, personal offices and other trappings of power, will diminish.

Truly flat organizations will be more responsive to social shifts and nimbler in meeting market demands because they will have fewer levels of decision-making and communication barriers.

Throughout this book, we have identified organizations that have inverted the pyramid and put employees first. They have recognized that the role of management is to support front-line employees and help them to generate value for the business. We have spoken to enlightened leaders who earn the respect and loyalty of their employees by listening to them and harnessing their energy. These businesses will adapt and thrive in the new world of work.

Employers will have to focus more on the employee as an individual as new generations enter the workforce, says Isla Ramos Chaves, head of business transformation and project management for Lenovo in Europe, Middle East and Africa, whom we featured in Chapter 5. 'Flexibility is the first step, but I think it's going to have to go much further than that,' she says. 'Everybody wants to be treated as special. Companies need to find a way to handle each individual and respond to what's important to them. The management style needs to be one-to-one. How you teach managers to do that is the big question, because that behavior does not come automatically to many of them.'[14]

This opens up a window of opportunity for the human resources function. Identifying the changes in organizational culture that are coming over the horizon is a key role for senior management. They will be looking to HR professionals for advice on how to make the shift to a 'Type B' culture and engage and invigorate the workforce. For many this will mean a transformation from holding back change and being risk-averse to becoming true business partners and leading the revolution in work practices.

Sustainable developments

The role of offices will shift from being workplaces to meeting places, as described in Chapter 6, and employees will increasingly be categorized by the flexibility and autonomy of their work. Definitions such as 'mobile', 'resident' and 'home-based' will become more common.

More people will work at least part of the time at home, or from work hubs built closer to people's homes, enabling them to work and connect without having to make long commutes.

Already there are significant examples of work hubs in the US and Europe, such as the network of over 100 'smart work centers' across the Netherlands, aimed at cutting traffic jams and pollution on the roads into major cities and increasing work flexibility and balanced lives.[15] The idea of flexible workspace is spreading elsewhere too. Regus, which provides serviced office space, opened its 1,500th business center in the world in Pune, India, in 2013, and said the country was a key growth market with its strong economy and growing demand for flexible working.[16]

Environmental sustainability will continue to be high on the agenda. Industrial Age work has left the planet dangerously polluted, and future work has to be different. In Chapter 6, we looked at how the move to a low carbon economy will drive greater use of remote working and how new office designs are promoting lower energy use and less waste, which in turn generates big cost savings.

As the next generation joins the workforce they will be asking more searching questions about why we work the way we do. They will challenge the need to commute daily and consume the planet's natural resources at the current unsustainable rate. They will be comfortable using videoconferences and video calls, instead of traveling to meetings. And they will be choosing their employers based on their green credentials.

The two young men whose stories we told at the start of this book are not only interesting examples of future work but also of the new generation's concerns about the future of the planet. They say they have grown increasingly aware that many of the world's problems are interconnected and that current economic systems will lead to more social injustice and environmental destruction.

'We have to change our basic assumptions and systems to keep the earth liveable,' says Martijn van der Linden. 'And this also relates to the way we work.'

Conclusion

We are still in the early stages of the transformation of work, largely because corporate cultures and management styles are not keeping pace with technological advances. This was why we embarked on this book: to help managers and organizations make the necessary shift to more efficient business, better lives and a healthier earth for the next generation to inherit.

Future work is one of those rare opportunities for all-round benefit. As we have shown through numerous examples in this book, it contributes positively to the bottom line while improving the lives of workers and helping to protect our fragile ecosystem. It is not an option for business any longer. It is a matter of staying competitive.

As Guy Laurence of Vodafone UK puts it, the leading organizations have adapted fast, but other companies will have to follow suit. The good news is that there are no technological, regulatory or security barriers that cannot be overcome, he says. 'Staff are happier because they don't want to go to the office, you kill fewer trees, and you serve more end-customers. I haven't found any genuine downside other than the dented pride of a few middle managers.'

This book is a call to action for those managers and the leaders of all organizations. If you don't bring your work practices into the twenty-first century, then your employees will react accordingly. The best ones will leave and the remaining ones will be disengaged. Your productivity will drop, and in a competitive world other organizations will replace you. If you do, you will not only enjoy bottom line benefits but also be contributing to the wider health of society and the environment.

In recent times, we have seen how Facebook, Twitter and other social media have played a pivotal role in exposing dictatorships in countries around the world, and we have watched as regimes have attempted to stifle free speech by controlling internet access. In the world of work, too, we should expect social media to be catalysts of change, helping to harness untapped resources of energy and creativity in the workforce.

Management in the new world of work demands a democratic approach in which managers agree the objectives with individuals, provide the resources and then trust them to take responsibility for getting on with it. The transformation of work is underway. With this book, we hope that you will be able to make the journey more easily.

Notes

Chapter 1: Time for change

1. Interviews with author, 2009, 2011, 2013.
2. Mayank Sharma: His illness and recovery, www.facebookstories.com/stories.
3. D. McGregor, *The Human Side of Enterprise* – Annotated Edition (McGraw-Hill, 2006), p. 6.
4. *Government at a Glance 2009*, OECD iLibrary.
5. A. Wittenberg-Cox and A. Maitland, *Why Women Mean Business* (John Wiley & Sons Ltd., 2009).
6. E. Galinsky et al., *Times Are Changing: Gender and Generation at Work and at Home* (Families and Work Institute, 2009).
7. *Working Better Report 2009* (Equality and Human Rights Commission), pp. 10, 20; and M. Shriver, *The Shriver Report: A Woman's Nation Changes Everything* (Center for American Progress, 2009), pp. 162, 415, 442.
8. S. A. Hewlett et al., *Bookend Generations: Leveraging Talent and Finding Common Ground* (Center for Work-Life Policy, New York, 2009).
9. *After the Baby-Boomers, The New Generation of Leadership* (Odgers Berndtson and Cass Business School, 2013).
10. Cass Business School video interview, *Leadership after the baby boomers*, May 2013.
11. P. Whitehead, 'Jobs are going back to the future', *Financial Times*, 22 March 2012.
12. R. Layard, *Happiness: Lessons from a New Science* (Penguin, 2006).
13. *City & Guilds Happiness Index*, www.cityandguilds.com/24635.html.
14. *Employee Engagement Research Report 2013* (BlessingWhite Inc., Princeton, NJ).
15. S. A. Hewlett et al., *Bookend Generations: Leveraging Talent and Finding Common Ground* (Center for Work–Life Policy, New York, 2009).
16. Health and Safety Executive data, published on Institute of Occupational Safety and Health website.

17. B. Pocock et al., *How Much Should We Work? Working Hours, Holidays and Working Life: The Participation Challenge, the Australian Work and Life Index 2010* (Centre for Work + Life, University of South Australia, 2010).

18. A. Maitland, 'When managers say: "Suit yourself"', *Financial Times*, 23 December 2008.

19. K. Joyce et al., 'Flexible working conditions and their effects on employee health and wellbeing', *Cochrane Database of Systematic Reviews*, no. 2 (2010), Art. No.: CD008009.

20. E. J. Hill et al., 'Workplace flexibility, work hours, and work–life conflict: Finding an extra day or two', *Journal of Family Psychology*, vol. 24, no. 3 (June 2010): 349–358.

21. *Employee Engagement Research Report 2013* (BlessingWhite Inc., Princeton, NJ).

22. Speaking about the 2013 Edelman Trust Barometer.

23. Interview with author, November 2010.

24. *After the Baby-Boomers, The New Generation of Leadership* (Odgers Berndtson and Cass Business School, 2013).

25. Cass Business School video interview, *Leadership after the baby boomers*, May 2013.

26. D. H. Pink, *Drive: The Surprising Truth About What Motivates Us* (Canongate Books, 2010).

27. OECD StatExtracts figures for 2011 (OECD September 2013).

28. OECD Observer No. 266 (OECD, March 2008).

29. Presentation to Henley Knowledge Management Forum, February 2011.

Chapter 2: How work has evolved

1. P. F. Drucker, 'Managing Knowledge Means Managing Oneself', *Leader to Leader*, vol. 16 (Spring 2000): 8–10.

2. G. Hamel, *The Future of Management* (Harvard Business School Press, 2007).

3. ONS, *Labour Force Survey*, 2013.

4. *Telecommuting Statistics* (Global Workplace Analytics, 2013).

5. *Crackberry Is the 2006 Word of the Year* (PRNewswire, 1 November 2006).

6. *Managing Tomorrow's People – Where will you be in 2020?* (PwC UK, 2010).

7. A. Richman et al., *Innovative Workplace Flexibility Options for Hourly Workers* (Corporate Voices for Working Families, 2009).

8. *Generation Y: Realising the Potential* (A joint research paper by ACCA and Mercer, July 2010).

9. Maternity at Work: A review of National Legislation/International Labour Office, Conditions of Work and Employment Programme Second edition (Geneva: ILO, 2010), p. 68.

10. *Failing Its Families: Lack of Paid Leave and Work–Family Supports in the US* (Human Rights Watch, 23 February 2011).
11. *Global Education Digest* (UNESCO, 2009).
12. *Women in Leadership* (Chartered Management Institute & Women in Management, White Paper, March 2013).
13. *Who's breadwinning? Working mothers and the new face of family support* (IPPR, August 2013).
14. *Breadwinner Moms* (Pew Research Center, May 2013).
15. E. Galinsky, K. Aumann, and J. Bond, *Times Are Changing: Gender and Generation at Work and at Home* (Families and Work Institute 2008 National Study of the Changing Workforce).
16. *Modern Parenthood: Roles of Moms and Dads Converge as They Balance Work and Family* (Pew Research Center, 14 March 2013).
17. *Working Better, Meeting the Changing Needs of Families, Workers and Employers in the 21st Century* (Equality and Human Rights Commission, 2009).
18. S.A. Hewlett et al., *Bookend Generations: Leveraging Talent and Finding Common Ground* (Center for Work-Life Policy, 2009).
19. *B&Q Case Study* (Agile Future Forum, 2013).
20. *What Are the Chances of Surviving to Age 100?* (ONS, March 2012).
21. G. Magnus, *The Age of Aging, How Demographics Are Changing the Global Economy and Our World* (John Wiley & Sons, 2009), p. xxii.
22. *Older Women Matter: Harnessing the talents of Australia's older female workforce* (Diversity Council Australia, with the Australian Human Rights Commission and Sageco, 23 May 2013).
23. Commenting on news of the death of a London bank intern on 21 August 2013.
24. Working Families conference, 3 July 2013.
25. Interview with author, June 2013.
26. Interview with author, July 2010.
27. Interview with author, July 2013.
28. Interview with author, August 2013.
29. Being an agent FAQ, LiveOps website, March 2011.
30. Interview with author, December 2010.
31. Interview with author, October 2010.
32. A. Maitland, 'The personal assistant I never see', *Financial Times Executive Appointments* (18 October 2012).

Chapter 3: Turning convention on its head

1. *Statement of Purpose* (The Alliance for Bangladesh Worker Safety, http://www.bangladeshworkersafety.org).

2. *Apple's Unkept Promises: Investigation of Three Pegatron Group Factories Supplying to Apple* (China Labor Watch, 29 July 2013).
3. Name changed to protect identity.
4. J. C. Ugrin and J. M. Pearson, 'The Effects of Sanctions and Stigmas on Cyberloafing', *Computers in Human Behavior*, vol. 29, no. 3 (May 2013): 812–820.
5. Chart adapted from *Enter the Timelords: Transforming Work to Meet the Future* (Equal Opportunities Commission/Equality and Human Rights Commission, March 2008).
6. T. Harnish and K. Lister, *Results Based Management* (Telework Research Network, 2010).
7. C. Ressler and J. Thompson, *Why Work Sucks and How to Fix It* (Portfolio, 2008).
8. H. Joly, *Best Buy CEO on Leadership*, StarTribune, commentaries, 17 March 2013.
9. M. Webb and C. Adler, *Rebooting Work* (Jossey Bass, 2013).
10. Response to request for information from author, July 2013.
11. *A Message from Steve Ferrara About BDO Flex* (BDO News, 4 March 2013).
12. Information provided by Ryan in response to authors' request, July 2013.
13. D. McGregor, *The Human Side of Enterprise* (McGraw Hill, 1960).
14. More information on W. L. Gore can be found in G. Hamel, *The Future of Management* (The Harvard Business School Press, 2007), pp. 83–100.
15. G. Hamel, *The Future of Management* (Harvard Business School Press, 2007).
16. D. Pink, *Drive: The Surprising Truth about What Motivates Us* (Canongate, 2010), p. 73.
17. R. Wooten et al., 'A Joint US–UK Study of Home Telenursing', *Journal of Telemedicine and Telecare*, vol. 4, no. 1 (1998): 83–85.
18. *Rebooting the PC: Using innovation to drive smart policing*, Policy Exchange, April 2013.
19. R. Semler, *Maverick* (Random House Business, 2001).
20. Interview with author, September 2013.
21. *The Happy Manifesto: 9 Steps to a Great Workplace*, 5 November 2010, http://www.happy.co.uk/the-happy-manifesto-9-steps-to-a-great-workplace/.

Chapter 4: Why it makes business sense

1. Business leaders call for more flexible working: letter in full, *Daily Telegraph*, 23 June 2013.
2. Interview with author, August 2010, updated 2013.
3. Case study in *Working Better: A Managers' Guide to Flexible Working* (Equality and Human Rights Commission, October 2009).
4. A. Maitland, 'When managers say: suit yourself', *Financial Times*, 22 December 2008.

5. Data provided by Chubb, 2008 and 2011.

6. *A New Way of Working, Insights from Global Leaders* (IBM Institute for Business Value, April 2010).

7. Data provided by Cisco, August 2010.

8. P. Thomson, *Working at Home: The Productivity Tool of the Future* (Telework Association, February 2010).

9. Microsoft 2010 US Remote Working Research Summary: National Survey Findings.

10. Interview with author, July 2013.

11. J. Thompson and Professor E. Truch, *The Flex Factor: Realising the value of flexible working* (RSA Action and Research Centre, July 2013).

12. N. Bloom, J. Liang, J. Roberts and Z. J. Ying, *Does working from home work? Evidence from a Chinese experiment*, 22 February 2013, http://www.stanford.edu/~nbloom/WFH.pdf.

13. *Flexible Working and Performance* (Cranfield University School of Management and Working Families, 2008).

14. Interview with authors, March 2011.

15. *Swine flu briefing (Business continuity planning section)* (Institute of Directors, March 2010).

16. M. Virtanen et al., 'Overtime work and incident coronary heart disease: the Whitehall II prospective cohort study', *European Heart Journal*, vol. 31, no. 14 (2010), 1737–1744.

17. S. A. Hewlett and C. B. Luce, 'Extreme Jobs: The Dangerous Allure of the 70-Hour Workweek', *Harvard Business Review* (December 2006). Also, S. A. Hewlett, 'Extreme managers need protection', *Financial Times*, 28 November 2006.

18. J. Sundquist et al., 'Psychosocial working conditions and self-reported long-term illness: a population-based study of Swedish-born and foreign-born employed persons', *Ethnicity & Health*, vol. 8, no. 4 (2003): 307–317.

19. A. Tsutsumi et al., 'Low Control at Work and the Risk of Suicide in Japanese Men: A Prospective Cohort Study', *Psychotherapy and Psychosomatics*, vol. 76, no. 3 (2007): 177–185.

20. Interview with author, June 2010 and June 2013.

21. J. Thompson and Professor E. Truch, *The Flex Factor: Realising the value of flexible working* (RSA Action and Research Centre, July 2013).

22. Interview with authors, July 2010.

23. *Green: Empowering People to Heal the Planet* (Cisco).

24. Telework Research Network, June 2010, www.teleworkresearchnetwork.com.

25. Lloyds Banking Group case study in *Understanding the economic benefits of workforce agility* (Agile Future Forum, June 2013).

26. *O2 releases the results of the UK's biggest ever flexible working pilot*, 3 April 2012, press release on company website.

27. Interview with author, August 2012, updated July 2013.

Chapter 5: Leaders for the new world of work

1. Interviews with author, August 2010 and July 2013.
2. Speaking at The Conference Board Diversity & Inclusion Conference, Chicago, 13 May 2009.
3. European Foundation for the Improvement of Living and Working Conditions, *Part-Time Work in Europe, European Company Survey 2009* (Publications Office of the European Union, 2011), p. 26.
4. Equality and Human Rights Commission, *Working Better: Meeting the Changing Needs of Families, Workers and Employers in the 21st Century* (EHRC, March 2009), p. 60.
5. www.timewisejobs.co.uk.
6. Maitland A., 'The part-timers are taking over', *Financial Times Executive Appointments*, 22 November 2012.
7. H. Ibarra and O. Obodaru, 'Women and the Vision Thing', *Harvard Business Review*, vol. 87, no. 1 (January 2009): 62–70.
8. ILM/MT, *Index of Leadership Trust 2010* (Institute of Leadership and Management, 2010), p. 11.
9. C. Mitchell and D. Learmond, *Go Where There Be Dragons, Leadership Essentials for 2020 and Beyond*, Council Perspectives (The Conference Board, 2010).
10. Interview with author, July 2010 and July 2013.
11. R. Fry and D'V. Cohn, *New Economics of Marriage: The Rise of Wives* (Pew Research Center, 2010).
12. Brookfield (formerly GMAC) 2010 Global Relocation Trends Survey.
13. Interview with author, July 2010, and August 2013.
14. Interview with author, July 2013.
15. www.timewisejobs.co.uk.
16. Interviews with author, 2012 and 2013. The author also wrote about Mike Dean in 'The part-timers are taking over', *Financial Times Executive Appointments*, 22 November 2012, and in 'The Part-Time Executive', *The Conference Board Review*, Winter 2013.
17. Interviews with author, December 2010 and July 2013.

Chapter 6: Changing workplaces

1. M. Webb, *Lay Off Your Buildings, Not Your People!*, http://changethis.com/manifesto/103.03.RebootingWork/pdf/103.03.RebootingWork.pdf.
2. Speaking during a visit to the Netherlands office, January 2010, and in subsequent online and telephone interviews with author, October 2010, updated in August 2013.

3. Microsoft video: http://mediadl.microsoft.com/mediadl/www/n/netherlands/pers/Film_Sevil_Peach.wmv.

4. *The Cisco Connected World Report* (Cisco, 2010), http://newsroom.cisco.com/dlls/2010/ekits/ccwr_final.pdf.

5. Interview with author, November 2010.

6. Interview with author, August 2013.

7. *Microsoft Continues Its Redmond Headquarters Expansion on a Grand Scale* (Microsoft News Center, 12 November 2007).

8. 'London West End now the most expensive office space in the world', *Property Magazine International*, 25 January 2013.

9. Interview by Janne Ryan for the Australian Broadcasting Corporation's By Design program, 16 September 2009.

10. Performance.gov: http://finance.performance.gov/initiative/manage-property/home.

11. Office of Personnel Management, *Status of Telework in the Federal Government* (OPM, 2009).

12. S. Losey, '1 Million More Teleworkers: Can Agencies Turn New Legislation into Reality?', *Federal Times* (29 November 2010).

13. 2012 Status of Telework in the Federal Government: Report to Congress, United States Office of Personnel Management.

14. Interview with author, August 2013.

15. Lisa Rein, 'The federal office space of the future? GSA's new floor plan eschews desk-jockey culture', *Washington Post*, 16 July 2013.

16. Interviews with author, December 2010 and July 2013.

17. http://www.linkedin.com/in/tomball2.

18. M. Dixon and P. Ross, *Agility @ Work* (Unwired Ventures Ltd., 2010), p. 14.

19. Interviews with authors, March 2011 and September 2013.

20. Interview with authors, July 2010.

21. 'Business Diary: Matt Brittin', *Financial Times*, 27 September 2010.

22. Nigel Oseland, *The Psychology of Collaboration Space* (published by Herman Miller, 2012).

23. Interview with author, December 2010.

24. Interview with author, June 2013.

Chapter 7: Culture is critical

1. V. Nayar, *Employees First, Customers Second* (Harvard Business Press, 2010), p. 169.

2. *Women Matter 2: Female Leadership, a Competitive Edge for the Future* (McKinsey & Co, 2008) and H. Ibarra and O. Obodaru, 'Women and the Vision Thing', *Harvard Business Review*, vol. 87, no.1 (January 2009): 62–70.

3. A. Wittenberg-Cox and A. Maitland, *Why Women Mean Business* (Wiley, 2009), pp. 2–3.
4. Interview with author, July 2013.
5. *Balancing Work and Family, A Practical Guide to Help Organizations Meet the Global Workforce Challenge* (HRD Press, 2010).
6. Interview with author July 2013.
7. K. Tong-hyung, 'Wireless Technologies to Allow Workers to Stay at Home', *The Korea Times* (20 July 2010).
8. 'S. Korea's working hours likely to be shorter than OECD average in 2021: report', *YonhapNewsAgency*,18June2013(http://www.globalpost.com/dispatch/news/yonhap-news-agency/130618/s-koreas-working-hours-likely-be-shorter-oecd-average-2021-r), and *Labor Productivity Levels in the Total Economy* (OECD, December 2012).
9. 'South Korean government promotes flexible working with videoconferencing', *Networks Asia*, 29 June 2012.
10. Interview with author, July 2013.
11. A. Wittenberg-Cox and A. Maitland, *Why Women Mean Business* (Wiley, 2009), pp. 193–200.
12. Interview with authors, August 2010.
13. OECD Labour Force Statistics for 2011.
14. Eurostat employment statistics August 2012.
15. Interview with author, January 2011.
16. Interview with author, January 2011.
17. *Working Better: Meeting the Changing Needs of Families, Workers and Employers in the 21st Century* (Equality and Human Rights Commission, UK, 2009).
18. Statistics from The Netherlands Institute for Social Research.
19. *Employee Engagement Report 2011* (BlessingWhite Inc, 2011).
20. Interviews with author, January 2011 and August 2013.
21. Interview with author, November 201, updated August 2013.

Chapter 8: Strategies for change

1. Speaking at the Linkage Inc. Women in Leadership Summit, 8 November 2010, and interviews with author, 2010 and 2013.
2. Interview with authors, March 2011.
3. Interview with authors, August 2010.
4. Speaking at a Swiss Re seminar, 1 November 2012.
5. Interview with authors, March 2011.
6. A. Maitland, *Working Better: A Managers' Guide to Flexible Working* (Equality and Human Rights Commission, 2009).
7. Interviews with author, 2010 and 2013, and data provided by company.

8. Interview with authors, August 2010.
9. P. Thomson, *Tomorrow's Leaders* (City and Guilds, 2007).
10. Interview with author, November 2010, updated June 2013.

Chapter 9: Making it happen as an organization

1. *Give people the freedom of where to work* (Richard Branson's Blog, 25 February 2013).
2. Interview with author September 2010, updated September 2013.
3. *Gartner Says Fewer than 30 Percent of Large Organizations Will Block Social Media by 2014* (Gartner Inc., press release 5 March 2012).
4. Interview with author, July 2013.
5. Interview with authors, August 2010.
6. Interview with author, August 2010, updated July 2013.
7. Interviews with author, 2012 and 2013. The author also wrote about Mike Dean in 'The part-timers are taking over', *Financial Times Executive Appointments*, 22 November 2012, and in 'The Part-Time Executive', *The Conference Board Review*, Winter 2013.
8. Interview with author, June 2010, updated June 2013.

Chapter 10: Making it happen yourself

1. Interview with author, May 2013.
2. Interview with author, June 2013.
3. Interview with author, May and September 2013.
4. R Hastings, *Netflix Culture: Freedom and Responsibility* (Slideshare, 1 August 2009).
5. J. McGregor, 'The catch of having an unlimited vacation policy', *Washington Post*, 13 August 2013.
6. *Understanding the economic benefits of workforce agility* (Agile Future Forum, June 2013).
7. *Give people the freedom of where to work* (Richard Branson's Blog, 25 February 2013).
8. Speech at The Conference Board Academy for New Diversity & Inclusion Leaders, December 2012, and interview with author, July 2013.
9. Email communication with author, March 2013.
10. *Volkswagen turns off Blackberry email after work hours* (BBC News website, 23 December 2011).
11. *Atos boss Thierry Breton defends his internal email ban* (BBC News, 6 December 2011).

12. Interview with author, November 2010.
13. Email exchange with author, August 2013.

Chapter 11: Looking over the horizon

1. Interview with author, February 2011.
2. ITU Statistics: www.itu.int/en/ITU-D/Statistics/Pages/stat/default.aspx.
3. P. Nicholas, *Linking Cybersecurity Policy and Performance: Microsoft Releases Special Edition Security Intelligence Report*, 6 February 2013.
4. Interview with authors, March 2011.
5. *Contingent Workforce Management: The Next-Generation Guidebook to Managing the Modern Contingent Workforce Umbrella* (Aberdeen Group, May 2012).
6. The State of Independence in America, MBO Partners, September 2013.
7. 'US – What will happen to staffing in 2018?' Staffing Industry Analysts, 5 March 2013.
8. Interview by email with author, December 2010.
9. P. Whitehead, 'Jobs are going back to the future', *Financial Times*, 22 March 2012.
10. Interview with authors, 3 July 2013.
11. Interview with author, November 2010.
12. Interview with author, August 2013.
13. D. Aron, 'The Future of Talent Is in Clusters', *Harvard Business Review* blog, 1 February 2013.
14. Interview with author, July 2013.
15. '"Smart work" could be key to green growth', *EurActiv Network*, 28 February 2011.
16. *Regus opens 1,500th business centre in Pune, India, a key focus for expansion* (Regus website, 26 March 2013).

Further Reading

Benko, C. and Weisberg, A. (2007) *Mass Career Customization*, Harvard Business School Press.

Birkinshaw, J. (2010) *Reinventing Management*, John Wiley & Sons.

Brake, T. (2009) *Where in the World Is My Team?*, Jossey-Bass.

Coplin, D. (2013) *Business Reimagined*, Harriman House.

Donkin, R. (2010) *The Future of Work*, Palgrave Macmillan.

Drucker, P. F. (1999) *Management Challenges for the 21st Century*, Butterworth-Heinemann.

Gratton, L. (2011) *The Shift*, Collins.

Hamel, G. (2007) *The Future of Management*, Harvard Business School Press.

Handy, C. (2001) *The Elephant and the Flea*, Hutchinson.

Heil, G., Bennis, W. and Stephens, D. (2000) *Douglas McGregor, Revisited*, John Wiley & Sons.

Lake, A. (2013) *Smart Flexibility*, Gower.

Layard, R. (2006) *Happiness: Lessons from a New Science*, Penguin.

Magnus, G. (2009) *The Age of Aging*, John Wiley & Sons.

Malone, T. W. (2004) *The Future of Work*, Harvard Business School Press.

McGregor, D. (2006) *The Human Side of Enterprise – Annotated Edition*, McGraw Hill.

Nayar, V. (2010) *Employees First, Customers Second*, Harvard Business Press.

Pink, D. H. (2010) *Drive*, Canongate Books.

Ressler, C. and Thompson, J. (2008) *Why Work Sucks and How to Fix It*, Penguin Group.

Semler, R. (2001) *Maverick*, Random House Business.

Semler, R. (2003) *The Seven-Day Weekend*, Arrow Books.

Shirky, C. (2008) *Here Comes Everybody*, Penguin.

Tapscott, D. (2009) *Grown Up Digital*, McGraw Hill.

Wittenberg-Cox, A. and Maitland, A. (2009) *Why Women Mean Business*, John Wiley & Sons.

Wittenberg-Cox, A. (2010) *How Women Mean Business*, John Wiley & Sons.

Index

Printed and bound in Great Britain by
CPI Group (UK) Ltd, Croydon, CR0 4YY